Research Beyond Borders

Research Beyond Borders
Multidisciplinary Reflections

Edited by
Anjana Narayan and Lise-Hélène Smith

LEXINGTON BOOKS
Lanham • Boulder • New York • Toronto • Plymouth, UK

Published by Lexington Books
A wholly owned subsidary of The Rowman & Littlefield Publishing Group, Inc.
4501 Forbes Boulevard, Suite 200, Lanham, Maryland 20706
www.rowman.com

10 Thornbury Road, Plymouth PL6 7PP, United Kingdom

British Library Cataloguing in Publication Information Available

Library of Congress Cataloging-in-Publication Data

The hardback edition of this book was previously
catalogued by the Library of Congress as follows:

Research beyond borders : multidisciplinary reflections / edited by Anjana Narayan and
Lise-Hélène Smith.
     p. cm.
1. Social sciences—Research—Methodology. 2. Humanities—Research—Methodology.
3.Qualitave Research—Methodology. I. Narayan, Anjana, 1976- II. Smith, Lise-Hélène,
1976-
   H62.R44719.2012
   001.4—dc23   2011042418

ISBN : 978-0-7391-4355-1 (cloth : alk. paper)
ISBN : 978-0-7391-4356-8 (pbk. : alk. paper)
ISBN : 978-0-7391-4357-5 (electronic)

Printed in the United States of America

Contents

Acknowledgments

We would like to thank Peggy Perry and Victoria Bhavsar from the Faculty Center for Professional Development at the California State Polytechnic University, Pomona for their support in funding this project in its initial and final stages. We would also like to thank Sharon Hilles, Dean of the College of Letters, Arts and Social Sciences, Liliane Fucaloro, Chair of the English and Foreign Languages Department and Laurie Roades, former Chair of Psychology and Sociology Department, current Associate Dean of the College of Letters, Arts, and Social Sciences, and Bandana Purkayastha, Professor of Sociology and Asian American Studies, UCONN for their continual assistance in the creation of this volume. We are particularly grateful to our graduate assistant Kelly Shimabukuro for her remarkable commitment to this project, from her drafting of the initial book proposal, her comprehensive reading, detailed feedback, and careful editing of each chapter, to her professional indexing. We could not have seen this project through without her steadfast dedication. We are also indebted to Jack Fong for his contribution to the collection, to Kent Dickson and Erin Carper for their meticulous, thoughtful feedback on the introduction and last chapter, as well as to our families for their unwavering support throughout the development of this book. We are also grateful to Julie Kirsch, Amy King, Lindsey Frederick, Melissa Wilks, and Samantha Kirk at Lexington Books, for their belief in our project and for their flexibility. Finally, we would like to thank all contributing authors for their expertise, enthusiasm, and patience.

INTRODUCTION

Onto the Front Lines

BY LISE-HÉLÈNE SMITH AND ANJANA NARAYAN

Few books address the tangible experience of conducting research away from one's home country. Most remain very discipline-oriented, dense or dry, lacking a personal touch that would provide nascent researchers with invaluable insights into what such a research process may actually be like.

The results of our efforts is an interdisciplinary attempt to assess the empirical, methodological, and practical implications of conducting research abroad, i.e. research that transcends national boundaries. Written by an interdisciplinary group of scholars from the humanities, social sciences, and sciences, this anthology presents the viewpoints of authors who specialize in diverse methods ranging from ethnographic and Indigenous methodologies, archival research, focus group surveys and interviews, to oral histories, statistical research, and case studies. Also are included insights drawn from both qualitative and quantitative data analysis and experiments employed by scholars that demonstrate how key ideas and methodologies can overlap in different areas of study. Given the ever-shrinking transnational spaces across which one can now migrate, we have compiled in this collection the scholarship and wisdom of those who have first-hand knowledge of conducting research in other parts of the world. Our collection is dedicated to the researcher-in-the-making in hopes of providing guidance to facilitate the undertaking of informed, innovative fieldwork overseas.

Many scholars have been moving beyond existing state-centric orientations that dictate how research processes unfold. Analyses of this trend reflect the need for researchers to use multidisciplinary transnational procedures so as to remain cognizant of the inequalities that continually inform intellectual practices. Moreover, with increasing globalization, researchers in varied disciplines increasingly find themselves being invited to join collaborative and/or comparative multinational projects. Yet, the inequality and asymmetry of power relationships is often overlooked when carrying out investigative studies overseas. Our collection constitutes a novel attempt to foster a more explicit and critical understanding of the politics of research aims, processes, and findings.

Indeed, the scholarly momentums contained within our collection were born from the desire to address the need for developing investigative approaches that are able to illuminate, analyze, and interpret cross-cultural phenomena as well as transnational dynamics as they affect researchers in the field. Our efforts are thus aimed at correcting one major shortcoming in social scientific and humanities research generally: namely the growing trend toward increasing specialization, a process that has resulted in disjuncted bodies of knowledge. Our concern is that researchers across disciplines generally treat their efforts as separate from other scholarly discourses, overlooking potential interlinkages among their findings that can tie various bodies of knowledge together. To remedy this, our collection presents an innovative attempt at methodological 'cross-fertilization'[1] in an effort to draw insights from scholars whose methods rely on key ideas and approaches that can be appreciated by practitioners of different disciplines.

In this book, we highlight practical issues and logistical dilemmas involved in conducting research in international settings. The spectrum of issues that this anthology illuminates include bureaucratic considerations of obtaining visas; foreign ministry clearance; politics of IRB requirements, such as informed consent; logistical considerations, such as time for travel; the daily rhythm of the local place; ethnic, language and religious barriers; and access to medicines and technology. Collaborative considerations are also highlighted, such as building trust with members of host communities, expanding shared research networks, obtaining research funding, and, most importantly, identifying dissemination avenues to present the results of research for the benefit of the participants, families, and communities touched by the research. Considerations related to the human condition are also highlighted from a humanities and social scientific perspective to attend to people whose lives are disrupted by war, poverty, malnutrition, or the natural elements, to name but a few. More importantly, we encouraged authors to reflect upon and examine the imbalances or biases that characterize their scholarly initiatives. It is our hope that our readers will derive from this collection a stronger sense of how knowledge is generated and shared.

RESEARCH IN INTERNATIONAL SETTINGS: HISTORICAL OVERVIEW

As noted by David L. Szanton,[2] American research in international settings only began at the end of World War II. Before then, the American isolationist policy of the 1920s and 1930s explained the negligible number of research studies conducted overseas. The United States' entry into the war in 1941 triggered a growing awareness of Europe; by 1945, most Americans were reasonably familiar with European politics, culture, society, and institutions.

Moreover, the establishment of the United Nations (UN) in 1945 coincided with the struggle for independence of many colonized nations. The UN took the initiative to provide field training and to organize social welfare and economic development programs in these non-Western countries. Consequently, the United States found itself in dire need of economists, sociologists, political scientists, and other specialists not only to promote democracy and social/economic development in African, Asian, and Caribbean countries, but also to protect American interests in these regions. With the consensus that the country needed larger long-term investment in international studies, prominent American research universities sought to develop these competencies through student/faculty scholarships, foreign language centers, research grants, and other initiatives. The establishment in 1950 of the Ford Foundation's Foreign Area Fellowship Program (FAFP) marked the culmination of these efforts. The FAFP subsidized the training of American students and scholars in area studies, emerging as the major funding source research in international settings. Federal legislation now administers some of the most successful and widely beneficial programs while private foundations have also been notable contributors.[3]

During the 1960s and the 1970s, intense criticism targeted the exportation of American models of "development" and "modernization" to the global South. This coincided with the war in Vietnam (1964 to 1975) and a growing spirit of anti-Americanism. The Reconceptualization Movement in the Social Work discipline, for instance, rejected the American model of Social Work in favor of a new one based on the Marxist doctrine of social justice.[4] The American model was perceived as being part of a political and economic system that maintained the status quo instead of challenging it. Consequently, this period witnessed the reemergence of indigenous approaches to conducting research which were more locally relevant. As a result, scholars and researchers in several disciplines undertook research in international settings that increasingly factored in socio-cultural contexts, from which two distinct methodologies emerged: the universalist approach and the cultural approach. The universalist approach was context-independent and assumed uncritically that the western context was general enough to be applicable at the universal level and that it could be adapted to other cultural contexts. By contrast, the cultural approach was context-centric and prioritizes specific social contexts and a particular country's unique cultural identity.

Both approaches regarded the nation-state as a necessary and natural representative of modern society. As Peggy Levitt and Sanjay Khagram note, recent scholars now challenge the assumption that the nation-state or even its contemporary borders defines the concept of methodological nationalism. Instead, they regard it as another form of "methodological unitism" that has a severely limiting effect on historiographic and ethnological studies and data sets. A research methodology that is restricted to the nation-state or its boundaries fails to detect and interpret identities and linkages that intersect or transcend this boundary. To overcome this limitation, scholars such as Levitt and Khagram call for methodological transnationalism, "which reformulates existing data and accounts, invents new kinds of information and evidence, applies investigative approaches in novel ways, and designs novel research tools and designs with which to analyze trans-societal and organizational phenomena and dynamics."[5] Similarly, Ulrich Beck and Natan Sznaider developed a concept of methodological cosmopolitanism.[6] Anna Amelina remarks that cosmopolitanism, or the concept that all humanity belongs to a single community, is an outcome of growing global inter-dependence and the consequent "ambivalence of multiple identities."[7] Cosmopolitanism recognizes that a person has several affiliations that are shaped according to various and multiple dynamics related to race, religion, nationalism, and culture. This approach rejects the "either/or" principle of methodological nationalism in favor of the "both/and" principle of methodological cosmopolitanism. Moreover, the "both/and" principle, Amelina argues, enables systematic and structured research. She uses Beck and Sznaider's argument that a fresh research methodology may overcome the challenges of transnational research and globalization by allowing researchers to move beyond the "global/local and national/international" approaches that characterized earlier nation bounded research strategies.

Accordingly, in moving away from methodological nationalism and its limitations, scholars are looking at more innovative and efficient data collection techniques. Wittel[8] notes that the "field" in fieldwork is no longer confined to a specific geographic region, nor can it be clearly demarcated or defined. Similarly, research in multicultural settings is grounded in a "global emergent context" and should move beyond studying the personal interactions between small local ethnic groups confined to a single region to researching social practices that simultaneously emerge in disparate locations. This shift in focus has been actively encouraged by the internet revolution, enabling researchers to observe and report on online communication between interactive and connected virtual entities in cyberspace.

Transnational studies that examine complex issues at the global level also have a local impact on research. The authors in this collection describe their experiences in different geographic regions, which will give readers a useful comparative framework in which the 'local' can be used to further explore dominant discourses and their links to wider social relations and practices. This collection also attempts to move beyond methodological nationalism in academic disciplines, through cross-disciplinary and cross-field theorizing. Today, there are many kinds of transnational activities and many rich areas of related social scientific inquiry. Yet, there have been few attempts to learn from, or through, approaches and analyses from one transnational domain to another, which is a major drawback. This book demonstrates how researchers can better utilize, draw from, or be intellectually stimulated by the concepts and methods available across disciplines.

PERSONALIZED EXPERIENCES IN THE FIELD

Whether to prepare fieldwork overseas or to conduct research nationally in a more cognizant manner, we hope that the cues provided by contributing authors in the following pages will demonstrate ways in which researchers can negotiate positionality and knowledge production successfully. Whether it addresses motherhood, sectarian violence, the vulnerability of children, or the United States itself as a site "abroad" for non-American researchers, to name just a few chapter topics, our collection showcases a variety of disciplines, methodologies, and contextualized experiences to impart its readers with a sense of what may arise or transpire when collecting data/doing research in a transnational context.

Many contributing authors explore questions of personal responsibility and perspective in the production of scholarship, as part I of our book entitled "Dialogues" seeks to highlight. In order to respect the integrity of the histories they relate, David Del Testa, for example, argues that historians should pay careful attention to the sense of ownership that develops when researching and writing history. He notes that in order to understand the biases and prejudices inherent in any recounting of history, historians must know very well the perspective of the people they study as well as that of other historians who have told the story before. Del Testa's insights are derived from his experiences collecting data in France and Vietnam as his research sought to situate a Franco-Vietnamese woman's diary into a historical context through interviews and fieldwork. In this subtle and complex process, Del Testa employs self-reflexive case studies to consider the intimacies and power of history, along with how historical anatomies are interwoven with the candid retelling of narratives that include both honesty and prejudice. Del Testa wisely cautions against disseminating history without sensitivity to the context of its reception, because intimate knowledge spread indiscriminately can have disastrous results.

Similarly, Mark Carey's chapter draws a distinction between the purportedly innocuous transnational researcher *vis-à-vis* those harnessed by multinational corporations, government agencies, NGOs, or even tourists, and cautions that the former is still vulnerable to extractive or exploitative research. Carey argues that one way for scholars to minimize this tendency is through a research diplomacy that engages researchers within the host country in collaborative links with locals and research participants during the investigation, and sharing research results at the field site and throughout the country with the groups. Carey shows that practicing research diplomacy improves scholarship because personal interactions with a range of people within and beyond libraries, archives, and fieldwork sites often facilitate access to data. In his chapter, Mark Carey shares wisdoms born from his environmental historical research with the Mayangna indigenous people inhabiting a nature reserve in Nicaragua by focusing on how indigenous groups have adapted to recent climate change and glacier hazards in the Peruvian Andes. His contribution illustrates the benefits of research diplomacy while demonstrating that beyond the procedural aspects of research lie the central reality of human relationships in all their interpersonal iterations.

It is precisely because data collection is often inseparable from its *ethos* or milieu that it should be treated as such, as Wiline Pangle makes clear. In her chapter, Pangle argues that the success of ecological research is highly dependent on establishing strong relationships with local communities, not only with the local villagers, but also with park authorities and the tourist community. She reminds us that it is a researcher's responsibility to acknowledge fieldwork data as the by-product of a cultural, ethnic and political context that cannot be ignored. Pangle's chapter presents the procedural steps and interpersonal diplomacies involved in ecological data collection abroad, from the planning to the execution. As a scholar of behavioral ecology, she conducted her doctoral research in Kenya during a sixteen-month field season, studying the behavior of large mammalian carnivores when faced with danger. On the one hand, her chapter presents the advantages of joining an established and rooted ecological field station such as benefiting from well-oiled procedures of visas and permits. On the other hand, her narrative also addresses its drawbacks, including challenges linked to time management. Because of her participation in an ongoing research project, Pangle stresses the importance of self-awareness, integrity, and cultural etiquette for the preservation of the larger group's reputation and presents some advice for young researchers considering similar field work.

In part II entitled "Insecurities," Jack Fong echoes Pangle's practical and ethical concerns in his considerations of the field researcher confronted with sectarian violence. Fong's chapter addresses a blind spot in ethnographic research that entails how to gather data and conduct field research in a systemic crisis context. His chapter outlines the wisdom of expediency and hyper-time in data collection between the two worlds of Thailand and Burma. He emphasizes the importance of fostering links with journalists during the data collection process, especially when a clear anatomy of field remains amorphous due to a protracted war. Fong illuminates the humbling consequences of attending to a population that is experiencing perennial life and death adversities to which the privileged scholar is only temporarily exposed in the field and from which he will depart at the conclusion of the research process. In such a dystopian context, Fong makes visible how data collection can capture the desperation of a people and nation as they seek to emphasize their existence in a devastated world. His chapter underscores the process of examining a people, the Karen ethnic nationality that has been subjected to a genocidal campaign by the notorious military regimes ruling Burma, while they are in "survival mode."

When conducting independent fieldwork in areas of the world torn apart by war or by extreme social or economic inequalities, trust can also become a necessity to handle uncertainty, risk, and vulnerability in relationships, as Mónica Ruiz-Casares' chapter outlines. Ruiz-Casarez examines the challenges of establishing trust when initiating research with orphans and vulnerable children in Namibia. She discusses the ways in which trust can play a crucial role in developing an effective research team, in gaining access to the setting for data collection, and in utilizing research findings. For Ruiz-Casares, trust entails coping in situations where trust is lacking as well as gradually building trust through prolonged local engagement and sensitivity to local values and practices. She describes strategies to promote trust with children, research assistants, and local institutions, and raises questions about different understanding of and attitudes towards privacy. Ruiz-Casares also explores the ways in which distrust may be at times functional and necessary yet emphasizes how researchers should nurture trusting relationships through open communication and by demonstrating integrity and benevolence. Her chapter concludes with an analysis of how power symmetry, asymmetry and interdependence in the context of entrenched hierarchies of power require a constant negotiation of children's voices.

While addressing such power asymmetry and dependency, Kristen Conway-Gomez discusses the considerations of the field-based discipline of geography and narrates her experience residing with people in the Amazon whose daily lives depend on natural resources. Conway-Gomenz explains the methodological flexibility required in the field: she shows how misunderstandings born from miscommunication and potential threats to her life forced her to redesign means to collect her data for tropical biodiversity conservation. Conway-Gomez's one-year stay in Bolivia, fraught with the never-ending specificities of a particular field site, reminds us to be cognizant of the unexpected research events that accompany field work.

Part III entitled "Encumbrances" opens on Cecily Jones' reflection on her experience of combining the roles of graduate student and single mother during a period of fieldwork for her doctoral thesis. Jones relates some of the financial and emotional challenges encountered while attempting to juggle fieldwork with parental responsibilities in a "foreign" society. She discusses how she addressed issues such as securing adequate funding, affordable housing, schooling and childcare; coming to grips with local bureaucracies; organizing time to conduct the research; and dealing with isolation in the absence of a support network. In the process, Jones reaffirms feminist critiques of traditionalist representations of fieldwork and the field as a masculinized space within which male researchers are abstracted from familial relationships, free to engage in the pursuit of knowledge construction and production, and unencumbered by the disruptive presence of dependents. Such masculinized representations of the research process reproduce the field as the embodiment of a public/private divide from which children and partners have been banished. Jones argues, however, that the presence of loved ones within the fieldwork process abruptly disrupts the neat but ultimately untenable theoretical dichotomous categories of private and public.

While the research process often lends itself to unexpected challenges or results, serendipitous events can also sometimes further expand the parameters of the field researcher. In her chapter, Rebecca Sammel presents the research process as quite random and outlines the ways in which omissive silences in archival holdings can be circumvented via unexpected emergences of relations within the texts in a given archive. Sammel argues that the original handwritten catalogs, rather than contemporary digital records, must be examined, for it is the marginal notations accumulated over the centuries that yield discoveries of unlooked-for revelations. Her chapter presents an *excursus* into the practical implications of archival searches, in light of the financial impracticality of such research for most students in the humanities today. Yet it argues that students accustomed to employing Google as the first step in their search for primary sources instead should be trained and funded to examine the primary materials themselves—the paper, vellum, or papyrus catalogs—since the record-keepers have left invaluable clues as to the justifications for the composition, omissions, and inclusions of a holding. Sammel notes that the process of discovery, particularly when consulting European archives of pre-sixteenth-century materials, can be so delightfully unexpected that it cannot be predicted by impressions gleaned by searching online catalogs, facsimiles, and databases of virtual holdings.

Similarly, conducting qualitative research in a region as rich, diverse and complex as the Sub-Indian continent presents unexpected, practical difficulties that may be difficult to overcome. In her chapter, Shweta Majumdar narrates her attempt to comply with IRB requirements and the difficulty of negotiating institutionalized and bureaucratic rules of research ethic boards in countries where such boards do not exist. Majumdar devotes her chapter to ethnographic reflections during fieldwork among Bengali widows in Vrindavan, a Hindu pilgrim city where widows, particularly from

West Bengal, migrate to spend their last days in hopes of attaining salvation. She explains that the stories of these "religious" widows have been globally circulated, presenting them as hapless and helpless victims of a traditional and backward culture. The author sets out to excavate the voices of these widows, who are seldom heard in these narratives, in order to get their stories "in their own words." While doing so, Majumdar also revisits the insider-outsider debate, arguing that although there are well-developed conversations in methodological accounts, the role of language and age are less frequently considered when discussing the outsider-insider dilemma. Majumdar reveals that even though she was an "insider" by most standards on account of her growing up in India, of her ethnicity, language and gender, she nonetheless found her convictions tested in the field. The author concludes by noting that power and privilege in field settings constitute dynamic and diffused entities that constantly call for renegotiations and that researchers must remain mindful at all time of how they are being perceived as well as how they are representing others.

Finally, in part IV entitled "Crossroads," Virginie Magnat links the crisis of representation in the social sciences to the postcolonial critique of the notion of "objectivity" in ethnographic fieldwork. She moves beyond cultural anthropologist Victor Turner's performance ethnography to make visible how a post-Turnerian paradigm and Indigenized research are not only challenging conventional approaches to conducting, writing and disseminating research, but are also provocatively redefining conceptions of terms such as "research" and "abroad." Situating her approach at the crossroads of performance studies, experimental ethnography, and Indigenous methodologies, Magnat discusses the cross-cultural research that she has conducted in Poland within the emerging field of performance as research, and examines how being engaged in this type of research has led her to develop a dialogical, reflexive, and performative pedagogical approach to teaching.

The last chapter of this collection continues to move away from dominant research methodologies by considering research that posits the United States as a "foreign" site. Sami Hanna and Mustafa Sever's chapter indeed explores how conducting research on or with one's own ethno-cultural population, but outside the boundaries of one's homeland, is conceptualized and manifested into actual research practices. Hanna and Sever focus on international graduate students residing in the United States who employ various modes of reflexive practices to rationalize their diasporic proximities to communities they study. They note how such proximities turn into epistemological claims, particularly with regards to the ways they position themselves as insiders or outsiders to their research participants. Yet the authors incisively note that presumed sameness or oneness with the communities under scrutiny glosses over other major differences between the researcher and the researched, differences which themselves could be treated as an important dynamic of the research processes had the research been conducted within the localities of the homeland. Additionally, Hanna and Sever discuss the ways in which the notion of "insiderness" is constructed on discursive or textual grounds and legitimized through spatial binaries of being *here* and *there*. They particularly emphasize the simultaneity of being *here* and *there* in a "foreign" territory, which can create novel meaning-fields for both researchers and the researched without conscious recognition of the transnational character of the loci.

When reading the following accounts in the authors' own words, it is our hope that our readers will keep in mind the aforementioned considerations, such as how to manage the political and ethical implications of research; how to remain aware of one's status in the field; how to address the stipulations of the review boards; how to respond to cultural and linguistic challenges that may arise during the research process; and how knowledge is assembled, managed, and disseminated to various audiences. We hope that our efforts will remedy the fact that a single source does not exist to guide nascent researchers who wish to test their intellectual mettle by undertaking research beyond borders.

NOTES

1   Steven Vertovec, "Transnational Social Formations: Towards Conceptual Cross-Fertilization," presented at Workshop on "Transnational Migration: Comparative Perspectives," June 30-July 1, 2001, Princeton University http://www.transcomm.ox.ac.uk/working%20papers/Vertovec2.pdf

2   David L. Szanton, "The Origin, Nature and Challenges of Area Studies in the United States," in *The Politics of Knowledge: Area Studies and the Disciplines,* ed. David L. Szanton (University of California Press, 2004), 10-11.

3   The Fulbright Program for Mutual Educational and Cultural Exchange, which was driven by the need to change the traditional American isolationist policy, is governed by the Mutual Educational and Cultural Exchange Act of 1961, while the National Endowment for the Humanities (NEH) is an independent federal agency established by the National Foundation on the Arts and the Humanities Act of 1965.

4   Lynne M. Healy. "International Social Work: Professional Action in an Interdependent World." New York: Oxford University Press, 2001.

5   Peggy Levitt and Sanjay Khagram. "Towards a Field of Transnational Studies and a Sociological Transnationalism Research Program," Hauser Center for Nonprofit Organizations, Social Science Research Network, Working Paper, no. 24 (2005): 16.

6   Ulrich Beck and Natan Sznaider, "Unpacking Cosmopolitanism for the Social Sciences: A Research Agenda," *The British Journal of Sociology,* 57, no. 1 (2006): 1-23.

7   Anna Amelina, "Searching for an Appropriate Research Strategy on Transnational Migration: The Logic of Multi-Sited Research and the Advantage of the Cultural Interferences Approach," *FSQ* 10, no. 1 (2010): 9.

8   Andreas Wittel, "Ethnography on the Move: From Field to Net to Internet," *Forum Qualitative Social Research* 1, no. 1 (2000) at http://www.qualitative-research.net/index.php/fqs/article/viewArticle/1131/2517

Part I

Dialogues

CHAPTER ONE

History Lessons from an Indochinese Diary

By David Del Testa

Researching and writing history can be exciting, but the privilege of recreating history through research carries with it important responsibilities.[1] It is important to recognize that the process of uncovering histories and writing about them can have consequences. This chapter discusses, from a personal vantage point, questions regarding the research process, the responsibilities surrounding it, its potential consequences, and encourages its readers to engage in healthy self-reflection on the act of doing historical research. It draws from the lessons that I learned in the process of trying to recreate a particular personal history as accurately as possible from a variety of sources and explores the personal avalanches that seemingly mundane acts of research can potentially cause. This chapter focuses on the research that I completed on a diary written in 1943 by Ms. Claudie Beaucarnot and the consequences of meeting with her and people mentioned in her diary. I have studied this diary because the community to which Beaucarnot belonged—Vietnam's French "mixed-race" population—walked between two cultures, exposing cultural exchanges between the French and Vietnamese that historians have otherwise not thoroughly examined for what was once known as French Indochina.[2]

I should explain what I believe historical research entails. Historians use texts, either singly or in comparison, and always relative to the larger history around the document (the "context"), in an attempt to reconstruct and interpret the past. A "text" can be anything that a historian can examine and interpret, such as a book, a form, an interview, a photograph, a building, or a map. Historians treat these texts in one of three ways: as primary, secondary, or a hybrid primary-secondary. A primary text originates in the time studied, like a letter written by Abraham Lincoln to his generals or a medieval castle on a hill; primary "texts" are often unselfconsciously historical, meaning that they were never meant to serve as a source of reflection in the future. A secondary text is generally a comment on, and analysis of, primary sources, like a book written about the Roman Republic, or a contemporary collection of historical statistics. A hybrid of the two concerns a secondary text that has become primary because of the insights it gives on the past. For example, a textbook from the 1930s remains secondary because it relates a history, but it may serve as a primary example of how educators wrote textbooks in the 1930s. In terms of interviewing people, the subjects of interviews are usually considered "primary" sources when they discuss their own experiences (an art historian reflecting on her days in college) and "secondary" when they discuss a subject in which they are expert (an art historian discussing a kind of art for which she has a great deal of knowledge).

Whatever sources a historian uses for her or his work, no right-minded historian makes claims for finding "the truth" in her or his recreations of the past. Such panoramic vision is impossible to achieve. However, anyone who calls him- or herself a historian focuses his or her energies on discovering as complete and accurate a representation of the past as possible. This means producing original work, giving credit to the work of others when used in support of one's own work, and following certain guidelines that encourage respect for history and its sources, living or dead, widely available or unique. Indeed, the two main associations of professional historians in the United States have detailed policies on fairness, accuracy, and accountability to which their members must adhere.[3] Additionally, scholars collecting oral histories generally follow guidelines adopted by either the Oral Historian Association or the American Anthropological Association, including acquiring written permission before starting an interview and providing the people interviewed with transcripts of their interviews from which they might demand corrections.[4] Most organizations—schools, hospitals, and laboratories—in which researchers conduct studies on living humans also have an Institutional Research Board (IRB) to verify researchers' compliance with accepted guidelines on research behavior. Following these guidelines provides an outline of behavior through which the researcher respects the rights of the informants, including that to privacy and to protection from having knowledge coerced from them. Similarly, it protects researchers from charges of history "theft." The apparently overweening concern professionals have for respecting historical sources is not without merit. One only need recall the Tuskegee Syphilis Experiment to understand why "informed consent" has become such an important component of modern research.[5] Likewise, as George Orwell had the Party cadre Winston say in *1984*, his fictional account of a totalitarian society, "He who controls the present, controls the past. He who controls the past, controls the future."[6] Leaders of oppressive regimes or those with extremist politics will go to great lengths to hide or alter history to make themselves look good, serve their political needs, or protect themselves from criticism in order to understand how powerful history can be as a tool or weapon. Examples include Turkish nationalists intentionally destroying archival records of the 1912–1915 Armenian genocide in the National Archives of the United States; Soviet photo artists editing out Leon Trotsky from a photograph of him seated with Josef Stalin and Vladimir Lenin during Stalin's rule (1928–1953) because Stalin came to oppose Trotsky; and the "Mission Accomplished" banner disappearing from behind President George W. Bush in White House footage of his "victory speech" aboard the aircraft carrier USS Lincoln on May 2, 2003. Fortunately, in most of the world, historians, both professional and amateur, abound, making their own observations and contributions, challenging stereotypes and accepted representations with fresh evidence and interpretations. Beyond the process of reconstructing history through an examination of "texts," historians also spend a significant amount of time analyzing the events or stories they have recovered, using evidence to recreate the image of the world they imagine existed. Usually, historians use the "historicist" approach, where they attempt to understand the people they study or the events they research, in relation to the time period and values in which they are set, although complete knowledge is impossible.[7]

In the "doing" of history, anyone should recognize that all historians have biases that they may not recognize but which influence their work. So, for example, I present myself as an employed, professional historian trained at an important state research university, with a broad focus on the history of modern Europe and a slightly narrower one on modern Asia. This means I often write in a certain way that my peers consider acceptably "scholarly." I chose to focus on France and Vietnam because two of my uncles had served as combat soldiers in Vietnam, and I wanted to understand why they had to travel to that nation to fight. As an undergraduate and then graduate student, I learned about French colonialism, studied French and learned Vietnamese in order to understand "both sides of the story." Sometimes focusing shared perspective also means that I do not have strong conclusions about one or the other's actions. I have spent the equivalent of four years abroad, two in France and two in Vietnam, where I improved my language skills and conducted field research in archives, libraries, and collected oral histories. People often shape themselves to fit their own points of view, discounting those parts of themselves and experiences that do not fit with their view of the world. By luck, I did my research during the early 1990s, when the archival records of French Indochina had for the most part become available to the public (that is, most documents were no longer subject to censorship for political reasons). In addition, archivists and librarians in both France and Vietnam had cataloged these records so that researchers could easily find the documents they might want to see. What is more, in 1986, the Vietnamese government embarked on the Đổi Mới (Renovation) program,[8] one consequence of which was foreigners' ability to conduct sponsored research in the country's archives and libraries, albeit with censorship.[9] Of course, some records had "fallen off the boat" on the way back to France from Indochina or had "disappeared in the chaos" during the wars in Vietnam, a euphemisms for the destruction of archival materials deemed by French colonial authorities or Vietnamese officials, respectively, as too sensitive to retain for posterity. But for the most part, a rich documentation had become available to researchers. One prejudice has both brightened my work and perhaps, some would say, weakened it. In all of my research, I have tried to find the voices of "real people" from 1920s and 1930s French colonial Indochina as a counterbalance to official reports and recent histories that I feel are not correct and as an excuse to get "close" to the history that I seek to study.

My research also coincided with the great period of "Indo-chic" in France and other Western-oriented consumer economies, during which a whole series of movies, books, and even restaurants, such as the chain restaurant "Indochine" in New York City, Singapore, and Vienna, and "La Coloniale" in Paris, attempted to recreate, through décor and menus, the supposed romance and elegance of France's colonial past. This "Indo-chic" paralleled and followed a fruitful period of research on the American Vietnam war. It provoked both enormous general and scholarly interest in colonial Indochina. Schools and foundations thus made financial support available for projects specializing on Vietnam and, to a lesser degree, Cambodia and Laos. In addition, Régis Wargnier's film "Indochine" and Jean-Jacques Annaud's film "L'Amant [The Lover]," both released in 1992, had so incensed the community of former residents of Indochina now living in France, that they responded by publishing scores of memoirs and monographs to challenge what they viewed as an incorrect romanticization and representation of the French colonial community as vain, perverted exploiters.[10]

LESSON ONE: ATTACHMENT ANXIETY

I learned multiple, intertwined lessons while researching the Beaucarnot Diary. One of the most important was that historians become important bearer of truths so that interpretation and contextualization become challenging. As a result, the researcher might end up having a "romance," in a sense, with the subject, even if there are no feelings beyond historical interest. He or she becomes a protector of the subject's intimacies and a bearer of trust, which constitute important components of any romantic relationship. At the same time, the sensitivity one has to the feelings of the informant can sometimes inhibit the criticality or "objectivity" of the scholar who needs to bring out their importance to a larger audience, thereby making the production of historical scholarship possible. The Beaucarnot Diary's author and I share an intimacy that makes it difficult for me to delve too deeply into the historical problems that surround her story, although they have stimulated much productive reflection, discussion, and scholarship.

I cannot remember who told me that I should look at the copy of a typewritten diary found in a box of materials on the economics of French Indochina, but I did so in November 1999 during a brief visit to the Overseas Archives in Aix-en-Provence, France (where the archives of France's colonies are stored).[11] In that box, I found a typewritten transcription from 1994 of a 1943 travel journal kept by a then nineteen-year-old Claudie Beaucarnot during an automobile vacation she took with her family from Hà Nội to Sài Gòn. A quick reading of the diary revealed it to be one of the more interesting primary documents originating from French Indochina that I had read. On the surface, the diary seemed like that of any teenager, recounting her summer days filled with travelling between Indochina's towns, with hiking, swimming, and shopping. Reading in-between the lines, however, reveals challenges to many common representations of French Indochina. First, Claudie wrote the diary in 1943. I knew that the Japanese had been present in the region from July 1940 to August 1945, and I had no idea that anyone would even think of taking a pleasure trip through Indochina in the midst of World War II. Second, the Beaucarnots were a métisse, or mixed-race, family and quite well off—a wealth that defies the common representations of colonial mixed-race people as impoverished and marginal.[12]

The history of Franco-Vietnamese contact is long, complex and filled with mutual admiration as well as disgust. For example, many French admired the Vietnamese dedication to learning, and many Vietnamese thirsted for the "modern" knowledge the French brought with them during their occupation of Vietnam between 1885 and 1954. Yet many Vietnamese despised the French for not educating them well and as equals. Their lack of apparent appreciation for the development brought made many French resentful. This combined affection and hatred often did not leave much sentiment in the middle for those who represented the mixture of France and Vietnam. As a result, mixed-race people were often objects of derision and discrimination for both the French and the Vietnamese. At the same time, they often served as valuable go-betweens and cultural messengers from whom the French and Vietnamese learned about one another. At moments of extreme political turmoil, when especially the Vietnamese had to express political allegiance or risk losing any form of protection from violence, mixed-race individuals became the targets of selective violence in order to eliminate the cultural dialogue for which they stood. It was their place as cultural mediators and barometers of tolerance in a colonial environment that interested me. Accompanying my initial excitement with the discovery of the diary was a crisis in confidence. While working on my dissertation, I indeed had faith that I was researching "the good guys," Vietnamese and Cambodian railroad workers who, after twenty-five years of relatively loyal service to the French, revolted spectacularly against colonialism and became important allies in Vietnam's struggle for independence.[13] Through the Beaucarnot Diary, I encountered a family in-between the categories of oppression and dominance.[14] I would soon discover that they in fact *exemplified* a growing demographic reality in Indochina whose threat to conservative French settlers and Vietnamese anti-colonial forces was so great that their community was targeted for violent elimination at the end of World War II. I would learn that following the harrowing experiences of World War I, Claude Beaucarnot, the diarist's father and a trained industrial ceramicist, had responded to a newspaper advertisement to serve as a manager for an industrial ceramics factory in Hà Nội. I wondered if he was supporting colonialism per se or if it was simply a job with nice perks, far from reminders of the war. Marcelle Gaspard, the diarist's mother, was the abandoned daughter of a French math teacher and his Vietnamese concubine. As such, she certainly was, in a sense, a victim of colonialism and because she spoke Vietnamese and remained in contact with her Vietnamese family, she walked between two worlds, those of the native Vietnamese and of the French colonialists. Their daughter Claudie, her younger sister Nicole, and her older half-sister Juliette (from Marcelle's previous marriage to a man who also, like her mother, abandoned her) were born into a situation I could not expect them to have challenged at the time. The family lived decidedly between the French and Vietnamese societies, probably because neither society fully accepted them and because they faced a certain level of discrimination that only their relative wealth allowed them to overcome. Could I expect a nineteen-year-old to challenge colonialism and all the pain it was causing? Should I expect the eighty-two year-old women I later met to suddenly become critical of her life in the colony—a life of which she was a product and which had made her family wealthy, at least during the colonial period?

I had another source of discomfort, in that I realized that I was already involved in a "romance" with the diarist, even though I had yet to meet her. While trying to find out if Ms. Beaucarnot was still alive, I sent copies of her diary to my academic colleagues. I proposed that we prepare a translation of the Beaucarnot Diary, accompany it with a series of chapters analyzing it, and publish it as a mixed primary source document and essay collection marketed to college students as an aid in teaching history, representation of history, and scholarly reflections on that history.[15] Although my colleagues responded quickly, I could not bring myself to pursue the proposals I received from them: they suggested that we address, for example, Claudie's Freudian (that is, latently sexual, after the work of the Austrian psychoanalyst Sigmund Freud) relationship with her father. These types of analyses in many ways reinforced the stereotypes of colonialism that I believed the Beaucarnot Diary challenged. Thus, I decided to go at it alone, reshaping my idea for the diary and its surrounding essays into an on-going project for use with my undergraduates and selfishly kept Claudie for myself.[16] I developed a rough draft of that vision in early 2005. I spent my spare time exploring the themes, places, and people of the Beaucarnot Diary, while at the same time wrestling with the "history of the slightly implicated." I had no idea where such an exploration would take me.

I had always had good luck in getting in touch with the former residents of Indochina. France is an easy country in which to do research, because the French have dedicated enormous sums of money to preserve their past, with laws codifying public access to records. Each French archive has published guides to its collections, and many can now be found on-line. Privately published guides to French libraries and archives also exist.[17] During my search for former residents of Indochina, if archival or library documents did not contain the names that I needed, and if I could not find additional leads in books dedicated to research in Vietnam,[18] I turned to colonial-era telephone books and tried to trace names back to France. I had scoured the cumulative catalog database of the United States available through most university libraries known as "WorldCat," and I had by then a good knowledge of the Library of Congress cataloging system that powers it. In various instances, I wrote to the publishers of those former residents who had produced books and asked either for their addresses or for the press to forward them a letter from me. Various groups associated with Indochina had published membership lists, copies of which were available in the various archives I visited. Another easy, but somewhat time-consuming method was to look up, from the United States, family names with an French on-line telephone directory once it became available on-line.[19] At times, I have sent two hundred letters in my attempts to find one individual, which may seem like a sort of historical direct-mail advertising, but usually the individuals who did respond were nice and tried to share what they knew.[20]

In the case of the Beaucarnot Diary, I asked the staff of the Archives d'Outre-mer to forward a letter to former resident of Indochina Yvonne Fontaine, who had started the project of collecting the memoirs of the former residents of Indochina for deposit in the archives, hoping that she would then in turn forward the letter on to Ms. Beaucarnot. This took place in December 1999, and I received a response in February 2000 from Ms. Beaucarnot, who was quite pleased to have received a letter inquiring about her diary. She kindly agreed to respond to whatever questions I might have, and expressed her surprise that it was an American who had found her. We began a lively exchange of letters, and I sought university support to travel to France to interview her in person.

The ways in which one presents oneself is essential in this process. I always make sure to send paper letters whenever possible because they imply a level of seriousness and time commitment that electronic communication does not, especially when the people I wish to contact did not grow up using the Internet. I always explain my intentions and goals clearly, and I do not hide my purpose. One line I have always included in all of my letters when requesting information is that I do not intend to "darken the history of France," a phrase I picked up from a form used to request limited-circulation materials in French archives. I do so honestly, because I do not intend to slander purposefully the actions of the French people I study, although readers of my scholarship may later interpret what I write according to their own biases. Indeed, I always try to present myself as an "honest historian," someone who does not judge but merely presents history, although I realize, perhaps with some cynicism, that to this generation, a young, open-faced, bespectacled American may appear both better intentioned and hopelessly naive in comparison with France's admittedly politicized scholars. Likewise, not 'darkening the history of France' also implies a certain pride in France, although one has to ask in this case, which France, and the France of whom? In short, I do my best to enter into a kind of moral contract with the participant and hold up my end of that contract, meaning that I will not simply take from the person with whom I am engaged as a historian but also give back, for better or for worse, the larger history I find out about that person to him or her.

Agreeing tacitly to a kind of moral contract can have its limitations. In my own case, I have succeeded in gaining access to a community to which I would have never had access if I had simply started writing about that community's members in ways that they would see as negative, although they may be popular with contemporary historians. For example, the website I created about the Beaucarnot Diary focuses on presenting the text and illuminating its parts, the act of comparing past with present, and nothing more. Over the course of six years, I have conducted four formal interviews with Ms. Beaucarnot, and each time, she and her daughters have cordially received me into their home as a guest. In addition to the website mentioned above, the questions I posed and answers I received form the basis of many of my papers, as well as those of several undergraduate senior honors theses. This is all plain for Claudie Beaucarnot to see through the website. It has also provided support for work done by my colleagues in their own research. As Claudie and I grew closer intellectually and emotionally, the level of trust between us grew as well, as did both her personal reflection and the depth of familial history that she relayed. This interaction also seems to have had a sort of therapeutic effect for Claudie. One day, in their kitchen, her daughter said to me, "You know David, you've done wonders for Mom. She was so sullen before, but now she is much more lively." Knowing this, I felt even more reluctant to attempt the kind of critical analysis scholars are trained to undertake, and yet I knew that in order to reveal the diary's importance, I had to analyze it critically. I understood that I had a professional responsibility to be critical of the colonial regime—in which Ms. Beaucarnot grew up and whose impact is still felt profoundly and universally. However, personally, I did not want to upset Ms. Beaucarnot because, on the one hand, she had been so nice to me, and on the other, I just did not see how focusing on her personally could produce any profitable analysis.

I questioned myself even more when, after I began to ask questions beyond her range of knowledge, Ms. Beaucarnot introduced me to her friends from Indochina. Many of them began to reveal information about her family, including the discriminated petty prejudices they say she faced, but that she herself had denied experiencing. In meeting her friends, I encountered a whole new set of questions linked to my responsibility when describing her family and the social and political context in which she lived in Indochina. All of these people more or less shared their personal stories with me, and added pieces to the larger puzzle of understanding French Indochina as viewed by French colonialists. As a solution, I decided that, at least for the time being, I could try to reconstruct the social world of Indochina's métis community and promote discussion about collaboration, complicity, and resistance inherent in colonial relationships without bringing Claudie into it. I was simply too close to her to talk about her in such a cold, clinical manner.

The lesson I hope young scholars glean from my experiences is to be careful when preparing oral histories and conducting historical research. One's initial detachment may end up developing into emotional attachment of which one needs to be aware and take into consideration when analyzing the data collected: only your own critical awareness can assist you in making choices about how you present your research, how you acknowledge your own biases when presenting such research, and what choices you make about its analysis and dissemination.

LESSON TWO: BRING SOUND TO SILENCE

During my interviews with colonial Indochina's former residents, a certain recurring phrase caught my attention: "We didn't talk about that when we moved to France." The universal refrain of all those who were repatriated after World War II from Indochina to France, a country some of them had never visited and for whom it may or may not have represented a physical or spiritual home, was that many French from France called them *sales colonialistes* (dirty colonists). Despite the pride they felt with regards to what they had achieved in the colony (in their eyes, turning "virgin" land into productive soil, endowing Vietnam with an infrastructure its people needed but were incapable of providing for themselves, and so on) and the suffering they faced during World War II, they were faced with the fact that no one in France cared about their stories or achievements. In the mounting human, financial, and moral costs of the *sale guerre* (dirty war) fought in Indochina from 1946 to 1954, or the *guerre encore plus sale* (even dirtier war) fought in Algeria, another French colony, from 1956 to 1962, silence rather than seeking recognition or acknowledgement about one's past was often considered the better choice, even between husband and wife.

In the midst of these unexpected revelations and the controversial questions they raised, I quickly learned to think carefully about how these former residents of Indochina saw themselves as political and social actors relative to France's colonial project in Indochina (that is, their *positionality*). To many people born and raised in Indochina, France itself was a place of dirty collective toilets, no hot water and little soap, little fresh fruit, no wilderness, cold weather, political bitterness and division, and, most of all, no possibility for creativity or upward mobility. In contrast, Indochina had the latest technology, with flush toilets and air conditioning, the best food, clean clothes, a bevy of servants, and little strife.

It is important to understand the conditions under which most individuals left Indochina. By the end of 1945, almost all of Indochina's European civilians and military residents had been in the colony since at least mid-1940, and more likely since the mid-1930s. No resupply of any kind had occurred since 1941 because of World War II. With the exception of a few products for which the colonial government had developed a local industry such as vaccines, rubber tires, and steel, no Western medicines, foods, or clothing were available. This had caused some discomfort, but the sheer deprivation imposed by and anxiety caused by the Japanese takeover of the Indochinese administration between March and mid-August 1945 was far worse. After the war, the settler population of Indochina departed while the military population vastly increased. Individuals went to France, regardless of their station of life in Indochina, without their positions, careers, or even educations, since metropolitan French universities did not recognize degrees granted by institutions of higher learning in Indochina (although the French Ministry of Education recognized high school diplomas for white French and a few Vietnamese who had received French citizenship). Thus, in some instances, educated French adults in their mid-twenties had to redo college. They also returned to a France devastated by the war—a country in which real reconstruction did not begin until the arrival of Marshall Plan aid in 1948.

At this juncture, I think it is also important to reflect on the differences of gender in the broader experience of "return." In general, all the men with whom I spoke returned from Indochina to develop or continue to develop professional careers within some branch of the French civil service, e.g. as hospital administrators, senior managers in the French rail company, senior diplomats, and chiefs of the Paris police. Most of the women, however, saw an abrupt stop to a life rich in opportunity and activity. Many had grown up in financial, emotional, and physical environments in Indochina that gave them plenty of opportunity to engage in sports, to love and work in fresh air, and to take leadership roles. They simply had enjoyed a great deal of social freedom. They may have flown airplanes in air clubs, managed plantations, or played on a women's basketball league. In France, they suddenly became housewives or simple employees isolated by social restrictions and a lack of opportunity for women—their stories silenced by the political climate and their ambitions hampered. Thus, for these settlers, I was the ear for which they had longed, into which they could tell their hidden story. It also helped that I am an American, because, for reasons I discussed earlier, the former colonists would not necessarily want to tell these stories to their fellow French. As Alice Kaplan wrote about her experiences, "A French person couldn't go see [the French anti-Semitic writer] Bardèche the way I was going; the visit itself would be a declaration of affinity."[21] As one engages in historical research, one must think carefully of the context from which history will emerge, or what has kept those stories from being told before.

LESSON THREE: MARCH 9, 1945, AND MY AMERICAN IDENTITY

An important part of doing historical research is recognizing not only the perspective the researcher brings to the period under consideration, but also how the history views him or her back. In this case, it is not the researcher's emotional attachment to the subject, or his or her position relative to the subject, but the subject's position relative to the researcher and how he or she views the researcher, which can influence the project's results.

I sat in Mr. Henri Riault's garage on a late spring day, looking through his small collection of unpublished colonial-era memoirs. I had met him through Ms. Beaucarnot, who, during our second set of interviews, referred me to him as someone with all of the answers on Indochina, a statement that proved quite true. A generous man, he seemed excited that someone had expressed an interest in his story. The son of an engineer who had worked in Indochina for over twenty years, Mr. Riault had fond memories of the colony, but he had also been brutally tortured by the Japanese at the end of World War II. Claudie warned me about this fact and I learned very quickly during our first visit not to ask him about his personal experiences, as he could become quite emotional.

During our second visit together, I asked Mr. Riault to show me his collection of published and unpublished memoirs, biographies, and autobiographies. As I flipped through an unpublished diary from the period of March to December 1945, I come across section heading entitled "Arrival of the Americans." I snickered at this, which caused Mr. Riault to turn to me and say with a deadpan expression, "That was the moment of our greatest disappointment." We moved on to examine sketches of Buddhist temples made in the 1890s, and made no further comment on the matter, but there was a slight chill in the air on a hot Spring day. My bemused reaction had not gone unnoticed. It is important to remember that the keepers of historical knowledge can interpret your historical detachment and emotional reflection on a topic they hold dear as, at best, a lack of seriousness or, at worse, an insult or callousness or both.

For years, I had read extensively about the arrival in Indochina of members from the Office of Strategic Services, a special combined civilian and military branch of the United States government dedicated to special or secret operations behind enemy lines during World War II. Eager to promote independent, pro-American governments in Southeast Asia, beginning in 1944 the United States began to use agents of the OSS (Office of Strategic Services) to support Hồ Chí Minh's pro-communist, anti-colonial guerilla forces. The professed nationalism of the group and Hồ's overt pro-American stance at the time went a long way towards encouraging US support. Such support was perhaps rightly perceived as anti-French at all levels of the French government that reclaimed France from the Germans after 1944. Hồ's guerillas, especially its mid-level leadership, indeed made no bones about their desire to remove the French from Indochina as soon as possible, through whatever means necessary. Mr. Riault's double disappointment of seeing Americans not only refusing to support the French but also arming and training the Vietnamese is understandable. At that moment, what I represented to Mr. Riault as an American crystallized for me. In Mr. Riault, I encountered some-one who obviously, within the context of that war, had very real reasons for not appreciating my Americanness or for what I hoped America stood.

In such a context, I could understand Mr. Riault's sensitivities to this subject as well as Claudie's, and those of the many other people with whom I had spoken. Yet, at the same time, each one of them received me cordially *because* I was an American. I was a guest, one both linked to and interested in their history, and perhaps Americans still retain the cachet of goodness with members of a certain generation. I sensed, without ever daring to ask, that, somehow, they saw me as a young American researcher who was more open to their stories and their collec-tive or individual interpretation than their own French scholarly community. I am sure that they expected nothing more from such community than the scorn and disdain they felt upon their return, and the mockery of their lives as they saw it in the "Indo-Chic" movement.

LESSON FOUR: WHERE *IS* THE TREASURE?

In researching history, the historian makes connections between the past and the present that may have been otherwise lost. Not only does history have con-sequences for understanding the past in order to provide lessons for the present, it also affects the production of behaviors in the present for which sometimes nasty precedents exist.[22] It is important to recognize, as the anthropologist Nancy Schepner-Hughes did after completing controversial fieldwork on mental illness in rural Ireland, that no matter how many precautions one takes, the researcher al-ways influences the local space through his or her conclusions. Schepner-Hughes wrote, and it is apt for history as well, that "[b]oth the danger *and the value* of anthropology [and one could read *history* here easily enough] lie in the clash and collision of cultures and interpretations as the anthropologist meets her subjects in a spirit of open engagement, frankness, and receptivity. . . . Anthropology is by na-ture intrusive and it entails a certain amount of symbolic and interpretive violence to the "native" peoples' own intuitive, though still partial, understanding of their part of the world."[23] In most instances, the results of making such connections are benign, but one can imagine that, sometimes, things can simply get out of hand. It is also quite important to think in advance of all the possible results of the history one uncovers, so that one is prepared to face situations that no one may have otherwise fully anticipated. Such was the case with my interviews of Mireille Lepique.

The Beaucarnots and the Lepiques had been close friends from the 1920s until after World War II. Although Claudie Beaucarnot introduced me personally to Ms. Lepique in 2005, we had already exchanged letters. In May 2004, I traveled from Hà Nội to the West of Hòa Binh, the site of the former plantation of the Lepique family. At the end the nineteenth century, Mr. Lepique, Mireille's father, chose to remain in Indochina after several years of service in the colonial military rather than return to France for reassignment, and took out a concession of land from the French colonial government (which eventually grew to eight thousand acres). He began a life of farming, ranching, and dairy production that endured for almost forty years. All went quite well for him and his family until March 9, 1945.

During the late evening of March 9, 1945, and morning of March 10, 1945, the Japanese forces stationed in French colonial Indochina staged a coup de force against the French colonial government, declaring Vietnam independent of colonial rule and under Japanese guidance; they immediately began a process of isolating the French.[24] The Japanese executed hundreds of French soldiers and imprisoned thousands of soldiers and civilians. The details that can explain these events are complex, but it is important to remember that since July 1940, France had been occupied or influenced by Nazi Germany while Imperial Japan had become indirectly allied to France through its mutual alliance with Adolph Hitler's Germany.[25] Thus, when Japan invaded and conquered most of Southeast Asia, the Japanese spared French Indochina from takeover. Instead, Japanese forces allowed the profascist government of the recently installed Governor-General for Indochina, the Admiral Jean Decoux (1884–1963), to continue its rule over Vietnam, Cambodia, and Laos.[26] Yet on March 9, 1945, the Japanese military in Indochina overthrew the French leadership.[27] Besides those French deemed essential to the functioning of the colony's infrastructure, all Europeans were isolated into a few urban centers, such as Hà Nội, Sài Gòn, Vinh, Huế, and Đà Lạt, and left to their own means, moving those Europeans who lived in the countryside to the cities. Everyone recalls this as a frightening and difficult period.

In an interview, Mireille Lepique told me that after March 9, 1945, her family had had some warning of the roundup from Vietnamese friends since the Japanese had taken awhile to send troops out of the major urban centers and into the countryside. They knew that when upon leaving their plantation, either the Japanese or the local population would loot their house. Mr. Lepique decided to bury the family's small collection of jewelry and extra money in the hills and to send his daughters, including Mireille, into temporary hiding. He dispatched into the hills surrounding the plantation a helper with three of his children, a box wrapped in oilskin, and some food and water. The helper and the three Lepique children traveled for many hours, deep into the hills. It was rough going, but soon they were alone. The helper took them to a cave with a narrow entrance, a horizontal slit in the side of a sloping hill that only he would recognize. They slipped into the cave and dropped onto a sandy floor below, hidden from view, where they remained for several days. The helper buried the box in the floor of the cave, where it probably remains to this day. The helper and the children returned to the plantation a few days later, to learn that although the Japanese had visited the plantation without incident, they had to travel to Hà Nội immediately. They would never return again, as shortly thereafter the area became the Vietnamese anti-colonial guerillas' "rear zone."[28]

As a group of Australian geographers have noted, the Vietnamese tendency to prefer "scientific" and prepared inquiries has meant that "questionnaires, surveys, and mapping are often preferred over semi-structured interviews, oral histories, participant observation and participatory research methods."[29] Asking common people for their opinion also clashes with the politics of history in Vietnam. As the historian Patricia Pelley has argued, consultations by communist historians with the larger populace ended there in the 1960s, when the communist historians in North Vietnam wrote a new, politically-acceptable history of Vietnam that became the historical canon for the whole country when the two parts of Vietnam were reunited in 1975.[30] Even today, with Vietnam opening up to the world, the government tightly controls certain aspects of society, especially its politics and representations of its history, which in Vietnam are also inherently political. Someone conducting scholarly research must have a government-linked sponsor who will supply him or her with a research visa. Research in Vietnam implies a certain responsibility to inform one's host of one's intentions and activities. France prepared me well for bureaucratic procedure. In Vietnam, a similar bureaucracy exists, but the results are not guaranteed because of a number of factors seen to a lesser extent in France, such as corruption, dislike of foreigners, and a lack of checks and balances. Sometimes, however, if introductions fail or do not materialize as promised, and believe I am doing something relatively innocuous, I have simply shown up at a locale and asked to meet someone or see something. I have transposed colonial-era maps onto contemporary maps to find the location of French colonial-era buildings and gone to them to see if they still exist, and have asked around to learn if anyone can tell about their past. The researcher, however, has to be careful as this kind of behavior is not recommended. For example, at rail yards outside of Hà Nội, an official asked for my passport, which I knew meant that I might have to "buy" it back from him. Fortunately, the agent's sidekick convinced him that I was just looking around and not doing anything wrong. "Foreigners like steam engines," he said.

I decided that I wanted to visit the Lepique plantation to see what had changed and if I might collect any memories of the Lepique family from the current tenants. My Vietnamese sponsors at that time did not really want me to go; I decided to go anyway. I felt a little like Alice Kaplan, as I knew that the security I enjoyed because of my status as an American, my financial reserves, and my professional status protected me to some degree from real problems (such as imprisonment for simply visiting a public location).[31] Through a friend who accompanied me, I rented an automobile and the services of a driver and traveled into the picturesque, hilly countryside in which the plantation had been located. The town with which it had been associated had grown for sure, but it didn't seem that things had changed all that much when compared to maps I had seen. Fields were green with rice instead of grass for cattle, and hills edged with apricot trees instead of coffee. It was a poor town but not destitute, with shops and houses lining each side of the district road, a garrison, and a sparkling new Communist Party headquarters. At the intersection of the road to the former plantation, we stopped at a kind of convenience store that sold fresh fruit, cold drinks, and other sundries, before asking around. Now, a foreigner, especially a big, hairy, perspiring one like myself in a small Vietnamese town in the former "rear zone" of the anti-colonial resistance, will certainly invite a great deal of attention. Soon we had lots of new friends milling around, asking who I was, pulling my arm hair, smiling, and so on. They seemed curious, but not suspicious. The idea was to move quickly, however, before the police found out we were there.

My friend found that the person who owned the part of the land on which the plantation was located lived across the street from the roadside store where we had stopped. We went to visit him, and I explained that I was a historian who had met the daughter of the former French owner of the land, and that I was writing a history for the family (not quite true, but genealogies make sense to the Vietnamese). The man said his family had been given land from the center of the plantation after the war, and much of the foundation and first floor of the house had survived. They only grew rice now as opposed to coffee as the Lepiques had done. The man said that Mr. Lepique was remembered favorably in the town and area, and that one of his sons had visited a few years ago to leave some money for the preservation of graves on the property, which the man said he had done. I had only rarely heard a Vietnamese person say anything favorably about a French colonist before, so these comments intrigued me.

It was agreed that it was probably better for me not to go to the property itself but that my friend would go and at least take some photos. I had a Coke* in the broiling sun and kicked a ball around with some giggling kids. A woman came up and said that the police were on their way, and that it was a good time to go. At that point, I really started to sweat but fortunately my friend and the current landlord soon returned, after taking a few hasty photos. I didn't relish the negotiating process of having to buy my passport back from the police ("Five thousand dollars! Okay, one hundred dollars! You are lucky today, my friend, forty dollars . . . let me buy you a beer so we can all laugh about it and leave as friends."). It would have been my fault in creating the opportunity for graft. We were going to get back in the car when the landlord asked me quietly, "Where is the treasure? Where is the gold?" My friend looked at me curiously as I looked at the man, and said that I honestly didn't know there was a treasure. The Lepiques had put everything into their plantation. The gold was the house, the ripped out coffee trees, and the mill, all of which were gone. The man looked at me quite hard, and then said he hoped we would come back when we could all go visit together, but that now was not the right time.

Why not tell the man about the shoe-shaped slit a full day's walk to the west? Was there any good in leaving an oilskin-wrapped box with some jewelry and now-mottled piastres in it buried in a cave? It was just the man, my friend, the driver, the woman fanning herself while pretending not to listen, some kids kicking a ball at my feet, and me. But, I knew my history; I knew the context that was important on this particular day.

The situation recalled the gold rush in nearby Nghệ An province in 1985, and it was clear to me what I had to do.[32] By 1985, the economic situation had improved in Vietnam since bottoming out in 1981, but the exigencies imposed by Vietnam's ongoing occupation of Cambodia and an enduring U.S. embargo plagued the country. Word of the gold had spread like wildfire. This was particularly true in Nghệ An province, which had suffered heavily during the 1964–1975 war, and even more as Chinese aid dried up and Soviet aid was heavily reduced. Tens of thousands of people suddenly tramped their way deep into the forested, elephant-filled mountains of western Nghệ An province to pan and dig for gold. This was illegal in several ways, as at the time travel of any sort required a permit, and access to border areas was strictly controlled. Although little is known and less said, hundreds died of disease, violence, and despair in search for gold. Already poor, most prospectors ended up with nothing, stranded in humid forests with improper equipment and little food. Conflicts arose between officials who told people to go home, and those desperate for gold. Some people had brought leftover weapons from the war with them in order to defend their claims. The government eventually deployed the army against the prospectors in order to eject them; soldiers and miners died in open battles using automatic weapons against one another, over nothing more than a few traces of gold in the cold waters and mud of the forested mountains of western Nghệ An.

Imagine what would have happened if, as I closed the door to the car and rolled down the window, I had told the landlord, "There's a box with some old bills and some jewelry in a shoe-shaped cave a day's walk to the west." He might think about going to look for it someday. But the kid with whom I had played a little soccer would run home and tell his parents, and the woman who had been eavesdropping would tell her brother, and soon all of Hoa Binh province would know and go tramping off to look for the cave. Maybe the police would arrest Mr. Landlord for talking with a foreigner. Somebody might slip on a rock and fall, hurting him- or herself. Some kid might step on an unexploded bomblet and die. A lot of people could get bent out of shape over what could become - like a giant game of telegraph where one giggling child tries to pass a secret ear-to-ear down a line to other giggling children, and the message changes completely by the end - two steamer trunks *full* of gold bars and precious jewelry, along with some weapons and, curiously, an old clock.

Instead, I said nothing and slumped in the seat as we drove forward into the town, to take another route back to Hà Nội. Everything was cool and the cops passed us by. I am sure, Mr. Landlord tells them, the foreigner was looking for the local hot springs. Okay, the police will say to him, no problem, it's just like crazy foreigners to be out driving around on such a *hot* day looking for *hot* springs.

History is not about finding The Truth, as most of us know, but about trying to describe a situation or people truthfully. Sometimes it's better not to tell the whole truth, because the truth can hurt. Was his father a concentration camp guard? Did he take drugs then? I don't know where the treasure is, and neither do you. No one ever will. This story is completely made up, really. The lesson is that history has consequences, and historians sometimes become the bearers of special knowledge. An old axiom is that those who do not know their history are doomed to repeat it. Perhaps a corollary of that axiom is that it is important for historians not to doom others to repeat the histories about which they have learned.

Conclusion

The Beaucarnot Diary was a privilege to find and I believe that bringing it to the public was a good and successful endeavor. Presently, my efforts concentrate on continuing to reconstruct and connect Indochina's métis community to the larger Vietnamese society in French Indochina. Unfortunately, some of my informants have passed on since I met them, and I feel an enormous burden to represent them fairly and conscientiously. I hope that the lessons I learned in meeting them will carry me forward to introspective conclusions of which they might be proud, even if they might not entirely agree with them. This is the most I can do for now.

NOTES

1   Unlike historians, anthropologists have spent much time agonizing over the responsibilities of their research, and they have even gone so far as to reflect on their own reflections! Lane Ryo Hirabayashi provides an interesting reflection on the fieldwork of Dr. Tamie Tsuchiyama in the Posten internment camp for Japanese Americans during World War II. See Lane Ryo Hirabayashi, *The Politics of Fieldwork: Research in an American Concentration Camp* (Tucson: The University of Arizona Press, 1999) and Gesa Kirsch and Liz Rohan, *Beyond the Archives: Stories About Research as a Lived Process* (Carbondale: University of Southern Illinois Press, 2008).

2   This "story within a story" originates from France's occupation and administration of what is now Vietnam, Cambodia and Laos as a colony known as French Indochina between 1858 and 1954.

3   See the various publications of the "Research Division" of the American Historical Association at http://www.historians.org/governance/rd/index.cfm. The organization to which many historians of the United States belong, the Organization of American Historians, has similar approaches described in articles such as "Historians and Archivists: Educating the Next Generation" available at http://www.oah.org/pubs/archivists/historiansandarchivists. pdf.

4   Among others, see the guidelines of the oral History Association at http:// omega.dickinson.edu/organizations/oha/pub_eg.html. The American Anthropological Association has a special publication on ethics available at http://www.aaanet.org/committees/ethics/toc.htm.

5   For forty years (1932–1972), public health researchers followed 399 poor
     African-Americans in rural Alabama who had contracted syphilis, but did
     nothing to inform them about or treat their worsening condition. See, among
     other excellent texts, James H. Jones, *Bad Blood: The Tuskegee Syphilis Experi-
     ment*, Revised Edition (New York: Free Press, 1993).
6   George Orwell, *1984* (New York: Everyman's Library/Alfred A. Knopf, 1949,
     1992), 260.
7   The opposite approach is "presentist" in which a scholar examines history
     from the perspective of today. For example, some scholars judge how men
     treated women in the past from the standards of today.
8   In 1954, after negotiations in Geneva ended French sovereignty in Vietnam,
     the northern half of what is now Vietnam came under the control of the Com-
     munist Party of Vietnam, and the Party's leadership embarked on a program
     of building a socialist planned economy, that is, where the state manages most
     of the large enterprises and industries and coordinates the activities of agri-
     culture through collective farming (as opposed to individuals farming their
     own land the produce of which farmers sell themselves on an open market).
     A mixed market and planned economy continued, with significant modifica-
     tion during the war years of 1964–1975, until 1977. In 1977, with Southern
     Vietnam reunified with the North into the Socialist Republic of Vietnam,
     the Communist government of Vietnam attempted to intensify state plan-
     ning and control of industry, commerce, and agriculture, with disastrous re-
     sults. Food production plummeted. Combined with the costs of an invasion
     and occupation of Cambodia that began in late 1978, a short war with China
     in 1979, and an embargo of trade promoted by the United States, Vietnam's
     economy imploded, resulting in true famine in the center and north of the
     country in 1981. Severe political oppression accompanied socialism and
     hardened over time, where even speaking with a foreigner could invite arrest
     and punishment. In 1986, the hard-line communist prime minister Lê Duẩn
     passed away, and his supporters within the Party lost power, giving room for
     those who sought reform the opportunity to advance the Đổi Mới program,
     through which farmers were more fully freed to farm what they wanted to
     farm and sell their product on the open market, state enterprises allowed to
     close, and foreign investment invited. As a consequence, Vietnam's economy
     has boomed, and individual freedoms have greatly expanded (although the
     country remains a one party state).
9   The Communist Party of Vietnam—in essence Vietnam's government be-
     cause no other viable political party is allowed to exist—remains quite protec-
     tive of the stories and myths it has constructed about itself, the relationship of
     the Party to the Vietnamese people, and the resistance to foreign occupation
     by the Vietnamese. For example, Vietnamese histories present the period of
     French colonial occupation as one of unmitigated oppression and misery. The
     story of complicity, collaboration, and resistance is much more complicated,
     of course, but a Manichean (good vs. evil) view has served the Party well in
     justifying itself and its own actions. Thus, while researchers may request ma-

terials in the archives, the archivists censor anything that may be perceived as threatening to the national story.

10 Régis Wargnier, "Indochine," 1992 and Jean-Jacques Annaud, "L' Amant," 1992.

11 Claudie Beaucarnot, *Diary*, March 1990, 1943.

12 At the time, my vision of mixed-race colonial subjects was limited to derogatory presentations of them in George Orwell's *Burmese Days* and its obsequious, semi-literate, and marginalized Eurasian characters Samuel and Francis. George Orwell, *Burmese Days* (New York: Harvest, 1934).

13 David W. Del Testa, "'Paint the Trains Red:' Labor, Nationalism, and the Railroads in French Colonial Indochina, 1898–1945" (PhD diss., University of California, 2001).

14 There are very few accessible primary sources from which an instructor might present to undergraduates in order to give personal insights into French Indochina. One example, Trần Tử Bình's *The Red Earth*, offers such insight, but there are no similar sources to balance it against. See Trần Tử Bình, David G. Marr, and Ha An, *The Red Earth: A Vietnamese Memoir of Life on a Colonial Rubber Plantation*, vol. 66, Monographs in International Studies, Southeast Asia Series (Athens, Ohio: Ohio University, Center for International Studies, Center for Southeast Asian Studies, 1985).

15 Because the diary was filed in a public portion of the archive, meaning its author or the author's agent, such as a child or lawyer, had deposited the diary as part of a larger public record, I knew that we could publish some of its sections without the author's permission. Still, I could make a good-faith effort and try to find Claudie Beaucarnot, to ask if we could reproduce longer sections. If the Diary had been a part of private collection of documents retained at the archives for controlled consultation, requiring the perhaps onerous permission of the main archivist, a government agency, or the people who deposited the documents, continuing such work would have been much more difficult, as access and reproduction of such materials would be more tightly controlled.

16 I had students translate the diary as a student project, and students have used the themes in the Diary as a basis for student research projects. See the web site dedicated their work at www.bucknell.edu/Beaucarnot/.

17 See, for example, http://archiveswiki.historians.org/index.php/Main_Page and Erwin K. Welsch, *Archives and Libraries in France*, with 1991 Supplement (New York: Council for European Studies, 1979/1991).

18 For examples of these guides in English and French, see Chantal Descours-Gatin et al., *Guide de recherches sur Le Vietnam: Bibliographies, archives et bibliothèques de France* (Paris: Éditions L'Harmattan, 1983) and Denis Gazquez avec la collaboration d'Agathe Larcher-Goscha, *Publications officielles de L'Indochine coloniale: Inventaire analytique (1859–1954)* (Paris: Bibliothèque nationale de France, 2004), *Commission française du Guide des sources de l'histoire des nations, sources de l'histoire de l'asie et de l'océanie dans les archives*

et bibliothèques françaises, 2 vols. (New York/Detroit: K.G. Saur; Distributed by Gale Research Co., 1981).

19 www.pagesjaunes.fr/pb.cgi.

20 Sometimes one gets involved in family romances. Once, when looking for the particular daughter of a prominent métisse family, I received an email response to my letter from a teenager. This young woman begged me not to tell her parents that she was writing to me, but she wanted to let me know that there was a rumor of someone who had gone to Indochina and married a local person. I eventually connected this young woman to a French colonial forestry official who abandoned his Vietnamese wife when his tour of service was up sometime in World War I.

21 Alice Kaplan, *French Lessons: A Memoir* (Chicago: University of Chicago Press, 1993), 189.

22 The German director Michael Verhoeven's 1990 film "Nasty Girl," a fictionalized account of an actual young woman researching her town's history during World War II, provides a good if quirky illustration of the potential consequences of researching sensitive and not so sensitive parts of the past.

23 Nancy Scheper-Hughes, "Ire in Ireland," in *Ethnographic Fieldwork: An Anthropological Reader*, ed. Antonius C.G.M. Robben and Jeffrey A. Sluka, Series Blackwell Anthologies in Social and Cultural Anthropology (Malden, MA: Blackwell Publishing, 2007), 208.

24 There are several autobiographies that address this period. Jean-Jacques Maitam, the son of a wealthy merchant and official in the French internal security bureau, and himself a Hà Nội police detective and diplomat, addresses his imprisonment with the Japanese. See Jean-Jacques Maitam, *A House Divided (Viet Nam)* (Greensboro, NC: Tudor Books, 2002). Mandalay Perkins recounts, romantically, the biography her stepfather, Michel L'Herpinière, and his imprisonment. See Mandaley Perkins, Hà Nội, *Adieu: A Bittersweet Memoir of French Indochina* (London: Fourth Estate, 2005).

25 Perspectives on this event are now multiple, fortunately. For a French perspective, see Philippe Grandjean, L'Indochine face au Japon: 1940–1945: Decoux-De Gaulle, Un malentendu fatal (Paris: Éditions Harmattan, 2004). For a recent American scholarly perspective, see Mark Atwood Lawrence, *Assuming the Burden: Europe and the American Commitment to the War in Vietnam*, ed. Fredrik and Christopher E. Goscha, Series From Indochina to Vietnam: Revolution and War in a Global Perspective (Berkeley: University of California Press, 2005).

26 Jean Decoux, *À la barre de L'Indochine: Histoire de mon gouvernement général (1940–1945)* (Paris: Plon, 1949).

27 Eric Jennings, *Vichy in the Tropics: Petain's National Revolution in Madagascar, Guadeloupe, and Indochina, 1940–1944* (Stanford: Stanford University Press, 2004).

28 Andrew Hardy, an Australian anthropologist, has a particularly good discussion of the process of research on colonialism in his book *Red Hills*. See An-

drew Hardy, *Red Hills: Migrants and the State in the Highlands of Vietnam* (Honolulu, Hawaii: University of Hawaii Press, 2003), especially the first fifty pages of the book.

29 Steffanie Scott, Fiona Miller, and Kate Lloyd, "Doing Fieldwork in Development Geography: Research Culture and Research Spaces in Vietnam," *Geographical Research* 44, no. 1 (2006): 31. This article provides one of the few reflections on doing fieldwork in Vietnam, and while I agree with its many observations and cannot know the precise experiences of the article's authors, I do feel that they expected a system that resembled their own and became grumpy when it wasn't that way.

30 Patricia Pelley, *Postcolonial Vietnam: New Histories of the National Past*, John Hope Franklin Center Book (Raleigh/Durham: Duke University Press, 2003), 25–26.

31 Kaplan writes of her new position as a professor conducting research as opposed to a graduate student: "This network [of friends, apartments newly acquired], the security of a salary, and the means to travel made me start to think of France as a living library, an enormous proving ground for my thesis." Kaplan, *French Lessons: A Memoir*, 186.

32 http://www.huynhtieuhuong.org/eng/about-hth.html.

CHAPTER TWO

From National Parks to National Archives: The Diplomacy of Research in Latin America

BY MARK CAREY

Yale University has finally agreed to return Inca artifacts that Hiram Bingham extracted from Peru nearly a century ago.[1] Bingham, a Yale professor, worked in Peru from 1911 to 1915, climbing mountains, looking for archaeological artifacts, and then locating the famously impressive Inca ruins of Machu Picchu, recently voted one of the world's Seven Wonders.[2] Bingham opened this Inca sanctuary to scientists and tourists worldwide—a triumph for science, tourism, and, more recently, the Peruvian economy. But Peruvian scholars, attorneys, and government officials see it differently. They have spent much of the last century arguing with Yale to secure the return of the five thousand artifacts they believe Bingham extracted unjustly. To Luís Valcárcel, a Peruvian intellectual involved with Bingham's field research in the 1910s, the control of Inca and other indigenous artifacts—and their retention within Peru—embodied not just a fight for museum exhibits. Possession of the artifacts also represented Peru's autonomy, its independence, and its right to its own resources, as well as Peruvians' power to write their own history. Critical emblems of Peruvian history and culture should reside in Peruvian hands, not North Americans.' As a Peruvian National Institute of Culture official recently pointed out, "What if Peru had George Washington's things? We would have to return them. They would mean something to the United States, not Peru."[3] To control research materials and data, then, is to exercise national sovereignty and to determine not only the past but also the future.[4]

The Bingham-Yale-Peru case illuminates pertinent issues for any scholar conducting research in a foreign country, especially U.S. and European scholars working in the developing world. Bingham may have conducted research nearly a century ago, but the contest over data, artifacts, and the right to write a country's history remain potent issues in the twenty-first century. In many regards, foreign researchers consume intellectual property, ethnographic information, and cultural relics just as eco-tourists consume Costa Rican national parks, or as mining companies exploit Chilean copper, or as pharmaceutical companies extract Brazilian medicinal plants (and the indigenous knowledge about those plants). In fact, many scholars continue to question whether it is even possible for North American or

European researchers to study Latin America without perpetuating the imperial gaze and "without replicating imperial practices."[5] But should we throw up our arms and abandon research in order to avoid these potential pitfalls of research abroad? No. Living in a vacuum would be worse. Instead we can implement strategies to avoid the Bingham model. While graduate students and professional scholars might construe their presence as more innocuous than those of Merck or even the camera-toting tourist on a rainforest canopy tour, these students and scholars must nevertheless take great care to avoid the extractive nature of research exemplified by the Hiram Bingham or Indiana Jones approach.

To minimize the imperialistic extraction of data and to conduct research as responsibly as possible, North American and European scholars researching abroad should adhere to a few critical guidelines: engage researchers within the country; collaborate with locals and research subjects during the investigation; and share research results in the field site and throughout the country. Following these research guidelines serve two purposes. First, it helps alleviate the Bingham problem by proceeding in a way that ensures local, regional, and national participation and shared control over the research agenda. Second, it ultimately facilitates information gathering and thus enhances and enriches the research outcome.

In short, effective, successful, and non-exploitative research requires *diplomacy*. Forming personal relationships, engaging with local and regional scholars, discussing research and scholarly approaches, exercising tact and cultural awareness, and showing respect for research subjects comprise the basic elements of what I call "research diplomacy." My own experiences conducting research in Nicaragua and Peru have helped me understand the need for and benefits of diplomacy during research. I learned several lessons while researching Nicaragua's Mayangna Indians in the late 1990s that I subsequently applied to my research approach and methods in the Peruvian Andes. For me, successful research has hinged on my ability to perform not only as a professional historian, but also as a diplomat—a researcher who builds transnational connections, fosters collaborative research, and thus minimizes the imperial nature of my research embedded in my identity as a U.S. citizen.

LEARNING RESEARCH LESSONS IN NICARAGUA

I had been warned even before the six-hour trip by dugout canoe into Central America's largest tract of tropical forest that, upon arrival in the Mayangna indigenous community, I should report promptly to the mayor. I had been studying Nicaragua's Mayangna Indians for more than a year when I arrived in the village in 1997, so I understood the issue: before conducting any interviews or recording any oral histories, I would first need the mayor's endorsement. As an environmental historian, I was examining the complex interactions of Mayangna land use practices, indigenous land rights, international conservation agendas, and the expanding agricultural frontier into eastern Nicaragua.[6] I was interested specifically in understanding the Mayangna's historical relationship with the area that in 1991 became a national protected area, the BOSAWAS Natural Resource Reserve. Environmental history offered an ideal way to investigate these past (and present) human-environment interactions. The field strives to uncover the role of climate, ecology, geology, biology, and other non-human forces in human history; it also reveals how societies thought about, used, managed, sold, fought over, and even invented "nature."[7] By the late 1990s, the field had also uncovered important new ways of thinking about relations between indigenous people and nature preserves. On the one hand, historians showed that indigenous people should not be romanticized as living in ecological harmony with land and natural resources because that view runs the risk of denying their historical agency.[8] On the other hand, scholars also revealed that conservation had historically been embedded in imperialist, even racist agendas that often displaced indigenous people from their homelands to set aside playgrounds for white, middle class urban residents from the industrialized countries of the North.[9] As such, environmental history offered important historiographical insights to my study on the Mayangnas in BOSAWAS.

Environmental history was also useful methodologically because it is uniquely interdisciplinary, requiring not only a mastering of history and natural sciences but also relying on a wide range of sources and data. Environmental historians often delve into untapped archives, read past scientific or engineering reports that scholars from the humanities have never analyzed, and generally proceed through research following quite different paths than many other historians. These research strategies would help illuminate Mayangna history. But gaining access to untapped data is both exciting and daunting. It is always complicated and frequently requires more research diplomacy than the scholars who mine more standard archives, libraries, and document repositories.

In Nicaragua, these challenges of doing environmental history affected my research from the outset. When I ventured by dugout canoe into the BOSAWAS Reserve in 1997, I was seeking more clarity about whether late-twentieth-century conservation agendas would help protect Mayangna autonomy by securing their rights to land inside BOSAWAS or if the policies would erode Mayangna autonomy by transferring control of the land from indigenous residents to the national government or to foreign-dominated conservation interests. Research suggested that it was critical for Mayangnas to retain their right to the land through the granting of formal land titles, which the government had promised but not delivered. Land, autonomy, and control over indigenous information were thus vital concerns for the Mayangna.[10]

Beyond archival and library research, I did not want to miss the opportunity to interview residents of local communities within the nature reserve. Their historical perspectives, their histories, and their beliefs about the natural world were crucial not only for my individual research interests, but also for evaluating the effects of government policies related to indigenous land rights, nature reserve boundaries, poverty, ranching, timber extraction, and other issues in Nicaragua. After flying on a small Cesna plane from Managua to Siuna, the plane circled over the town to alert residents that they needed to clear cattle and children from the landing strip, which doubled not only as a runway but also as a road, marketplace, pasture, and playground. Once on the ground, I spent a week discussing my research with

BOSAWAS officials. They helped arrange my trip into the nature reserve where I would interview residents in various Mayangna communities.

By the time I arrived in the first indigenous community, I had done enough research to know Mayangnas were "isolationists." They lived a half-day hike from the closest roads and had no electricity. Many explained that they preferred the isolation to preserve their land and way of life, though most went regularly to towns for supplies, education, or short-term work. I had first visited a Mayangna community in 1995, when I went as a journalist from Costa Rica's *Mesoamerica* news report and was directed by my brother, who was a Peace Corps volunteer in Siuna. Returning two years later for thesis research, I was much more aware of Mayangna history and understood their isolationist past. But I did not think a graduate student compared with a seventeenth century Spanish missionary, who Mayangna groups had attacked and repelled in that region, or with Johnny Shols, who collected a gold nugget in the region in the 1880s and triggered both the arrival of U.S. mining companies and the creation of the PisPis Mining District comprising the towns of Siuna, Rosita, and Bonanza. I even believed my research was more benign than that of conservationists arriving first during the 1970s to create Saslaya National Park and later to establish the BOSAWAS Reserve. Despite my own rationalization, I was still an outsider to Mayangnas. And the mayor, who I met with promptly after arriving, did not necessarily see the difference between me and those other foreigners from previous decades and centuries. In fact, he initially startled me by quickly cutting to his most pressing concern. As he saw it, I would compile information in his village, then take it to the United States where I would use the data to publish articles (in English, which would never arrive in Nicaragua), advance my career, and potentially gain fame. "What do Mayangna people and my community get out of this?" he asked with polite apprehension. He clearly recognized the potential for research to go the way of Hiram Bingham's. As we sat on the riverbank behind the Moravian Church, I explained that in addition to my own research I had two other goals. First, I hoped my research could be used to illuminate historical context for contemporary discussions about Mayangna land rights; their history was not widely known even to professional historians and anthropologists. Second, I was working with both Nicaraguan research institutes, mainly the Research and Documentation Center of the Atlantic Coast (CIDCA), and with conservation NGOs in Managua. All of these organizations worked closely with Mayangna and Miskitu communities in the region. The mayor accepted my explanation and I began to collect oral histories over the next week.

As I researched, I also showed my interest in the community, demonstrating that I was not solely interested in the extraction of material from them. I played soccer with everyone on Sundays, when they chased the pigs off the field and refastened the bamboo goalposts. I could not entirely fit in, of course: I was a good foot taller than the next tallest player and they all broke out laughing when I won every head ball. But they appreciated my playing, chided me for scoring goals, and enjoyed my participating in their own customs and activities. I also took photographs of families, of a guitar player, of the iguana caught for a soup, and of the community leaders posing in front of their newest building. I had to go to Managua, two days away, to develop the photographs in this era before digital photographs became widespread. I then sent photographs back to the community so they could have what for some were the only pictures they had of themselves. Effective research required these friendly community interactions as well as a reciprocal exchange rather than a one-way extraction of data.

Back in Managua, I encountered a different set of challenges, many of which turned into formidable obstacles. Technically, a letter of presentation written on official stationary—typically from the researchers' university and signed by a department head or graduate school mentor—is enough to initiate archive access in Latin America. Different archives and libraries have various other entry requirements, such as fees, passport-sized photographs, photocopies of passports, laptop and digital camera registration, and even payment for the electricity used by a laptop in Peru's National Library. But in Nicaragua, I encountered a whole range of "invisible" requirements as well. The national archive, for example, was difficult to access due to holiday closures or the "restricted" collections. In one division of the national archive an archivist implied that I needed to contribute financially to see some materials. When I replied that I could not, I suddenly discovered that only a few published materials were available. At a periodicals archive, the director told me that my entrance would require the creation of an agreement (*convenio*) between my university and his archive. When I explained that I was a Fulbright Scholar with no university affiliation, and that the U.S. embassy overseeing the Fulbright program would likely not formalize an agreement or commit to financial support, I quickly learned that the archive was "too disorganized" for me to use. Public libraries proved significantly more accessible than archives. But for historians, unpublished materials in archives usually offer the most important resources and the best data. My research suffered. I suffered. At the time, I simply did not recognize that I had to be a diplomat at every stage and in every aspect of the research process—whether in the national park, the indigenous community, or the national archive.

In the end, my scholarship would have been stronger if I had understood what those Nicaraguan archivists were actually saying when they said that "no," I could not enter the archive because it was closed, too disorganized, or under-funded. I suspect that "no" often did not mean no; rather, "no" was likely a delay tactic or some other diversion. I now understand that, for archivists in many areas of Latin America, "no access" often means "no, not today." Or it can mean "come back and talk again so that I know you're serious." A "no" may convey, usually accurately, that the archivist is overworked, without adequate resources to do his/her job, or less inclined to help a foreigner than complete the boss' assignments. With perseverance, with effort to understand archivists' positions, and, like in the Mayangna community, with a demonstration of how research can help the archive and the country, then archivists might be persuaded to open more doors. Officially or unofficially, access to archives in Latin America is often a privilege, not a right.

My lessons negotiating Nicaraguan archives were numerous: perseverance in entering, compassion for the archivists, building trust with the archivists, providing documentation to prove my status as a serious researcher, and giving names of well-known national scholars whom I had met to demonstrate that I was known locally. Obviously, the actual carrying out of historical research—that is, the analysis of documents—depended on first overcoming a host of other research challenges that involved locating and seeing the documents in the first place. These challenges associated with the access to data are the ones we rarely, if ever, learn about in graduate school.

At the culmination of my year of research in Nicaragua, I presented a lecture at the Central American University, where I learned yet another valuable lesson about the diplomacy of research abroad. At the conclusion of my lecture, a member of the audience rose to ask the first question. "I disagree with everything you have said," he charged. "You cannot understand Mayangna history because you do not speak our Mayangna language." Initially surprised, I grew even more perplexed when this audience member, a Mayangna Indian, explained his position. He reiterated my precise arguments about the historical link between land and indigenous rights, as well as the need to secure rights for Mayangna Indians inhabiting the BOSAWAS Reserve. If he agreed with my interpretations, I wondered, why was he so adamantly opposed to me and my lecture? In hindsight, I realized the true reason for his critique: he was frustrated not with what I had said, but rather with the way he perceived my research. Because I had not worked closely with *his* Mayangna community in eastern Nicaragua or with the Mayangna intellectuals in Managua, of which he was a part, he saw me as an outsider. Worse, he believed that I, a North American gringo historian, was writing his and his people's history—and he did not even know me. I had followed the appropriate channels to secure research clearance and support in the communities where I conducted field work, but I remained unknown to this critic at my lecture. Though impossible to meet every person during research, the critic reinforced the importance of diplomacy and outreach during the research process and of engaging the present-day intellectuals among those groups we study. I now recognize that my response to my critic's "question" should not have focused on Mayangna history or on my research results, as I explained it to him at the time. Rather, I should have instead provided a detailed explanation of my research *process*, including my résumé of personal connections, Mayangna contacts, and alliances in the indigenous communities where I had conducted research.

When I left Nicaragua, I took several key research lessons with me. Most importantly, what I previously believed to be the primary components of historical research—archival research and oral histories—turned out to be incomplete because they fail to detail how the historian finds those materials in the first place. Further, the emphasis on data analysis lacks the crucial personal interactions necessary for successful research abroad, especially indigenous history. Scholars produce better scholarship, with more relevant results, if they engage people both within and beyond the archive. This diplomacy also helps avoid the one-way extraction of data without tangible benefits for the study site.

APPLYING THE LESSONS IN PERU

Research diplomacy must be carried out before, during, and after research. When I embarked on my next major research project in 2001, the doctoral dissertation in history, I applied lessons learned from Nicaragua. My research goal was to examine Peruvian environmental history, and specifically I wanted to study the societal aspects of past climate change and water use in the Andes. I had learned in Nicaragua, however, to leave the topic someone open-ended before initiating field research abroad. The relatively moldable topic was easy because I was at an early stage of research; I was still in the first years of my PhD studies so this trip to Peru truly was an exploratory trip—something I would recommend strongly for all first and second year graduate students. I remained convinced that the most relevant, grounded, and important research topic would be one that did not emerge entirely from the French theorists or U.S. historians I was grappling with in graduate seminars. Those were of course vital. But I needed to follow my own interests as well, and I was determined to develop a topic that Peruvians cared about. I did not want to repeat my Nicaragua experience where I arrived with research questions already set.

My objectives for initial research thus centered on having conversations with Peruvians to achieve two goals. First, I sought their understandings of the most pressing environmental issues in contemporary and historical Peru. Second, I solicited feedback on my research ideas to determine whether my interests in climate and water were relevant to them. Before arriving in Lima, I had collected contacts from colleagues and U.S. researchers, accumulated Peruvian scholars' names from the published literature, and searched the Internet for relevant NGOs. Once in Peru, I followed through with those contacts, and increasingly made new ones. I talked with professors and graduate students, spoke with people after lectures, visited NGOs, met scientists and government officials, and spoke with archivists and librarians at the various repositories I combed for published and unpublished data. I even tried to engage non-professionals, such as taxi drivers running red lights, hotel and store owners scouring for change for hundred Nuevo Soles, and passengers sitting next to me on cramped busses swerving through rush hour traffic. Affiliation with an NGO provided additional contacts in rural *campesino* communities, giving me a way to meet with leaders and community members without arriving as a completely unknown outsider.

As I followed every lead and spoke with dozens of people—all with the goal of building a network and refining my research topic—I accomplished several objectives beyond topic selection. For example, I learned to navigate Lima's impossibly expansive layout, I practiced and thus improved my Spanish by talking with so many people, I cultivated new friendships, and I developed professional contacts, including some with archivists who later opened their doors and with scholars who subsequently supported my affiliation with their institutions. Some eager researchers might view my initial two months in Peru, in which I did little archival research but met dozens of people, as a waste of time or a distraction from the key to historical scholarship, archival research. I view it as just the opposite: these invaluable two months paved the way for more rapid, efficient, successful, and relevant research when I returned for major dissertation research. What's more, my final dissertation—and the subsequent book manuscript—emerged with significant input from Peruvians.[11]

By the time I left Peru after those two months, I had narrowed my research topic to a unique angle on an important issue in Peru and elsewhere: the historical effects of melting glaciers on nearby societies, especially those adjacent to Huascarán National Park and the Cordillera Blanca mountains. As a former park ranger at Mountain Rainier and Glacier National Parks in the United States, I knew a lot about glaciers. But until I spent time in the Andes and learned about the importance of Peru's more than three thousand glaciers as water sources, I never saw how I could integrate glacial ice into human history. A conversation over coffee with a Peruvian environmentalist from Cuzco—one of those key meetings—led me to this topic. Then, as I visited the Cordillera Blanca, the country's most glaciated mountain range with approximately six hundred glaciers, I also learned through interviews and contacts that melting glaciers had unleashed several cataclysmic outburst floods and avalanches since the 1930s.[12] Nearly thirty thousand people had died in this valley from melting glaciers, a process driven largely by global climate change. Further, as glaciers melted many different groups, including local farmers, industrial irrigators, government agencies, and international hydroelectric companies, worried about the loss of water stored in the Andes. After two months of following leads and meeting with Peruvians, I had developed a dissertation topic that fulfilled several criteria: first, it examined Peruvians' struggles with natural disasters, climate change, and water resources—key issues both past and present; second, it merged my interests in glaciers, water, and environmental history in the Andes; and, third, it contributed to the nascent field of Latin American environmental history and brought a fresh approach that linked environmental history with the history of science and technology. I would examine how Peruvians struggled with and overcame the natural disasters from melting glaciers, the science and technology involved in those processes, the economic obstacles different entities faced, the power struggles among affected social groups, and the efforts of a country and its peoples to live with—or die from—global climate change during the past several decades.[13] Without my exploratory research trip that involved dozens of interviews with Peruvians, I may never have settled on this topic.

But effective topic selection is only part of the research process. To avoid an extractive research process and outcome, I needed to learn how best to study and then share results with Peruvians. Securing Institutional Review Board (IRB) permission for research with human subjects, or as many prefer, research participants, also helped ensure that my research would not be exploitative or dangerous to Peruvians. Historians in the United States have been arguing with the federal Office for Human Research Protections for more than a decade to make oral history exempt from IRB approval.[14] Most historians believe that oral history methods and approaches are distinct from those of the biomedical and behavioral sciences, where concern about human subjects research originated. Historians maintain that IRBs unfairly scrutinize oral history and historians because members of these overseeing boards are usually not historians or familiar with the field's objectives and methods. Approval from IRBs, many historians contend, thus endangers historical research.

Cumbersome as the process of IRB approval might be—and it was—I found the process helpful for conducting research abroad because it made me much more aware of potential risks imposed on research participants. Institutional Review Boards are worried about how research could affect people in the study site, and I learned more about this through the IRB approval process than I did from historians who often ignore IRBs. Many historians have never even heard of human subjects. But I see valuable benefits of the process because what I might have construed as innocuous information could in Peru become highly political—and has already in my research area as water shortages and community conflicts have already arisen beneath melting Andean glaciers. The IRB approval process showed me prior to conducting the investigation how to protect informants so that they would not later become victims of political repercussions. Further, the process forced me, at an early stage, to think more concretely about how I would get information and what questions I would ask research participants. It taught me to be a better research diplomat, and more historians should be aware of such a process even if they feel that IRBs restrain and potentially conflict with oral history objectives.

Once I had IRB approval, my research agenda in Peru involved three stages: (1) locating materials; (2) accessing materials; and (3) sharing research results.[15] First, the search for data can pose significant obstacles, especially with less traditional topics or more recent topics, in which case researchers cannot rely entirely, or even mostly, on national archives and major libraries. The personal contacts gained during preliminary topic selection and reconnaissance helped identifying private and non-public government archives, as well as finding people for oral histories and interviews. In Peru, many national government documents generated after 1950 are not stored in the national archive. Therefore, finding them buried in the ministries and state agencies that produced them requires significant legwork and hunting. Personal contacts provide a crucial network for locating these collections. Once inside the archive, however, scholars must keep working to find the relevant materials. And in this endeavor, archivists make crucial allies. Friendly interactions with them, though not too obsequious, can speed up this process. Researchers who take five minutes to chat with them, invite them for lunch or coffee if it seems appropriate, and treat them as research collaborators will avoid the repeated mantra I heard in Nicaragua: "no, I'm sorry, but that collection is closed." Respectful, friendly interactions with archivists—accompanied by professional and diligent research—will help locate new information, sometimes even from closed or uncatalogued collections.

After finding research materials, the second research step involves securing permission to actually view and analyze the information. Again, diplomatic relations with archivists, librarians, and bureaucrats can expedite this process. I personally experienced the value of consistent, friendly interactions with an archivist in Huaraz, Peru, where I was looking for historical newspapers. When I first arrived, the archivist offered a common initial explanation: the newspaper collection was too disorganized for anyone to see. Without funds from Lima, and without adequate personnel or space, the archive had never possessed the resources to catalogue and organize these national, regional, and city newspapers that dated to the 1870s. Frustrated with the archive's inaccessibility, I nonetheless persevered with the archivist's suggestions of alternative collections to find my data. But I also recognized the "no, the collection is closed" response from my days in Managua. So, after several weeks and dozens of friendly, professional conversations with the archivist, I was gratified but somewhat unsurprised when she pried open the squeaky door of the newspaper collection and granted me full access. She was right, though, about its state of disorder! Mountains of newspapers strewn among broken light fixtures, wheel-barrow tires, and a ripped blue tarp that dangled loosely from the ceiling all offered a challenging environment for systematic research. I developed a sore back from weeks on the rickety chair in that room, but I successfully mined the collection for buried treasures that illuminated critical periods of my historical study. In one case, I found a September 1962 newspaper article that summarized research on Mt. Huascarán, Peru's highest peak. Two U.S. mountaineer-scientists suggested that a glacier could potentially generate a cataclysmic avalanche that would destroy several towns in the valley below.[16] Tragically, the dire warning became reality eight years later when the avalanche they foresaw swept into the valley and killed nearly 15,000 Peruvians. Finding the 1962 newspaper article in that archive testified to the political nature of natural disaster prevention—and countered claims that the 1970 avalanche came completely unexpectedly. Many other Latin American historians offer similar stories about how they found unorganized, supposedly closed archival collections that ultimately yielded important data for their research. Such stories, however, are most likely to come from scholars who spent the time and expended the effort to cultivate good relations with archivists.

Research access to non-public government archives or to individuals for interviews and oral histories generally involves an equally challenging process. Access may entail a meeting (or six) with high level bureaucrats, while access to private collections or company archives often requires conversations with the owners themselves. Judges, priests, corporation owners, business managers, mayors, private citizens, engineers, scientists, and bureaucrats approved my requests for research clearance at various sites. In all of those meetings to secure permission, my success—just like with the Mayangna mayor in Nicaragua who grilled me about my research and its importance for his indigenous community—hinged on my ability to communicate respectfully and to convince people that my research was important to *them*, or at least relevant for reasons they could readily grasp. This convincing involved explaining in plain language why my research was pertinent to their institution and in their country, how the data in their archives was crucial, how their important institution filled a vital niche and was doing essential national projects, and how I planned to utilize and share their data after completing the research. In short, finding the materials is a key step, but securing permission to analyze the documents sometimes proved more challenging.

The third stage for successful, non-extractive research involves sharing the results. Giving lectures, conducting workshops, participating in conferences, publishing articles in the native language, meeting with the media, reviewing books, guiding graduate students (and writing letters of recommendation for them), and distributing copies of published work, even if it is in English—all of these activities show a willingness to share while simultaneously indicating a level of transparency about the research process that someone like Hiram Bingham did not provide. I will never forget how surprised and gratified the many Peruvians were when I returned to their homes or offices with article reprints and a copy of my dissertation for them to keep. These visits, when I simply wanted to give them a copy of my work as a tiny token of my appreciation for their support, often turned into extended conversations over coffee (or rum). Hours later, they could not stop thanking me for returning and for sharing. These collaborative interactions ultimately produced an exchange of ideas, which is—or at least should be—the end goal for all research. It is the maintenance of these personal connections and the sharing of research results that distinguish our twenty-first century research methods from those of the nineteenth century colonists and neo-imperialists. If we fail to share, then we commit the same errors of the past. Diplomacy, after all, involves listening and negotiating, not unchecked or unanalyzed intervention.

Foreign scholars who arrive abroad with funding, technology, theories, and other resources can unintentionally flaunt their almost unimaginable assets—and power—over most Latin Americans. Thus, when archivists deny access to special collections or when indigenous residents fabricate stories about their past, they may be attempting to reconfigure the geography of power relations that place white, foreign researchers in the dominant position. By inverting the power dynamics, locals can hope to thwart the exploitative, imperialistic extraction of cultural data that has marked the history of the developing world and extended into so many other realms of their societies, economies, and politics. Scholars, too, can help balance the power discrepancies. Researchers who exercise genuine diplomacy that involves cooperation, collaboration, and sharing will help minimize the imperialist agendas inherent in foreign research projects conducted abroad. Diplomacy smoothes the way for efficient research, it generates the most incisive scholarship, and it involves the people themselves in the production of and control over their past, present, and future.

NOTES

1   Randy Kennedy, "Yale Officials Agree to Return Peruvian Artifacts," *New York Times*, Sept. 17, 2007.

2   For good analyses of Bingham in Peru, see Christopher Heaney, "Bonesmen: Did Yale Plunder Peru?" *The New Republic* (Oct. 23, 2006): 14–19; Deborah Poole, "Landscape and the Imperial Subject: U.S. Images of the Andes, 1859–1930," in *Close Encounters of Empire: Writing the Cultural History of U.S.-Latin*

American Relations, ed. Gilbert M. Joseph, Catherine C. LeGrand, and Ricardo D. Salvatore (Durham N.C.: Duke University Press, 1998), 107–138; Ricardo D. Salvatore, "Local versus Imperial Knowledge: Reflections on Hiram Bingham and the Yale Peruvian Expedition," *Nepantla: Views from the South* 4, no. 1 (2003): 67–80.

3   Quoted in Christopher Heaney, "Finders Keepers? After Almost a Century, Peru Revives the Drama of Hiram Bingham, 5,000 artifacts, and Machu Picchu," *Legal Affairs* (March-April 2006), http://www.legalaffairs.org/issues/March-April-2006/scene_Heaney_marapr06.msp (accessed Nov. 21, 2007).

4   Margaret MacMillan, *Dangerous Games: The Uses and Abuses of History* (New York: Modern Library, 2009).

5   Sophia A. McClennen, "Area Studies Beyond Ontology: Notes on Latin American Studies, American Studies, and Inter-American Studies," *A Contracorriente* 5, no. 1 (Fall 2007): 174. Also see Mary Louise Pratt, *Imperial Eyes: Travel Writing and Transculturation* (New York: Routledge, 1992).

6   Mark Carey, "La influencia Mayangna en la historia de la Costa Atlántica nicaragüense," Revista de Historia 14 (2002): 73–88; Carey, *Separate but Integrated: A History of Isolation and Market Participation Among Nicaragua's Mayangna Indians* (MA thesis, University of Montana, 1998). Field research in Nicaragua was funded by the Inter-American Foundation and the Fulbright Program.

7   Ted Steinberg, "Down to Earth: Nature, Agency, and Power in History," *The American Historical Review* 107, no. 3 (June 2002): 798–820; Douglas R. Weiner, "A Death-Defying Attempt to Articulate a Coherent Definition of Environmental History," *Environmental History* 10, no. 3 (July 2005): 404–20.

8   Kent H. Redford, "The Ecologically Noble Savage," *Cultural Survival Quarterly* 15, no. 1 (1991): 46–8; William Cronon, "The Trouble with Wilderness; or, Getting Back to the Wrong Nature," in *Uncommon Ground: Rethinking the Human Place in Nature*, ed. William Cronon (New York: W.W. Norton and Company, 1996), 69–90; Shepard Krech III, *The Ecological Indian: Myth and History* (New York: W.W. Norton & Company, 1999).

9   Ramachandra Guha, "Radical American Environmentalism and Wilderness Preservation: A Third World Critique," *Environmental Ethics* 11 (Spring 1989): 71–83; Louis S. Warren, *The Hunter's Game: Poachers and Conservationists in Twentieth-Century America* (New Haven: Yale University Press, 1997); Roderick P. Neumann, *Imposing Wilderness: Struggles Over Livelihood and Nature Preservation in Africa* (Berkeley: University of California Press, 1998); Sterling Evans, *The Green Republic: A Conservation History of Costa Rica* (Austin: University of Texas Press, 1999); Mark David Spence, *Dispossessing the Wilderness: Indian Removal and the Making of the National Parks* (New York: Oxford University Press, 2000).

10   Peter H. Herlihy, "Indigenous Peoples and Biosphere Reserve Conservation in the Mosquitia Rain Forest Corridor, Honduras," in *Conservation Through Cultural Survival: Indigenous Peoples and Protected Areas*, ed. Stan Stevens (Washington, D.C.: Island Press, 1997), 99–129; Sarah M. Howard, "Land

Conflict and Mayangna Territorial Rights in Nicaragua's Bosawás Reserve," *Bulletin of Latin American Research* 17, no. 1 (1998): 17–34; Anthony Stocks, "Mapping Dreams in Nicaragua's Bosawas Biosphere Reserve," *Human Organization* 62 (2003): 65–78; Anthony Stocks, Benjamin McMahan, and Peter Taber, "Indigenous, Colonist, and Government Impacts on Nicaragua's Bosawas Reserve," *Conservation Biology* 21, no. 6 (2007): 1495–1505.

11 Mark Carey, *In the Shadow of Melting Glaciers: Climate Change and Andean Society* (New York: Oxford University Press, in press).

12 Alcides Ames Marquez and Bernard Francou, "Cordillera Blanca glaciares en la historia," *Bulletin de L'Institut Francais d'Études Andines* 24, no. 1 (1995): 37–64; Georg Kaser and Henry Osmaston, *Tropical Glaciers* (New York: Cambridge University Press, 2002); Marco Zapata Luyo, "La dinámica glaciar en lagunas de la Cordillera Blanca," *Acta Montana* (Czech Republic) 19, no. 123 (2002): 37–60.

13 Mark Carey, "Living and Dying With Glaciers: People's Historical Vulnerability to Avalanches and Outburst Floods in Peru," *Global and Planetary Change* 47 (2005): 122–34; Carey, "The Politics of Place: Inhabiting and Defending Glacier Hazard Zones in Peru's Cordillera Blanca," in *Darkening Peaks: Glacial Retreat, Science, and Society*, ed. Ben Orlove, Ellen Wiegandt, and Brian Luckman (Berkeley: University of California Press, 2008), 229–40.

14 See Arnita Jones, "AHA Statement on IRBs and Oral History Research," American Historical Association (AHA), 2008, http://www.historians.org/perspectives/issues/2008/0802/0802aha1.cfm (accessed Aug. 17, 2009); Linda Shopes, "Oral History, Human Subjects, and Institutional Review Boards," Oral History Association, http://www.oralhistory.org/do-oral-history/oral-history-and-irb-review/ (accessed Aug. 17, 2009).

15 I have briefly discussed some of these research steps in "Beyond the Archive: A Practical Guide for Research in Latin America," *Brújula* 5, no. 1 (Dec. 2006): 173–6. Dissertation field research was funded by the Social Science Research Council, American Meteorological Society, and the Pacific Rim Research Program of the University of California.

16 "Jornadas libradas por los montañistas norteamericanos," El Departamento, 29 de Setiembre de 1962.

CHAPTER THREE

Studying Wild Spotted Hyenas in Kenya: Challenges and Implications

BY WILINE PANGLE

INTRODUCTION

Seven hours had already passed, and Serena still had not done much other than roll on her side and follow the shade around the *Acacia* tree she had selected for her afternoon nap. My computer batteries had died on hour three of this cheetah watch, and the combination of light intensity and heat made it difficult to continue working in the car. Serena would become the ninth cheetah data point in my comparative study of carnivores if she allowed me to witness her kill and feed that day. Named after the tennis player, Serena was a prime female in her fourth year easily recognizable by her face markings and tail rings. She and I often crossed paths on the plains of the Masai Mara National Reserve in Kenya, where I had been collecting data for my doctorate research.

I had arrived in Kenya in the summer of 2005, full of energy and ready to start my doctoral research studying the behavior of East African mammalian carnivores after many months of planning this field season. At present day, the world is faced with the increasing disappearance of these majestic animals, yet their conservation is crucial to the maintenance of stable ecosystems.[1] In order to manage carnivore populations effectively, understanding their behavior is key to assessing their vulnerability and best prevent their extinction. Most behavioral studies on mammalian carnivores focus on their role as predators rather than as preys, which results in a lack of understanding of the mechanisms that such animals have developed to deal with sources of danger. Filling this gap in knowledge is what got me interested in studying carnivore behavior and what led me to the graduate program of Michigan State University and to the lab of Dr. Kay. E. Holekamp.

Like most dissertations, mine proposed a multifaceted approach, tackling a central question from different angles. The first facet on which I concentrated was a comparative study of the vigilance behavior of East African carnivores, both to assess their levels of vigilance while feeding as well as resting, and to identify predictors for this behavior. Vigilance, defined as a behavior that increases the likelihood of detecting stimuli such as approaching predators,[2] is an easily quantifiable variable that is often used in studies of threat-sensitive behaviors. Vigilance in many mammals involves a common set of motor patterns (e.g., an animal lifting its head and scanning the environment), which facilitates comparisons between species, and thus allows scholars to gain insight into how this behavior contributes to survival among animals that confront contrasting sets of challenges in the wild. I decided to examine carnivores of a range of body sizes: dwarf and banded mongooses, black-backed jackals, wild dogs, cheetahs, leopards, spotted hyenas, and lions. The first goal of my research was thus to establish the general characteristics of the threat-sensitive behavior of East African carnivores.

This comparison across multiple species could not, however, allow me to gain precise insights on how exactly carnivores monitor their environment. When looking at several species, I could not determine for instance how the presence of conspecifics (other individuals from the same species) affected an individual's vigilance levels, or how age changes this vigilance. I decided to devote the rest of my dissertation to one particular carnivore to fully explore vigilance behavior. I chose to work with spotted hyenas (*Crocuta crocuta*) because this particular species offers several advantages as a model organism in which to examine the antipredator behavior of large carnivores. Spotted hyenas are keystone predators in most sub-Saharan ecosystems,[3] and they are the most abundant large carnivores in East Africa.[4] Relative to other large carnivores, spotted hyenas are extraordinarily flexible in their behavior and ecology. For example, they breed throughout the year, they may be either diurnal or nocturnal, they occupy a vast array of habitat types, and they eat carrion as well as live prey that range in size from termites to elephants.[5] Their responses to environmental challenges could therefore represent very conservative indicators of how other top predators, including those that are rare and endangered, are likely to respond to these challenges.[6] Although hyenas are top carnivores in the food chain, they encounter serious threats throughout their lives, and most die of violent deaths inflicted by their two main predators, lions and humans.[7] One would expect that natural selection promoted mechanisms to reduce the impact of those mortality sources. The second goal of my doctoral research was to identify those mechanisms and understand their importance.

Such a research project involved watching hyenas, as well as various other carnivores, in their natural habitat. For that purpose, I arrived at Fisi camp in the Masai Mara National Reserve (MMNR) in Kenya in May 2005. Fisi camp (named after the Swahili word for hyena) is a research site that was first established in 1988 by Dr. Holekamp with the financial support of the National Science Foundation.[8] This reserve constitutes the upper most part of the Serengeti savannah ecosystem. Fisi camp is set on the territory of a clan of hyenas (a social group consisting of up to ninety individuals), called the Talek clan after the closest town, that has been monitored daily ever since 1988. When I arrived in Nairobi in 2005, I was getting ready to collect all the data necessary to answer my research questions, but I was also joining a much larger, long-term hyena project. In this chapter, I present some of the advantages and disadvantages of joining an ongoing research project and living in a research camp; I then explore the importance of establishing strong relationships with local communities to ensure the success of fieldwork; I end by reflecting on some of the ethical and practical issues that emerged during my research abroad.

PART 1: PLANNING AND EXECUTING A FIELD SEASON

Although joining the Holekamp hyena project as a graduate student provided me with a research site where I could pursue my dissertation research, I still had to determine specific research questions for which I could collect the necessary data in the field to write my thesis. In addition, I also had to write grant proposals to acquire funding to implement this research. I quickly realized that I was putting together a project which involved collecting data on a species that I had yet to watch in the wild; this abstract dimension of my project made its creation quite a daunting task. I immersed myself in every book, scientific article, video and documentary that I could find, and bothered many patient researchers who had previously worked with hyenas and large carnivores. Slowly, I started to get a mental image of the types of data collection that were possible to pursue in Kenya, and those that were simply not feasible. This process was quickened by my advisor handing back to me proposal after proposal with the note scribbled on top "Very interesting, but not possible to carry out on hyenas in the wild!" These research proposals usually necessitated intensive experimental manipulations, such as controlling the number of hyenas feeding at once or controlling the identity of the hyenas feeding, knowing the location of lions relative to hyenas feeding, or collecting daily behavioral data on a given hyena. As with all projects involving data collection on wild species, we, as researchers, cannot interfere at any level in the lives of hyenas, but only observe what they are doing or what is happening to them. This is not only to respect the natural environment of the hyenas, but also to preserve the integrity of the research: if we are exploring ways in which hyenas have adapted to their environments, such as trying to understand their incredible immune system, yet give them antibiotics when we dart them, we would highly affect their biology and the results of our findings. This means that as researchers, we cannot treat a sick hyena, nor help a hyena escape from a deadly encounter with a lion, or feed a cub whose mother has just died; we simply witness their lives unfold in nature.

After understanding my role as a field researcher/observer and the conditions under which such observations must take place, I finally formulated a feasible research plan. This consisted first in conducting in-depth observations of vigilance while various carnivores, including hyenas, feed and rest to assess general patterns in mammalian carnivores. Second, I would devote my time specifically to hyenas to assess their responses to predators at various stages of their lives. I had become aware that, among hyenas, fewer than 50 percent of cubs survive to adulthood,[9] which indicates that youngsters might be significantly more vulnerable than adults to competition and predation. This suggests that hyenas might adopt different threat-sensitive tactics during different stages of their life history. I proposed to study the effect of ontogeny, the development through life of given individuals, on vigilance by observing whether hyenas respond differently to lions, their main predators, when at their most vulnerable stages.

My doctoral research required not only that I observe young hyenas' vigilance in various contexts, but also that I conduct some experiments to test their reactions to lion roars, at various ages. I used playback experiments, which consist of playing previously recorded lion roars back to the hyenas. Such playbacks have the advantage of being non-intrusive for the focal animal, which is always a key component when working with wild populations. Moreover, conducting actual experiments in addition to observations would allow me to restrict potentially confounding factors: the strength of an experiment lies in the fact that nothing but the actual factor being tested varies. In my case, I would attempt to test hyenas always in the same situations; the only varying factor would be the actual age of the hyena. Any differences in behavior between hyenas of various ages could therefore be attributed to their age rather than to the many factors that cannot be controlled when basing conclusions on observations. As with any experiment, I would use controls to make sure that the hyenas' reactions to the lion roar were not based on the fact that I was simply playing loud sounds coming out of a car. Finding the appropriate control sound proved quite difficult: I needed a sound that hyenas hear in their natural habitat, but do not associate with either threats or food; knowing that hyenas eat about anything moving on the savannahs highly restricted my possibilities. In this case, I used baboon wahoos, a loud vocalization that baboons make to find where others are located, to rule out the actual experimental design as the cause of the hyenas' reactions. [10]

Finally, I wanted to quantify naturally-occurring variation among two hyena populations subjected to varying human pressures and evaluate the effects of human presence on the activities of large carnivores. In order to do so, I took advantage of the fact that Dr. Holekamp's lab is currently monitoring two clans (each containing fifty to seventy-five individuals), which are exposed to different human pressures: one group is located on the edge of the MMNR and is heavily disturbed by humans due to pastoralists entering the park daily with their cattle;[11] the second group is located deep inside the same reserve, resulting in very low disturbance by humans. I hypothesized that humans not only persecute hyenas by directly killing them, but also lead hyenas to monitor their environment more intensely to ensure their safety,[12] which could result in a decrease of feeding or resting efficiency. I tested this hypothesis by using both observations of hyenas in various contexts and playback experiments—this time playing cow bell sounds (which hyenas in the disturbed area hear on a daily basis) as the main treatment sound, and church bells as the control sound. The cows that the pastoralists bring in the park to graze wear bells that have a distinctive sound and can be heard from a long distance. This playback experiment therefore tested whether hyenas in the disturbed area have associated the cow bell sound with the presence of one of their predators and react accordingly. I recorded the church bells I used for the control sounds in my hometown with the help of my family, and it was oddly comforting to hear familiar church bells in the middle of the African savannah.

My research proposal was ambitious, particularly because it involved watching multiple species of carnivores feeding, and because it relied on experiments whose success would depend on finding hyenas in just the right situation. For playback experiments to be successful, I needed hyenas to rest alone and undisturbed, so that the reactions observed could be attributed to the actual playback experiment. I also needed to minimize exposure to the sounds, since hyenas could learn to associate the car and speaker set up with a false alarm. Finding hyenas resting alone can prove difficult, since hyenas are social animals that like to congregate. In addition, I needed multiple samples for each experiment to be able to reach conclusions for those studies. Simply finding the right opportunities of carnivores feeding on the savannahs could require hours of driving around the plains, looking for predators, and waiting for them to make a kill. I intended to stay in Kenya for a year and a half, but I had enough material to keep me busy for about twice as long and I had planned this purposefully. Once on site, I would be trying experiments out to test my hypotheses and based on the comments from my colleagues, I anticipated at least half of them to fail due to the lack of time and appropriate opportunities. In addition, setting up and successfully conducting experiments is a time-consuming process. I was aware that I would need back-up plans, such as solid alternative tests already designed that I could run in Kenya at a moment's notice, were I to run into obstacles that I had not anticipated.

Once my research project had been articulated came months of preparation to make it happen: I had to obtain the necessary visas and equipment, and secure funding to carry out the experiments. I left the United States at the Detroit International Airport to spend over a year in Kenya with suitcases filled not only with personal items, but with hundreds of blank mini-DV videotapes, video cameras, piles of scientific articles that I intended to read while in the field, and enough passport pictures of myself to cover a whole wall, or so it felt. I had in hand a simple tourist visa for Kenya. Only when I arrived in Kenya did I fully realize the chance that I had to be part of a well-oiled research project. My colleagues, who had already been in Kenya for several years, immediately took me around to all the necessary stops and introduced me to Kenyan bureaucratic paperwork. With their assistance, I soon acquired all the necessary permits, a multiple-entry visa was on its way, all the health care insurances were taken care of, and off I went to the research site, Fisi camp. Had I not been part of this research project, I would have had to spend several months in Nairobi, the capital of Kenya, scrounging for the necessary permits and various signatures to authorize my research. Instead, all was resolved within a week with no time and resources wasted, thanks to the knowledge and advice of my colleagues that had been passed down from cohort to cohort and that was now being passed on to me. I quickly had in my possession a whole notebook filled with names, addresses, and phone numbers of various contacts so that I may be in the position to help the next researcher arriving a few months later.

Fisi camp is located inside the Masai Mara National Reserve, on the shore of the Talek River. Invisible from road or air to respect the environment, the camp is tucked away in the midst of large fig trees that provide welcomed shade. The camp is composed of tents only without any permanent structures. It includes tents for common use (the dining and the kitchen tents), for research purposes (storage tents), as well as for living quarters (each resident at the camp typically sleeps in his/her own tent, separated from others by bushes that allow a minimum of privacy). The camp is not surrounded by any fence and animals roam in and out freely, unless they are actively destructing some of the infrastructure. I have been woken up by the sounds of ruminating giraffes chewing the bush less than three feet from my tent, and to the sounds of roaring lions whose silhouettes I could see from my bed under the moonlight. Over the months, I developed this psychological sense that nothing could happen to me when I was in my tent, zippers down, and my tent came to represent a safe haven against rain and cold, but also against predators and mosquitoes. This false sense of security was shattered the day I saw a snake that, without hesitation, found its way inside my tent; the fact that the snake was not venomous was lost on me at the time . . .

I remember with mixed emotions the few months that followed my arrival at Fisi camp. I remember my amazement at discovering the African savannahs, of not only observing the wildlife around me, but also studying it. I remember the first time I met our study hyenas after hearing so many stories about them over the course of the two years I had been at Michigan State University. I was amazed by how comfortable the hyenas were around our research car, the hyena cubs coming to sniff it and chew on any wire sticking out. I remember the first hyena social interactions I witnessed over a kill, and how blown away I was by the intricacy of the interactions that were happening right in front of me. I still remember the first hyena I learned to identify by her unique spots; her name was Gucci and she was a one-year-old hyena whose mother had been killed only a few weeks earlier. There were also frustrations that I had not anticipated, such as how much our research was dependent on the weather. During the rainy season, I spent hours both pushing the research cars out of deep mud holes and counting hours in my tent when I could not work due to the lack of power (all our camp is powered through solar panels, which is a bit of a strain when it has been raining for seven days straight!). I had also not fully grasped how long my training for the camp's large scale research project would take before I could carry out all of its aspects once the previous cohort of students left to go back to the States. This process involved learning tools that ranged from figuring out how to dart hyenas and collect blood and various body measurements, to learning how to cleanse a dead hyena skull, to learning how to diagnose various mechanical car issues. And most important of all, I had to learn to identify, solely based on unique spot patterns on their furs, the 120 hyenas that we were observing. Having never taken part in a project like this one before, it took me months to successfully recognize each hyena, and I still remember dreaming about hyena spots during countless agitated nights.

Like all students before me, I was also learning to be patient. I had to refrain myself from collecting data for my thesis right away and first learn the essential ropes of the hyena project. Before arriving at Fisi camp, I had never really considered the consequences of joining an ongoing research project. I had this amazing opportunity to study mega fauna without having to worry about the immense costs involved with maintaining a research camp of this size. My advisor provided all funding revolving around the camp including the personnel she employed, the cars she put at our disposal, and the equipment she provided, all from which I was benefiting. All I had had to worry about was acquiring the small amount necessary to run my specific project, which was mostly based on filming carnivores in various contexts. To balance the costs of my living at the campsite, like every student, I gave some of my time by helping with the long-term data collection of the project. The collection of a set number of variables over long-term projects is extremely valuable, allowing researchers to answer powerful questions. Participating in the camp's long-term study for me involved learning how to collect types of data with which I was not familiar. These data included collecting demographic data on the populations of hyenas we were following, but also behavioral data (who is doing what where at any time of the day) as well as morphological data (through darting hyenas and taking various body measurements and samples).

Once I felt comfortable with the many tools necessary for the hyena project, I was faced with the balancing act between collecting long-term data for the project and collecting my own data that had to remain original. I struggled for several months with finding the right balance, trying various combinations to most efficiently split up my time. I would, for example, spend mornings collecting long-term data for the hyena project, and evenings collecting my own data, before switching my schedules for a week or two. I quickly realized, however, that I could not be so regular or methodological in the way I organized my time, and that I had to seize opportunities when I surprised hyenas in various behaviors so that the data collection remained unbiased. Indeed, I would tend to most often see hyenas feeding in the mornings, and then resting on the plains in the afternoons. Keeping track of how much time I devoted to each project became essential and I learned to prioritize the hyena project without falling behind in the data collection for my dissertation. As I became more familiar with the site and our hyenas, this process reached a certain equilibrium and the pile of filled videotapes started growing in my tent. Eventually, I learned to recognize each hyena instantaneously, based on the smallest facial marks, on the way they would carry their body, and each hyena became its own entity, with its own stories and personality traits.

Getting to know not only all hyenas, but also all carnivores in the area so intimately, as well as every feature of the landscape, is an amazingly rewarding feeling. I had never spent so many hours in a restricted environment such as that one, spending day after day transecting the same area. Every landmark feature had its own name to facilitate communication between researchers, and quickly, each feature also had its own story. There was the tree in which I saw my first leopard, the rock that looked to me just like a hyena laying down in the distance, the hole in which the research car got stuck in the mud for the very first time when I was alone, the exact spot on a hill where one could see the entire territory of our hyenas, and so many more. Slowly, I started to feel as though I belonged there, as though I were not simply a passing visitor anymore. And along with this feeling came a realization of the responsibility at hand.

PART 2: IMPLICATIONS OF CONDUCTING RESEARCH ABROAD

Being part of such a large research facility establishes a presence in the community. Although we, behavioral ecologists, study animals, our project far from relies only on our relation to the spotted hyena, the object of our study, as I discovered within weeks of my arrival. Our research is highly dependent on our relationships with the local villagers, the park authorities, as well as the entire tourist community surrounding us. As part of a larger research site, one needs to exercise caution when interacting with these local communities as one's individual actions have repercussions for the group as a whole and bear consequences that can negatively impact the long-term data collection. Self-awareness, cultural etiquette, as well as the preservation of the group's reputation and integrity is paramount at all times.

I vividly remember my first skull retrieval expedition, which happened within days of my arrival at Fisi camp. Our cellular phone, which we hang on the only branch of the only bush in our camp in the hopes of getting a signal, would ring sporadically, as we received text messages a few times a day when our only signal bar would moodily decide to appear. I had already learned how dependent we were on those cell phones for communication—cheaper than radios or satellite phones, cellular phones were revolutionizing the whole area, allowing people to connect with each other in a somewhat reliable fashion. That day, our cell phone started to beep around lunch time—our night guard Steven had just found out that one of our study hyenas had been killed the night before. Villagers had found the radio collar with which we equip some of our adult hyenas to locate them at any given time. Over the years, we have been collecting hyena skulls of hyenas from our study clans so that graduate students from our lab may examine the ontogeny of the feeding apparatus in hyenas. Our sample sizes for known-aged skulls are restricted, so new skulls from hyenas who have been killed are extremely valuable. After hearing about a skull having been found somewhere, I always had mixed feelings: on the one hand, I looked forward to our collecting one more skull for the study; on the other hand, I would see the image of all the hyenas with collars flash before me, think about which one I had not seen in the last day or so, try to figure out which animal we had just lost, and secretly hope that it was not one of my favorites. A tedious search for the precious skull would usually ensue, which could take all day without the help of the Maasai. The villagers had learned of the value of these skulls, and would often help us in locating them. Their aid was invaluable, especially if the hyena we were looking for did not have a radio-collar, making it all the more difficult to locate.

We relied on villagers not only to locate skulls, but also to help us with about every aspect of our research project. The help of locals has been essential to the viability of our research site, whether it be concrete aid, such as giving us a hand to maintain the camp or helping us push cars out of the mud on a daily basis during the rainy season, or more technical aid, such as providing information on the whereabouts of hyena dens outside the reserve or helping us collect information on hyena depredation of livestock. What is more, our camp would not be located where it is if it were not for the hospitality of the local population. Historically, the MMNR is the ancestral land of the Maasai people, whose rights to the land are still strong.[13] The MMNR is different from most national parks in that, by being defined as a reserve, the revenue goes back to the Maasai. The park is in the authority of Maasai, and the Elder's council takes part in all decision making regarding the reserve.[14] Since our camp is located inside the reserve borders, the villagers could easily pressure the park not to allow our presence in the area anymore if they decided to do so. As researchers on site, we never forget that we remain guests and that the Maasai's hospitality should never be taken for granted.

A trusting relationship with local authorities is a key ingredient for the success of a large scale research program. As guests in a country and on a land, it is up to us, foreign researchers, to build a personal relationship with the locals, to gain their trust through actions rather than words. There are many ways in which researchers can do so, which often represent precious resources for the local population. Most individuals in our research camp get involved with the local families according to their expertise and interests. In my case, I contacted local primary schools upon my arrival in the area and volunteered at schools to talk about the environment, about hyenas, and to instruct children about nature. I also spent many hours with the women of the community discussing possibilities for education to help them pursue their schooling. As a group, we provided assistance in other aspects of daily life: for instance, cars remain a luxury in this part of Kenya so we often became the ambulance service by driving injured or sick people to the nearest clinic. We also provided first aid to villagers surrounding our camp and we were considered a "regular clinic," like most research camps overseas.[15] Through small gestures such as these, we slowly got to know the families around our camp, the teachers, the local doctors, and worked on building a trusting relationship with them, although it takes time to establish such ties and to start feeling integrated within a community. Over the years, the relationship between the villagers and our research camp has strengthened, and it has allowed for some wonderful collaborations, of which the skull expeditions is but one small example.

Our research is not simply embedded with the local community, but also with the park authorities and the tourism industry. The park authorities have been fundamental to the maintenance of our research camp. Without permission from the park officials, we would not be able to collect any data on hyenas inside the MMNR. When a section of the reserve was closed off to tourist vehicles a few years ago to help restore the vegetation, it would have been disastrous if the park authorities had extended this order to researchers: the section closed to the public happened to be right in the middle of the territory of one of the hyena clans that we study. Collaboration with the park allowed us to continue working in this closed section, while keeping the park updated on the restoration progress of the area in question. When dealing with park authorities, diplomacy seems to be the key word for me. Over my time in Kenya, I had multiple interactions with the various wardens of the park, and I always kept in mind that respect and communication were crucial, despite cultural and sometimes language barriers. As Westerners, we often arrive in areas like the MMNR with pre-conceived ideas of how such an area should be managed, usually based on Western examples. Management is a tradeoff: it is as much about the human dimension and policies as it is about biological dynamics.[16] In Kenya, biological processes are similar to Western processes but the interfaces between the people and their environment differs. This became highly apparent to me during a large drought that I witnessed. Maasai are pastoralists who keep live stocks on which their survival depends; yet during a drought, the live stock does not have enough grass on each Maasai's local land to remain healthy. The MMNR, however, has plenty of grass that would allow the livestock to last until the next rains. The park managers have to decide on whether to let the livestock enter and graze in the reserve, which would impact the wildlife, but allow thousands of people to remain healthy. Such decisions are often very difficult ones to make.

Although its role remains quite controversial in many parts of the non-Western world, tourism plays a large economic role in Kenya and became the third community with which we interacted on a daily basis. The savannah is an amazing ecosystem that supports a varied and abundant animal community, thus attracting tourists from all continents. Our hyenas were being watched daily not simply by us, but also by many tourists traveling in vans from the surrounding lodges. Our research camp was highly dependent on these lodges both for resources and communication with the outside world. As such, the presence of lodges, which rely on the tourist industry for their existence, was crucial to the functioning of our research project. Most lodges have a battery of cars and thus usually have a garage employing full-time mechanics. They are often the closest and most reliable mechanics in the area, and I spent many hours learning the ropes in their company. Such help is vital for our work: we rely heavily on cars, and our cars go through very rough terrain which leads to many breakdowns that can take hours or weeks to fix without the proper part, knowledge, or experience. Without mechanics close-by, we would often be deprived of our vehicles, which would be disastrous for our daily observations of hyenas. Moreover, lodges represent a contact with the outside world: thanks to their phone lines that connect to the internet, I was able to download my emails once a week and to receive much awaited news from my husband, my family and colleagues alike. I would also cherish the rare letters that would make it to me through the mailing address of the closest lodge. In compensation for these services, I spent many hours discussing hyena behavior with tourists over a drink and served as a natural history expert whenever they were interested in learning about the carnivores they had observed on their game drives. I got to know lodge managers and staff well, and it was always pleasant to stop by and pay them a visit. The lodges became a new social anchor: they constituted a place where I would receive news from loved ones, where I was always welcomed when storms kept me from reaching the camp safely, where tourist guides, air balloon pilots, and researchers could discuss endlessly the state of the wildlife, the latest sighting of rare species or the latest behaviors observed. Exchanging anecdotes with members of such a specific community who could relate to these stories and who had their own sets of stories to share, from witnessing the birth of an animal to hallucinating about the worst junk food possible, was truly a privilege. I had not foreseen the importance of this connection, both in terms of the actual resources it could offer, but also in terms of the social environment it fostered. A warm conviviality emerged from these interactions, one that became crucial support for all of us confronted with the isolation of the field.

PART 3: REFLECTIONS ON CONDUCTING RESEARCH ABROAD

There are some important ethical considerations to ponder when conducting research in non-Western countries, especially when one uses local infrastructure and research material for the benefit of a thesis and a career that will most likely be Western-based. Local communities do not usually gain from this intellectual merit, besides the few jobs provided by the presence of a research camp in need of labor. The responsibility that comes with this dimension, the taking or utilizing of local resources, becomes particularly acute when one is in the process of conducting research and faced with daily contradictions which can lead the researcher to question his role or purpose. I had not fully anticipated how present this concern of exploiting local resources would be in my mind throughout my stay and I was far from being the only one who felt ill at ease: most individuals I know, who have spend a considerable amount of time abroad and have come to know a community, voice similar concerns. We all addressed our discomfort according to our personalities and skills. For my part, I visited local primary schools to teach groups of children and I spent long hours at the local clinic talking with the local doctor to help him identify resources in Europe.

Both types of interaction grounded my stay in Kenya. Because of the isolation commonly experienced while conducting fieldwork, it is easy to get caught up in daily activities and lose perspective of one's purpose: it is for example easy to let a silly argument determine your mood for several days or to start believing that your missing data point will determine the success or failure of your entire thesis. Every time I got discouraged during the research process because I seemed to be acquiring data points at a crawling pace, I reminded myself to expand my limited world to that of the villagers around: their daily struggles, their humanity or lack of understanding kept me in check and reminded me that my research efforts were relational and could not become exploitative of an environment. There are multiple ways in which a given research program can give back to the community, which commonly involves training local university students or making its skills available to the community that enables the research program, whether it involves educating, assisting with daily tasks, or fund raising.

As a researcher in an ecosystem threatened every day to disappear, I also felt the responsibility to remain a steward of conservation. Over my stay, I had countless conversations with other scientists, researchers, students, tourists, and wardens on the status of the wildlife. There are multiple factors to consider when discussing conservation. Far from being a clean-cut process, acting on the issue of conservation is heavy with consequences that can positively or negatively impact the lives of thousands of people. While immersed in an environment in which conservation is a daily topic, I grew as a scientist more than I expected and realized not only what is at stakes, but also the multiple facets of conservation problems through witnessing incidents such as the drought I mentioned and how the park managers dealt with it. As active researchers living in the park, we were often asked to provide opinions and points of view. Although we were always careful about what we would state, we were also eager to share what we observed on a daily basis. I often felt that my role was to inform, to let others, whether tourists, students or lodge managers, know what we were witnessing, to share our discoveries both large and small, and to ultimately get people interested in their surroundings. Conservation often stems from interest and knowledge—natural steps once someone has become aware of the issues that define them. I witnessed several tourists give up the "best-picture-race safari" approach according to which only seeing more than one's neighbors seemed to matter, to become concerned citizens who are truly worried about the state of the wildlife they are viewing after a simple one hour conversation with them. This transformation from exploitative to preventative behavior alone is for me a reward like no other.

CONCLUSION

As Snow points out, there exists a gap between the humanities and the sciences that threatens to become a "gulf of mutual incomprehension."[17] Such a gap needs to be bridged and a dialogue re-established between what he calls "the two cultures"[18] as these academic disciplines are closer together than they might seem, if not in content, at least in their objectives and methodology. Such incomprehension leads to the inevitable fragmentation of knowledge which can prevent the advances of these disciplines together and separately.[19] Although there has been a growing recognition of such a gap, increased efforts to bring these fields closer together,[20] and greater value placed on sharing knowledge and collaboration, much remains to be done. What is more, we, as scientists, have a responsibility to improve our communicative skills to share our research results, including informing the general public of our findings, to reflect on the ethics of research and, last but not least, to educate our students on the nature of science. It is in this state of mind that I responded to a call for papers proposing to create an interdisciplinary collection of essays from the humanities and social sciences devoted to personalizing overseas fieldwork in order to help future scholars in their research endeavors. This chapter is my attempt at reconciliation and self-reflexibility, both of which were by-products of my research in the field.

I came back to the United States in August 2006 after sixteen months in Kenya. I dealt with the culture shock by taking as many hot showers as I could justify, enjoying running water and constant electrical power, eating a lot of junk food, and sleeping in until an ungodly 7a.m. after months of my alarm clock ringing at 4:45a.m. even on Sundays. I would spend three hours in the grocery store because I could not make up my mind about what to buy when faced with all the shopping options suddenly available to me. But I had successfully completed my doctoral field season. I had brought home enough data for my thesis and, as I soon realized in the months following my return, probably more data than I could actually use. I had planned to carry out six studies: one comparative study of vigilance in multiple carnivores, two playback experiments (one with lion roars, one with cow bells), two observational studies of vigilance in hyenas (one for cubs, one for adults), and one experiment testing how cubs learn about danger. My data collection in the field was fairly smooth, much smoother than I anticipated. I did have equipment issues, such as cables that failed for the playback experiments or car problems that made it impossible to watch hyenas on a daily basis, but overall, nothing too drastic. I spent so many hours filming hyenas and other carnivores that my data collection happened faster than I expected, especially for data on adult hyenas. The more data, the better for any research, but there comes a point where one needs to stop and assess whether the data collected is sufficient to answer one's original questions, which is what I did in July 2006 when I decided to come home. In the end, I managed to carry out five studies to completion and I only had to give up on the last experiment because it would have required a few extra years of data collection. For some of those studies, I have small sample sizes, which restricted my data analysis to some extent, but despite the sample sizes, I can still answer the questions I had posed in the very beginning.[21]

The time I spent in Kenya profoundly changed me in ways I would have never expected. I grew not only as a scientist but also as a human being when confronted to situations that I could never have imagined. One of the main skills I learned was to stay strong mentally: in such isolation, it is very easy to lose perspective on one's research. As Packer writes, when in the field alone, there is "nothing to fix your mind on, nothing to distract you from whatever might be troubling you. Magnifying whatever bothers you into a major source of anxiety."[22] For me, there were definite lows and highs, but I learned over time to keep them from becoming too extreme. I came to think about my field season as a marathon whereby one is aiming for the long-distance and cannot get burnt out within the first few weeks. I learned to ground myself in reality, both in my surroundings and in my life back home; to stay in contact with loved ones; and to fight isolation by seeking news from the outside world despite the fact that it all felt "strangely irrelevant."[23] But there were also so many rewards. I remember distinctly the moment when I realized that I was becoming a part of the community, the day that I attended the wedding of our night guard, Lesingo. I drove him, his new wife and his whole wedding party from the parents of the bride's home to their new home. This slow drive will probably be engraved in my memory for a long time, with the songs ringing in my ears, the excitement, the smells of the new animal skins proudly displayed in the car that had been remodeled for the occasion. I bring home with me not only this cultural experience, but also a myriad of vivid images of the nature that surrounded me for all this time, images of pure wonder that will never cease to amaze me. How can one forget discovering sixteen lion cubs under a month of age, fluffy and joyful, playing, rolling, biting each other's tails? Like many people who have worked in Africa, I have developed a love-hate relationship with her: in few other places in the world can one discover the beauty of Nature with the abundance of its fauna, yet the discovery of such beauty is inseparable from a political system loaded with corruption, from researchers' paranoia about mosquitoes to avoid catching malaria, and from a general physical discomfort at all levels.

Since my return, I have often been asked what advice I would offer to student researchers going to Africa. Besides approaching the trip like a marathon, I would advise them to think about what is important to them: if they cannot start their morning without a cup of coffee, then bringing coffee along becomes essential! Despite the fact that living for such a long time abroad is an experience in which one should immerse oneself, bringing along the small things that help you stay grounded can create a psychological comfort that makes adjusting to a new culture easier. Over the numerous months that I spent on site in Kenya, I came to realize the importance of educating oneself on the conditions in which fieldwork in Africa will be conducted to shape one's expectations. Africa is often presented as this exotic, even romantic country evoked in tourist scenes that could be taken straight from "Out of Africa." Although I did experience moments that could have rivaled with those depicted in the movie, day to day life constantly breaks this stereotype and can make reality seem much harsher: there is first the reality of living in the wilderness with involves at times dangerous encounters with wildlife and constant vigilance to prevent contracting various diseases; second there is the inevitable encounter with politics and corruption, which one might not be used to seeing or navigating; and lastly, there is the modernization that one might not expect. Reading accounts written by Westerners who have sojourned in Africa for extended periods of time, whether they be travelogues, scientific reports, or memoirs, probably constitutes one of the best psychological preparation for undertaking research in countries drastically difference from one's own, for breaking stereotypes and rectifying cultural assumptions, and for getting an idea of what to expect in the field. Otherwise, my advice remains practical: back up all your data, use common sense, think twice before speaking up, be polite at all times, learn the local dialect as much as possible, keep promises made to the local community, and take the time to enjoy the experience. Finally, it is important to remember that field research is a locally and culturally grounded endeavor and that data collection is the product of its environment; field research is relational and contextualized. Ultimately, it is up to each researcher to act in ways that are favorable to the maintaining of good relations with nearby communities and to acknowledge that his or her fieldwork data are the by-products of at once a cultural, ethnic and political context that cannot be ignored.

NOTES

1   Raffaelli, David. "How Extinction Patterns Affect Ecosystems." *Science* 306, no. 5699 (November 2004): 1141–1142.
2   Dimond, S., and J. Lazarus. "The Problem of Vigilance in Animal Life." *Brain, Behavior and Evolution* 9, no. 1 (1974): 60–79.
3   Hofer, Heribert., and East, Marion L. "Population Dynamics, Population Size, and the Commuting System of Serengeti Spotted Hyenas." Pp. 332–63 in *Serengeti II: Dynamics, Management, and Conservation of an Ecosystem,*

edited by Anthony Ronald Entrican Sinclair and Peter Arcese. Chicago: University of Chicago Press, 1995.

4   Mills, M. Gus L., and Heribert Hofer. *Hyaenas: Status Survey and Conservation Action Plan.* IUCN/SSC Hyaena Specialist Group. IUCN, Gland, Switzerland and Cambridge, 1998.

5   See for additional information on spotted hyenas the following references: Kruuk, Hans. *The Spotted Hyena: A Study of Predation and Social Behavior.* Chicago: University of Chicago Press, 1972; Mills, M. Gus L. *Kalahari Hyenas: Comparative Behavioural Ecology of Two Species.* London: Unwin Hyman, 1990; Sillero-Zubiri, Claudio., and Dada Gottelli,. "Feeding Ecology of the Spotted Hyaena (Mammalia: *Crocuta crocuta*) in a Mountain Forest Habitat." *Journal of African Zoology* 106 (1992): 169–176; Holekamp, Kay E., Laura Smale, R. Berg, and Susan M. Cooper. "Hunting Rates and Hunting Success in the Spotted Hyena (*Crocuta crocuta*)." *Journal of Zoology* 242, no.1 (May 1997): 1–15; and Holekamp, Kay E., Micaela Szykman, Erin E. Boydston, and Laura Smale. "Association of Seasonal Reproductive Patterns With Changing Food Availability in an Equatorial Carnivore, the Spotted Hyaena (*Crocuta crocuta*)." *Journal of Reproductive Fertility* 116, no. 1 (May 1999): 87–93.

6   Arcese, Peter, and Anthony R. E. Sinclair. "The Role of Protected Areas as Ecological Baselines." *Journal of Wildlife Management* 61, no. 3 (July 1997): 587–602.

7   For information on sources of mortality in spotted hyenas, see: Kruuk, *Spotted hyena*; and Frank, Lawrence G., Kay E. Holekamp, and Laura Smale. "Dominance, Demography, and Reproductive Success of Female Spotted Hyenas." Pp. 364–84 in *Serengeti II: Dynamics, Management, and Conservation of an Ecosystem,* edited by Anthony Ronald Entrican Sinclair and Peter Arcese. Chicago: University of Chicago Press, 1995.

8   See Dr. Kay E. Holekamp's lab website for more information on the Mara Hyena Proejct at http://hyenas.zoology.msu.edu/

9   Frank, *Dominance.*

10   See for example: Kitchen, Dawn M., Robert M. Seyfarth, Julia Fischer, and Dorothy L. Cheney. "Loud calls as Indicators of Dominance in Male Baboons (*Papio cynocephalus ursinus*)." *Behavioral Ecology and Sociobiology* 53, no. 6 (May 2003): 374–384; Fischer, Julia, Dawn M. Kitchen, Robert M. Seyfarth, and Dorothy L. Cheney. "Baboon Loud Calls Advertise Male Quality: Acoustic Features and Their Relation to Rank, Age, and Exhaustion." *Behavioral Ecology and Sociobiology* 56, no. 2 (June 2004): 140–148; and Sapolsky, Robert M. *A Primate's Memoir.* New York: Simon & Schuster, 2001.

11   Boydston, Erin E., Karen M. Kapheim, Heather E. Watts, Micaela Szykman, and Kay E. Holekamp, "Altered Behavior in Spotted Hyenas Associated With Increased Human Activity." *Animal Conservation* 6, no. 3 (August 2003): 207–219.

12   Pangle, Wiline M., and Kay E. Holekamp. "Lethal and Nonlethal Anthropogenic Effects on Spotted Hyenas in the Masai Mara National Reserve." *Journal of Mammalogy* 91, no. 1 (February 2010): 154–164.

13 For information Maasai history, see: Rutten, M. M. E. M. "Parks Beyond Parks: Genuine Community Based Wildlife Eco-tourism or Just Another Loss of Land for Maasai Pastoralists in Kenya?" London: *International Institute for Environment and Development*, Issues paper no. 111, 2002; and Rutten, M. M. E. M. *Selling Wealth to Buy Poverty - The Process of the Individualization of Landownership Among the Maasai Pastoralists of Kajiado District Kenya, 1890–1990*. Saarbrucken-Fort Lauderdale: Verlag Breitenbach Publishers, 1992.

14 Rutten, *Selling Wealth*.

15 Sapolsky, *Primate*.

16 Bolen, Eric G., and William L. Robinson. *Wildlife Ecology and Management*. 5th edition. Benjamin Cummings Publishing Company, 2002.

17 Snow, Charles P. *The Two Cultures and a Second Look: An Expanded Version of the Two Cultures and the Scientific Revolution*. Cambridge: Cambridge University Press, 1964.

18 Snow, *Two cultures*.

19 Wilson, Edward O. *Consilience: The Unity of Knowledge*. New York: Vintage Books, 1998.

20 See for example: Wilson, *Consilience*; and Gould, Stephen J. *The Hedgehog, the Fox, and the Magister's Pox: Mending the Gap Between Science and the Humanities*. New York: Harmony Books, 2003.

21 Pangle, Wiline M. "Threat-sensitive Behavior and its Ontogenic Development in top Mammalian Carnivores." PhD diss. East Lansing: Michigan State University, 2009.

22 Packer, Craig. *Into Africa*. Chicago: the University of Chicago Press, 1994.

23 Packer, *Into Africa*.

PART II

Insecurities

Methodological and Positional Considerations of Crisis Field Research: The Karen Revolution Example

BY JACK FONG

Conducting one's first field research is often viewed as an important rite of passage for the qualitative sociologist. Yet field research must now attend to the consequences of the information age where individuals and groups have become larger repositories of in-depth information about selves, communities, and histories. In a globalized world where information technology and the fluidity of national boundaries influence knowledge production, how then, will field research appear in a transnational setting? Fortunately, Michael Burawoy and his colleagues were able to make visible new ethnographic parameters in two important works, *Ethnography Unbound* and *Global Ethnography*.[1] For Burawoy, this meant following and acquiring data at different sites. Thus, the Burawoyian method becomes for ethnographers an endeavor that crosses international boundaries, space and time. The sociological field researcher must attend to a greater expanse of local and global cues from more abundant cultural and political reservoirs, swollen with information on new, recovered, and revisited articulations of identities. However, many distinguishing features of field research have not changed, namely the "messiness," the emotional, physical, and protracted nature of data collection in the field.[2] Field research also continues to be extremely dangerous in certain settings. This chapter attempts to make visible a key paradigmatic blind spot in global ethnographic methodology: how one conducts field research in the context of crisis. The discussion that follows explores the practical and positional considerations of field research in such a context.

Although ethnographers have certainly conducted research in or about environments fraught with danger, little has been written on important methodological, interpersonal, personal and positional considerations of the researcher engaged in what I term *crisis* field research.[3] Because crisis sites, or what Gill and Avruch generally refer to as "insecure contexts" and "conflict zones" respectively, contain tensions and conflagrations, the sociological field researcher of the globalized age is exposed to more challenging methodological considerations, relatively speaking, than those faced by field researchers of the fin-de-siècle.[4] The emergent positivism of the late nineteenth-century did not have yet to attend to the hyper-data generated by the late twentieth-century's information age, nor was there a consciousness of *positionality*, the awareness that knowledge is produced from the observer's social location and position in society. As Gill notes, the academic culture revolving around fieldwork tends to place fieldwork training at a low priority, thus relegating the importance of being "street-smart" from fieldwork discourse, and quietly accepting that "unfortunate experiences are . . . a rite of passage for the ethnographer, part of the accepted vulnerability of being a newcomer" that includes "getting mugged or catching malaria."[5]

I hope to contribute to a refinement of the aforementioned issues by beginning with a discussion of crisis as it will be approached in this chapter. The concept of crisis that I evoke is not derived from a critical perspective as employed by Jurgen Habermas in his *Legitimation Crisis*,[6] nor will I treat it aesthetically as a concept in stasis to be deconstructed to the *n*th degree. Instead *systemic crisis*, or systems experiencing crisis, can be understood within the context of development discourse as well as in the ways people express their life experiences in a failing social system. Thus, the process of systems experiencing crisis refers to the literal physical breakdown or obliteration of social infrastructure that, under non-crisis circumstances, would provide social stability, a modicum of social order, and the capacity to distribute resources such as food, clean water, health provisions, education, and shelter. Take for example an important finding regarding systemic crisis and famine. Economist Amartya Sen demonstrated that famine is due to mechanisms of food distribution that fail to respond to demotic needs when natural events intersect with poorly implemented distribution policies and institutional inadequacy.[7] China's botched Maoist-inspired Great Leap Forward, the great Ethiopian famines affecting the Wollo and Harerghe peoples in 1973–1974, as well as the 1974 famine in Bangladesh, are prominent examples of such failing systems.[8] By contrast, Sen noted that India, with the establishment of a functioning democratic bureaucracy and system, has not experienced a famine since its independence from Britain in spite of its regional poverty. The context where a system is experiencing crisis will serve as the context or backdrop for discussing crisis field research and its many considerations.

Under non-crisis circumstances, culture is reproduced with minor social disjunctions and dislocations. Systemic crisis, on the other hand, is intimately linked to humanitarian crisis as dysfunctions in the former result in dramatic changes for social relationships in the latter. One of the greatest generators of systemic crisis is protracted warfare, which shifts people toward survival mode as physical properties of their world crumble around them: schools are destroyed, hospitals no longer exist or exist without adequate medicines, the economy is in shambles, lives are lost, and the ecosystem that allows people to be units of production rather than units of consumption is acutely compromised. People become internally displaced and/or refugees in the process as they, in development parlance, experience *maldevelopment*, or the onset of socially limiting conditions. In this regard, crisis sites in war-torn regions need to be understood and scrutinized as a unique type of field site.

The Karen ethnic group of Burma is experiencing the brutal consequences of protracted warfare.[9] The Karen, the next largest ethnic group after the majority

Burmans, has been contesting ethnic cleansing campaigns implemented against them by various pro-Burman military governments. Engaged in the longest and most underreported ethnic conflict of the twentieth-century, and one that continues into the twenty-first century, the Karen National Union (KNU), the political body of the Karen State of Kawthoolei—along with Shan, Mon, Chin, Karenni, and Arakan ethnic allies as well as Burman democracy activists—desire to establish a federalist and democratic Burma. Sixty years after the start of the Karen Revolution and close to half a million deaths later, prospects for Karen self-determination and a democratic Burma continue to decline precipitously.

I had the privilege of conducting my field research with Karen people during the first half of 2004. This moving experience inspired me to rearticulate methodological considerations for a crisis field research capable of capturing the human condition of people in survival mode—of a people in systemic crisis. The considerations delineated in this chapter were cautiously derived and extrapolated from my stay with the Karen: I will introduce the circumstances that led to my immersion with the Karen, narrate my own experience in the field, and finally discuss issues related to knowledge production and epistemological awareness. It should be noted that a great deal of advice shared in the following pages does not originate from any intuitive prescience prior to entering the field but was rather gained through hindsight and reflection.

I was visiting Thailand during the summer of 2003 and had been exploring the many ruins of the fourteenth-century Siamese capital of Ayutthaya. I also spent time with childhood friends with whom I grew up prior to my family's move to the United States. It was during this period that I found myself having dinner with childhood friend, Jane Ritdejawong,[10] who at the time had established herself as a successful and quite famous television and radio news producer in Thailand, having honed her skills as a journalist with the Associated Press in years past.

After recounting my trek through central Thailand visiting ruins at Kamphaeng Phet, Sukhothai, and Ayutthaya to Jane, I commented that I had no idea Burmese invasions from centuries past had resulted in the numerous ruins visible in the central part of the country. I thought they had been abandoned and became ruins naturally. Jane informed me that Ayutthaya's invasion was far from an isolated incident and that Burma's militarized governments still subscribed to violence as a political discourse, resulting in their notorious aggression against its minorities. I was completely fascinated. In fact, Jane described for me one a large battle that occurred in 1995 when the pro-Burman military government launched a massive offensive against the Karen *ethnic nationality*, in the political parlance of the region, fighting the regime. "In 1995, the Karen capital of Manerplaw was captured and I was sent to cover Karen refugees that fled to Thailand by the thousands," Jane recalled. Trained as a political sociologist who explores ethnicity and race issues from a development perspective, I was awestruck as I listened to her recount her experiences reporting on the Karen. Jane concluded, "The people fleeing were like zombies. They were so tired and they carried so many things as they arrived in Thailand." She continued, explaining how various military regimes of Burma have been engaged in the ethnic cleansing of its ethnic nationalities for decades.[11] The

Karen were living in a perennially increasing state of destitution due to war; they were living in systemic crisis.

At the time, I had little knowledge of the Karen. I vaguely remembered childhood stories that painted Karen tribes as fierce mountain warriors but knew nothing of their political struggle against the various pro-Burman military regimes that ran the country. Nor was I aware that Burma had so many ethnic nationalities subjected to ethnic cleansing, against which the Karen have fought the longest and have suffered the most as a consequence. As our conversation continued, it became clear that the politics of Burma have always been and continues to be *ethno* politics of the most unresolved order. I became deeply moved by the Karen condition of humanitarian crisis. Jane's descriptions had a profound impression on me, resulting in my decision to research the Karen self-determination struggle for my dissertation. Prior to our dinner, I was equipped with theories and models; after that evening, I knew I had a *bona fide* case study. She continued her time-compression, ultimately stating, almost too casually, "Well, I know a colonel of the KNLA.[12] I had interviewed him before and we've become friends. I'll give you his number. Call him and say you're my close friend."

During the spring of my third year at the University of California, Santa Cruz, I had successfully defended my field statements on political sociology and the sociology of development. As aforementioned, although theoretically equipped in my sociology, I had no case study. Little did I know that during our fateful dinner at one of the many noisy and unpretentious restaurant in Bangkok, more generally referred to as *Krung Thep* by the Thais, just a few feet from the main street choked with automobiles, buses, and the famous *tuk tuk* auto rickshaws—far away from the surreal and atmospheric Ayutthaya landscape—serendipitous and unexpected possibilities burst forward. The immediate urban stimuli of Krung Thep—its noise, gridlock traffic, and swarms of people getting off work—were no longer in my peripheral awareness. Instead the night continued with a series of concentrically expanding intellectual parameters as the anatomy of my dissertation began to emerge. They came in waves as Jane told me of her associations with key members of the KNU. "Reporters, writers, human rights folks are welcome there; heck, they want the world to know about their fight!" she exclaimed with alacrity. Not surprisingly, I slept very little that night. I knew I had found the topic of my dissertation. I also realized that the implications of such a research would be quite profound for me as a human being and scholar.

Before leaving Thailand, I asked Jane *not* to contact her KNLA colonel and friend, Colonel San Htay, regarding my intentions. I still needed approval from my dissertation committee—and more dauntingly—from the Human Subjects Review Board (HSRB). I also needed to draft a prospectus that would delineate my field research and how it would unfold. Upon returning to the United States, I began reading on Karen and Burmese history. There were many texts and most were of very high quality. My favorite was Jonathan Falla's *True Love and Bartholomew*, a rich ethnography written by a nurse who trekked into the Kawthoolei to attend to the health of the Karen people.[13] Thanks to these texts and my newly acquired knowledge, I drafted the proposal for my committee, declaring my intentions to research the Karen struggle from a development and political sociological orientation, and to do so by collecting data at the frontlines. My committee members liked the topic but were quite apprehensive about the methodology. After a few tense but constructive exchanges with the committee and the HSRB, they approved my proposal. The compromise was to remain within the "orbit" of Thailand, ideally within refugee camps inside Thailand, and to base my research on interviews with participants within them.

My research on the Karen struggle would be analyzed using an alternative development perspective derived from the ideas of Rodolfo Stavenhagen.[14] As a development and international relations discourse, Stavenhagen's ethnodevelopment is ultimately a critique against failed multiculturalisms that have in their wake acute ethnic inequality. Stavenhagen argues that multicultural states experiencing sectarian violence need to have development policies specifically designed for minority groups. Since international aid and development strategy tended not to question the premise or validity of the state, aid is often technocratic and economistic in nature, and channeled to the group in power, that is, the group that controls the state apparatus and its cultural production. For Stavenhagen, this is an undesirable trajectory since the dominant ethnic group in power, the *ethnocracy*, often exhibits oppressive and deculturalizing tendencies, frequently denying aid to peoples at the cultural and political periphery. For Stavenhagen, *ethnodevelopment*, or development policies specifically designed for minority groups, remedies this multicultural asymmetry.[15] As such, ethnodevelopment views development qualitatively and culturally, beyond state-centric economistic growth models and the arithmetic of GNP and GDP, measures that gloss over intra-state cultural differences, political climate, and people as conscious actors in the construction of their own history. Stavenhagen argued that the ethnocratically-controlled governments could be made to support ethnodevelopment of its periphery if international pressure, e.g., via the United Nations, explicitly sloganeers the need to improve the human rights of the region. The developing periphery and the central polity can then reach some sort of conflict resolution thereafter.[16]

Matters were substantially messier in Burma. The militarized Burman ethnocracy has been intransigent toward international pressures encouraging the democratization of the country and the cessation of ethnic cleansing of its ethnic nationalities, of which the Karen are part and parcel. International aid to military-ruled Burma as a means toward conflict resolution has always been ineffective because the Burman ethnocracy hoards the funds for their own stratum while meting out maldevelopment upon the Karen and other Burmese ethnic nationalities. As a result, the Karen had to develop themselves economically, culturally, and politically by removing socially limiting conditions, irrespective of the central state. Their revolution for self-determination made me realize that a revision of Stavenhagen's ethnodevelopment was in order.

In spite of the theoretical complexities I would have to attend to, the expedient task was to determine the exact site where I could employ Stavenhagen to "read" the Karen struggle. One or some of the numerous refugee camps that dotted the Thai-Burma border appeared to be viable options since over 120,000 Karen refugees, along with many thousands of other ethnic Burmese nationalities, reside in the region. One camp, Mae La, housed over 45,000 refugees at the time when paperwork for my dissertation was being processed. Moreover, the United Nations High Commission for Refugees (UNHCR) had two offices in Thailand: one was in Krung Thep, but more significantly, the other was at the Thai border town of Mae Sot, only a few kilometers from the Burmese border. The Mae Sot UNHCR would provide a quasi-international setting to invoke my U.S. citizenship status should complications arise during my research. Indeed, Jane had warned me that refugee camps were not safe sites. Human rights reports by various pressure groups such as International Crisis Group, Human Rights Watch, and local non-governmental organizations like the Karen Human Rights Groups frequently document how the camps have been shelled by Burma's army, infamously known as the *Tatmadaw*, because they believed Karen refugees at the camps were pro-KNU. In addition, the Thai soldiers that guard the camps are few in number. On many occasions, corrupt soldiers would be tipped off about an impending Tatmadaw attack and abandon their posts, leaving the unprotected refugees to fend for themselves. Many important Karen refugee camps during the late1990s were tragically razed to the ground in this manner. I elected camp Mae La as my research site and hoped for the best.

By October of 2003, I was ready for Jane to contact Colonel San Htay on my behalf. From Santa Cruz, I called Jane in Krung Thep to inform her of my readiness. About two weeks later, Jane sent me a short email with Colonel San Htay's contact information. Her only reminder was not to be discouraged if I had a difficult time reaching him: "he might be in the jungle, at the frontlines. He can't be reached if that's the case," wrote Jane. "Only when he gets back to Mae Sot will you be able to reach him." Nervousness overwhelmed me, preventing me from making the call for a few weeks. Instead, I contacted another Karen with the information provided by an important website managed by diasporic Karen in the United States. After delivering a formal letter to her on Santa Cruz letterhead with names of faculty references, Hser Kri Paw responded via email. I called her with less apprehension and we arranged to meet. A week later, I drove to Bakersfield, California, to meet Hser Kri Paw and her family.

It turned out that Hser Kri Paw was a Karen activist living in California. Her husband was a KNLA commander of high rank and she in fact traveled yearly to the frontlines to see him. When they married, Colonel San Htay, his brothers, and their father, the legendary KNU rebel leader Bo Mya, all attended the lavish jungle wedding. With much enthusiasm, I asked to see photographs of San Htay. She obliged and proceeded to show me many pictures of her wedding, attended by villagers and important Karen guests. This is how I first saw San Htay, a somewhat rotund man with what appeared to be a kind countenance. After consulting with Hser Kri Paw for many hours, I began acquiring an impression of San Htay and of the type of fieldwork for which I had to prepare myself. Only after our candid meeting did I feel capable of calling San Htay.

San Htay and I finally spoke for the first time in November of 2003. Although our conversation was brief, I sensed that Jane had put in a good word for me. In a moving moment, San Htay said calmly and in fluent English, "Thank you, Jack, for caring about the Karen and our struggle.[17] We welcome you to our state. Call me when you get to Thailand. We will take care of you."[18] San Htay's kindness stayed with me and somewhat disarmed my multiplied anxieties when we finally did meet in at Mae Sot. He arrived quietly in a blue Toyota SUV at noon in early January 2004. We met me on the poorly manicured courtyard of my mosquito-infested, smelly, and dilapidated hostel. He looked just like the photographs Hser Kri Paw had shown me and smiled warmly as we shook hands. Sensing that I might have had a long trip to Mae Sot, which included a slow ten-hour bus ride up the mountains in the company of chain-smoking Buddhist monks, undocumented Burman and Karen laborers, children with faces etched by patinae of mucous, and uneasy examinations by soldiers at Thai military checkpoints, San Htay took me to lunch at a bustling Mae Sot market.

San Htay was a serious, religious, and private individual, often reflecting on personal matters. Perhaps such is the existential state of a rebel leader. I knew he was a powerful figure by the deference the restaurant proprietor, workers, and later his subordinates, granted him. As we conversed, the mood of our lunch remained serious. San Htay, however, was poised and calm, a disposition I could rely on given the intrigue that exists in uncertain political and military climates. After warning me that we were likely being photographed by spies,[19] we then came up with an informal schedule: I would return to Mae Sot again in one week. From Mae Sot, San Htay would drop me off at one of the refugee camps and assign people to keep an eye out for my welfare. I would be going in and out of the camps at his and other prominent Karen's recommendations. It would be in these settings that I would collect qualitative data for my dissertation. In the afternoon, I contacted Jane and excitedly told her of the healthy dialog generated during my meeting with San Htay. That evening, I took an overnight bus back to Krung Thep to plan and pack. My research had found traction and the reality of it was beginning to dawn on me.

Prior to my exposure to Jane's association with the Karen, upon arriving in Krung Thep, the city's constant stimuli—the noise, pace of life, and overall intensity common to urban centers in Asia—had given me sensory overload. Yet this was no longer the case when I returned from Mae Sot to again wander the streets and night markets of Krung Thep. The capital city, in all its pollution, brightly and sometimes garishly lit marquees, skyscrapers, and slums—now had a dreamy, surreal narrative as if it stood in denial of the suffering and humanitarian crisis taking place only a few hundred kilometers away. But the landscape of denial was also metaphysically a comfort zone, and I now embraced the city's arrogance and beauty, for I knew I would soon be forced to face humility in ways that would be new to me. In Krung Thep, my spirit transcended something, which to this day remains vague and unclear to me. In the following days, I made copies of my passport and left the original with a close friend. I also organized medication to take with me per the suggestions of my university's health center, which included the antibiotics Doxycycline and Ciprofloxacin, the latter to be used for dysentery. My remaining days and nights were spent conjuring up crisis scenarios to mentally prepare myself to accept the metaphysical and existential experience to come. The night before returning to Mae Sot, I called my folks to let them know that all was

well and kept my conversation with them short to avoid worrying them with unnecessary details. On our bumpy truck ride northwest from Mae Sot, I was accompanied by San Htay's elder brother and a radio operator known as "Signal,"
as well as Signal's wife, to whom I was not introduced, but who was breastfeeding
her baby next to me in spite of suffering from malaria and breaking out in cold
sweats. In the bed of the truck were large sacks of chili, food stuffs, and *muer-
toos*—Burmese cigars coveted by many peoples in Burma. To keep the wind from
blowing away the lighter foodstuffs, two Karen sat atop the supplies in the bed of
the truck. Everyone seemed in a festive mood for the approaching January 31st
Karen Revolutionary Day celebrations.[20] During our trip, San Htay talked about
his father, Bo Mya, while others quietly listened. I had read a great deal about
Bo Mya and knew he exemplified the tough mountain warrior that had repulsed
decades of Tatmadaw onslaught. Even as we arrived at a Thai military checkpoint,
the flow of San Htay's conversation was not interrupted by soldiers examining our
truck. The Thai troops gave us a casual salute after making eye contact with all
onboard and let us through, much to my relief.[21] Yet my anxieties were not allayed
with the passing of the checkpoint, but amplified as San Htay surprised me with an
alternative plan.

San Htay recommended that my itinerary be the same as his entourage, all of
whom were heading to the KNU/KNLA base at the 202 battalion *inside* Kawthoolei. There is a larger safety margin at the 202 base as San Htay echoed Jane's
assessments that refugee camps are areas highly vulnerable to Tatmadaw attacks.
San Htay's decision for me to reside with the KNLA rebels was pragmatic: should
anything go wrong at the 202 the KNLA could assist in my departure. Moreover,
at the KNU's Mu Aye Pu headquarters/base, I would be introduced to villagers,
guerillas, and commanders of the KNLA 202 battalion. Finally, San Htay added
that I would meet Bo Mya as he was scheduled to arrive the afternoon before the
January 31st festivities for Karen Revolution Day. Additionally, accompanying Bo
Mya would be prominent KNU and KNLA members from other battalions, reporters, and charity representatives. San Htay said this was a "good time" for me
to go to the base because the KNU and the Tatmadaw were engaged in ceasefire
talks.[22]

When our truck stopped to drop off Signal's wife at Mae La camp, where I had
thought I would get off as well, I had a few minutes to reflect as Signal walked his
family toward the camp entrance with their supplies and foodstuffs. San Htay's offer was simply too fortuitous to refuse. Although this meant that I had to deviate
from plans to remain at refugee camps, being situated at the 202 also meant that
a more diverse population sample would be available to me since villagers, KNLA
guerillas, refugees, veterans, and KNU officials would all be congregated at one
site.[23] I quickly learned that, in the field, impromptu decision-making, modifications to the itinerary, and flexible time management are realities with which the
researcher must negotiate. One must balance his/her judgments and realize that
this flexibility, blessed by serendipity, often means taking calculated risks that affect not only the researcher, but the social concentrics of the researcher's local and
global network. Realizing that I had made the most risky decision of my young

adult life by opting for a site my dissertation committee deemed least desirable, I left the camp that could have welcomed me and we continued northwest toward the 202 base. After about three and a half hours on the road, our truck descended to the banks of the Moei River. Across the Moei, which during the dry season was about forty yards wide, appeared the KNU/KNLA 202 battalion atop a forty foot cliff.[24] The supplies were immediately unloaded onto a long and colorful river boat. I took some deep breaths as the ferryman started the engine and brought us across the short expanse of the Moei. Upon arriving, we climbed the dusty incline while KNLA guerillas on duty kept watch. This was the beginning of Kawthoolei, a world of rebels, and, at the time of my arrival, a world that had been in rebellion for over fifty years. Beyond this epic view, however, were Karen villagers scurrying back and forth while some guerillas were playing an afternoon game of soccer; Falla would have recognized this world.

San Htay took me to a large red wooden barrack and showed me my room. I would be staying in what was Bo Mya's shelter at the 202. I was quickly introduced to a handful of Karen. Another handful of villagers gathered to see the new arrivals. We began our acquaintance with a discussion of practical matters, such as areas of the Moei where one could bathe and do laundry. My excitement continued to grow as I realized that these were the folks I would talk to and get to know. San Htay then invited me for an afternoon swim in the Moei where we talked about life, his hopes, and his dreams, or as he himself put it: "I'm a simple man Jack and one day I'd like to have my farm here." These words would remain embedded in my memory as a mantra that I was certain many Karen would have understood. The intensity of the day had left us exceptionally hungry and fatigued. As San Htay and I welcomed the evening, goat meat was served with rice and fish; we ate heartily. I did not sleep my first night due to the cold and sheer fright.

Thus began my field research with the Karen, whose world ended at the frontlines, a few hours trek away from the 202 where the KNLA faced off entrenched Tatmadaw troops. Next came the gradual acclimation to the infrastructural realities of Karen life at the 202: they virtually lived with no electricity—our base had one long fluorescent bulb powered by a car battery that was charged during the day by a generator, requiring me to summarize my field notes every night by candlelight. There were no refrigerators, televisions, or schools that I could see, no industrialized infrastructure made of concrete, no roads, and no telephone lines. What was viscerally present was the thick jungle, poverty, landmine survivors—some of whom attempted to hide their maimed lower extremities and prosthetics by wearing sarongs—malnourishment, and villagers and guerillas afflicted with malaria. I also witnessed effects of post-traumatic stress and fatigue on the Karen villagers and the KNLA, as well as their grit and toughness. By the end of my research, I had become sadly familiar and touched by the world of the Karen Revolution and its people.

I did not remain continuously at the 202 and accompanied many other Karen, per Burawoy's recommendations, to different data sites: a Karen pastor and previous member of the KNU Central Committee befriended me and exposed me to the Karen world of public relations and activism that acquired international aid and donations. His staff of young students was internet savvy and had created an underground Karen "base," as they jokingly referred to it, on the outskirts of the northern Thai city of Chiang Mai. There, news of the Karen struggle was relayed to the local and global community of the Karen diaspora. Those visits also allowed to me to come into contact with individuals such as pro-KNU pastors who administered a Karen church and inculcated young Karen to love their country and struggle. On another occasion, I conducted a tape-recorded interview of the pastor as he was receiving a haircut at a Mae Sot barber shop while plain clothed KNLA bodyguards stood outside. I also met KNU personnel when they accompanied Bo Mya for his diabetes treatment in Krung Thep, and English charity representatives from churches based in the United Kingdom. Outside of Kawthoolei, far from the 202, some of my interview sites included large restaurants, hotel lobbies, and food courts in Krung Thep's superstores. In these various locales, valuable data were provided through conversations, documents, pictures discs, and/or documentaries.

There was no set schedule during my time with the Karen, only one's ability to manage hyper-time: on a moment's notice, I would be on my way to northern Thailand's city of Chiang Mai or asked to go back to Krung Thep, back to Mae Sot, or back to the 202. My dissertation was thus compiled from very rich, yet highly segmented data. This segmentation resulted from inconsistent interview times that varied with different participants, filtered responses as a result of interventions by interpreters when communication with participants was unintelligible and required translation, as well as travels to a variety of different settings. My research concluded with the application of a sociological *bricolage* that employed the patina of history, human rights reports, and general statistics to close the gaps between segmented and qualitative data "chunks" to assess, evaluate, and document the Karen struggle.

Initially, I had hoped to provide more neutrality by streamlining the interrelationship among truths, embellishments, controversies, and intense feelings that make Karen and Burmese ethnopolitics so labyrinthine and complex. I had to assess in terms of degree some credibility issues experienced by the KNU in the form of landmine use, organizational corruption, and the employment of child soldiers by juxtaposing them in ways that made visible how the credibility pitfalls of the various pro-Burman military regimes were by far more severe, protracted, and insidious.[25] The task was more made challenging due to two intense types of Karen sentiments in the field. The first, understandably, echoed of war fatigue by some Karen civilians, with sentiments such as "if the Burmans only laid down their weapons and came in peace the Karen would embrace them," according to Hser Kri Paw.[26] Karen die-hards, on the other hand, continued to sloganeer Ba U Gyi's[27] Four Principles of the Karen Revolution: (1) there shall be no surrender, (2) the recognition of the Karen State must be completed, (3) the Karen shall retain their arms, and (4) the Karen will decide their own political destiny. For the latter group, Karen nationalist ideology was ingrained to the point that disentangling potentially scripted answers from ideological fervor was impossible. Additionally, in spite of the sometimes contradictory tensions that existed in the self-determination trajectory of the Karen, many Karen were hopeful and relied on their faith[28] to claim the moral high ground. It was in essence a righteous fight for the vast majority of them, especially for the younger Karen. Indeed, in the spirit of Weber and Dilthey's *verstehen*, it was my empathy for their liberatory sentiments that finally oriented my sociological imagination beyond capturing objective or neutral regularities of the Karen human condition.[29] The Karen struggle has a non-rational and passionate dimension that is difficult to read with objective reasoning; I found comfort in existentialist Edward Tiryakian's sentiment on objectivity, namely that it has "certain boundaries beyond which it cannot go in its quest for knowledge" and as a result, the understanding of human beings in its fullest expression is "impervious to scientific research" for "the realm of science is the realm of objectivity, but this does not exhaust all of being." Furthermore, he states, "The social sciences (in particular, psychology and sociology) are always confronted with their limitations in studying man . . . hence the task . . . is to illuminate the various aspects of existence, not to objectively describe it."[30]

By this point in my research, which had been inductive and open-ended, a Karen revolutionary trajectory emerged that was conducive to the construction of an alternative ethnodevelopment model. My field data were merged with an articulation of a model that turned Stavenhagen's ethnodevelopment upside-down: I noted that the Karen Revolution is itself a development process, a process which I designated as *liberation ethnodevelopment*.[31] Whereas Stavenhagen argued that ethnodevelopment from the state and international context can serve to alleviate destitution among ethnic minorities, this *top-to-bottom* approach assumes that the state is charitable or diplomatic enough to attend to peoples at its political and cultural periphery. In the case of Burma, two decades of condemnations against the country's various regimes at the international and domestic level—the latter context of which is most well known through the efforts of pro-democracy supporters and Burman activist and 1991 Nobel Peace Prize winner, Aung San Suu Kyi—have failed to destabilize the Tatmadaw's power base. Instead, the Tatmadaw's *Four Cuts* offensives have perennially increased in severity during the last decade, and continue at the time of this writing: China, India, and Thailand are now courting the regime while they superficially sloganeer a superficial and generalized indignation against the military government.[32] Liberation ethnodevelopment, on the other hand, is a *bottom-to-top* approach that accepts *revolution as development* if the group in question has developed institutions of a prototypical state to contest ethnic cleansing by the ethnocracy, the latter of which is the source of Karen systemic crisis. My exposure to the organs of the KNU, the health and education departments, the KNLA, as well as their swidden economy and the informal riverine economy based off the Moei and Salween rivers, represented what were clearly ethnodevelopment on Karen, not Burman, terms. Indeed the dynamics of the former were in structural opposition to the Tatmadaw and geared toward attaining some form of liberation from the pro-Burman military dictatorship.

When conducting crisis field research, it is important to keep practical and epistemological considerations in mind. There is a logistical side to research, after all. These considerations, if under attended or ignored, can dramatically hinder the researcher's data collection or perhaps even prevent the researcher from gathering his or her data altogether. The crisis field researcher should entertain the following methodological and interpersonal considerations when working on crisis sites caused by sectarian conflict: the field researcher should be up to date with vaccinations and have proper documentation to verify them; researchers can start at their universities' health centers as they will issue such verification. The researcher should also gather the appropriate medicines for the field and prepare to self-medicate if necessary. One can visit the United Nation's World Health Organization website to get up-to-date information on diseases and epidemics in areas of interest. The field researcher should also understand the ways in which seasons unfold regionally as weather is intimately linked to different kinds of disease and illness outbreaks. If in a rural area, always be aware of wildlife and protect yourself accordingly. If in an urban area always be aware of careless motorists and the intensity of traffic. In addition, the field researcher should always have good maps of the research site and study the topography of the area. If funding is available, purchase a satellite phone with global positioning system (GPS) for identifying your longitudinal and latitudinal coordinates at all times. A good micro-cassette recorder and a digital camera powered by Lithium batteries are highly recommended as is the acquisition of a bounded journal for entering field notes. Having these items is more realistic than assuming there will be electricity at a crisis site. Anticipate that electricity at a crisis site may only be available intermittently at best, and at worse, not available at all.

At the interpersonal level, if the crisis site is under the human rights radar, there will be journalists in the field. The field researcher should get to know some of the journalists since many are savvy with connections and contacts, possess good survival instincts, are frequently up to date with information, and can be well informed with the dynamics of the area. If possible, keep in touch with this contingent during the research process for the sake of being able to be privy to inside information. Ask journalists to recommend a good interpreter if one is needed. Schedule specific dates so that you can contact social networks outside your field research site. Make sure your contacts know the location of your embassy of domicile so that they can report any scheduling anomalies to the personnel. As a general rule, the field researcher should cherish contacts and never view them as episodically expendable. Moreover, if a snowball sample is the only feasible sampling option, every contact will matter *exponentially*. Friendships in the field can save a life. Respect of anonymity is also of utmost importance. When interviewing anyone, the field researcher should assign pseudonyms for his participants and keep the pseudonyms' relations to actual names discreetly stored away. If possible, the field researcher should try to mnemonically commit the pseudonyms to memory for the list of actual names must be the first destroyed should undesirable authorities attempt to thwart the data collection process. The only exemption to this rule might be if a personality is a well-known public figure (e.g., well known in the press), in which case assigning a pseudonym may not be necessary if the party in question grants permission for the researcher to exhibit transparency.

Any researcher should be exceptionally careful of when, how, where, and with whom currency transactions occur. If one normally conducts transactions with the U.S. dollars, remember that the greenback is one of the world's most stable currencies and that it will be highly coveted by many segments of the population. People in survival mode are clear and desperate in their needs and will often bluntly ask for money. If the field researcher does not have the wherewithal to engage in currency transactions, then by all means one should explicitly leave currency transactions out of all interpersonal relationships. Crisis sites are filled with a subtle chemistry between people that must be carefully cultivated through trust and patience. Money transactions may destabilize such chemistry.

The researcher in crisis sites must be especially aware of gendered patterns of communication insofar as whether it is shaped and configured along matriarchal or patriarchal centers of social relations. Rape and violence against women, and even men, are frequently used as psychological weapons in times of desperation and war, a fact that the crisis field researcher should never forget. If one senses the dangers of explicitly interviewing traumatized survivors, then err on the side of intimate speculations that should not be construed as data nor extrapolated to explain generalized patterns of gendered violence. I cannot overemphasize that one should never underestimate the subtexts of gender articulations by people in survival mode. Being able to "read between the lines" when people are not as forthright as we are used to in our culture allows us to streamline interpersonal relationships that is shaped by how others perceive us on the basis of our female or male status. Keep in mind that knowledge production is always relational, situated in cultural scripts that may be unfamiliar to you as a crisis field researcher, scripts that are dramatically affected by whether you are a female or male researcher, further complicated by whether your sample is male, female or both.[33]

In addition, the crisis field researcher should always exhibit poise, professionalism, and transparency during all interpersonal communications. Be aware that as a researcher, you are not only an individual, but also a representative of your university, department, and dissertation committee. Field researchers are also "ambassadors with long-term relationships in mind, considering outcomes for informants and compensating them for knowledge extracted."[34] Field researchers should display gratitude, humility, and respect toward all participants and interlocutors. Manners are free—anyone can have them—there is no excuse for not displaying decorum and professionalism in all instances of social interaction. Finally, never feel *entitled* to privileges as a scholar for trust, ever important for data collection, is built and solidified through humility, manners, and transparency, not through self-righteousness or hubris. The issue of how a researcher can earn the trust of and accessibility to participants in the field is, for Gill ensured by staying at a research site for a longer duration. This is not a new insight, of course, as Boas, Mead, Benedict, and Malinowski—the greats of anthropology, did just this. In hindsight, one of the mistakes I committed was my inability to develop long-term trust with one segment of the Karen population, namely the KNLA guerillas. A small minority, about a dozen, warmly received me; the remainder, however, viewed me with indifference. Much of their sentiments can be attributed to my nomadism, resulting in a *too* transnational field methodology within a short time-span. Simply stated, I did not "stay put" long enough at the 202 to appease their sensibilities as I often traveled to different sites, as aforementioned, to collect data. I was also frequently in the company of the 202 leadership. By being in the company of KNLA colonels and the late Bo Mya, my status was affected to a degree that compelled the guerillas to keep a quiet deference and distance.

A corollary to Gill's wisdom is that although time may warm the ties between the researcher and his/her participants, the context of systemic crisis and the hyper-time conditions of war may just as well shift certain people toward relying on their instincts to question the motives of the outsider. As noted by Gill during her stay in the Dominican Republic, the social networks exhibited by the Karen— more so in Kawthoolei than transnationally—also contain diffused cues shaped by "an elaborate system of spying and gossip" that protect "people from suspicious characters."[35] These should not be ignored, nor, and I emphasize, be viewed as anomalistic by the crisis field researcher. Demotic experiences and adaptations to systemic crisis justify demotic fears; the key is not to let those who explicitly resent and distrust the presence of a field researcher intimidate his/her ability to collect data (since distrustful sentiments are themselves qualitative data in the larger scheme of things). When faced with the inability to gain a group's trust, the researcher is responsible for compensating the segmented data by employing historical details to streamline data clusters, that is, to close gaps that manifest as epistemological blind spots.

Rest assured that the researcher will ultimately be "taken in" by one group. Fortunately, the contingent that took me in had many Karen participants that spoke rudimentary to good Thai and English, obviating my need to retain my interpreter, although I did have one assisting me during the first month of my stay.[36] My association with this circle had its benefits and disadvantages. The main benefit was that this circle consisted of important political actors that had a direct role in improving the lot of disadvantaged Karen, i.e., they were directly instrumental in shaping Karen public policy. Yet this same circle, upon their cooptation of me, narrowed the horizons of my data collection, limiting me to mostly a non-demotic, elite Karen circle that may or may not have shared similar sentiments with the most disadvantaged Karen, thus the need for bricolage that included historical data and human rights reports to eliminate some one's analytical blind spots.

The crisis site researcher also needs to be aware of how emotions are exhibited in the midst of others. Participants in crisis areas are often products of direct violence and brutality. Many will disclose the traumatizing experiences that have befallen them. The crisis field researcher should be cognizant of how the participants' emotions affect data collection. Finally, the crisis field researcher should not exhibit the kind of fear that can ruin one's composure and poise. If reckless confidence is not always the crisis field researcher's best ally, neither is fear. About two weeks into my stay at the 202, I was left with the realization that I was having a genuine peak experience, one that spoke to my passions as a human being and as a scholar. It was an experience that allowed me, if not to embrace, then at least to be comfortable with the unknown. To a great extent, this allowed me to transcend my fear. Upon this realization I was filled with a quiet peace that helped me cope with the very intense world of the Karen Revolution.

Epistemologically, there is also the issue of how the crisis field researcher negotiates his/her positionality, especially when axes of race, gender, politics, and privilege intersect with local and diasporic articulations of stress. Positionality informs how the researcher collects data, recounts a story, and projects a trajectory. In short, it influences how the researcher recovers and reconstructs the human experience in crisis situations. Positionality is a critical self-consciousness that points to how the researcher is *aware* that research is being conducted from his/her gender orientation, ethnicity/race, and/or political perspective. This methodological awareness is important lest the ethnographer colonizes or affects the voices of participants in the field through ethnocentric and overarching generalizations. Data should be viewed as outputs of social relations, not as dogmatic and/or reified facts.[37] Indeed my positionality—being an Asian American male that has inherited identity legacies borne from certain less than desirable chapters of the American experience—influenced my fascination for the Karen struggle, my interaction with participants, the determination of what data were deemed good data, as well as the telling of the Karen epic.

In this regard, I found myself an advocate of Karen liberation. My desire to see Karen self-determination and their fight for "freedom" realized, constituted an important example that could further inform my theoretical views on social justice, citizenship, and state formation. Given the degree of genocidal onslaught and maldevelopment meted out to the Karen by the Tatmadaw had gone on for many decades, my sense of responsibility shifted toward the Karen in ways that Avruch so presciently anticipated of field researchers, namely that "some of them . . . have always been self-consciously politically engaged with their people, for better or worse."[38] It has allowed me to make visible the Karen struggle within a human rights discourse—a discourse that Avruch incisively noted has made a tremendous impact on shaping the motives of the researcher in the field. Another crucial point to consider is whether a positionally grounded approach to crisis field research is too subjectivist and relativistic. The more complex, and in my opinion, constructive approach is to let participants' *indigenous conceptions of stress* and their local knowledge tell the story, as often as possible;[39] or as Hays-Mitchell remarked of her stay with various Peruvians in the context of civil war, "they taught me that, despite my best efforts, I simply cannot know poverty, violence, or war as they do and that I must therefore trust them."[40] The complexity of the researcher's position is further complicated by the fact that delineating one's own positionality does not mean that participants in the field will understand it. De Tona noted the influence of the "race of interviewer effect," where being seen as sharing or deviating from the identity of participants in the study is an issue that must be considered.[41] This effect relates to the comfort zone with those that consider or do not consider you part of their ilk, as greater cultural distances could potentially affect the depth of data disclosed by your sample. Nonetheless being aware of one's position has one important advantage: it compensates for ethnocentrically erroneous assumptions and overarching generalizations to a great degree if one does not belong to the same ilk of the people under examination. Through a compilation of different readings by various ethnographers on the same subject, "a mirror of . . . different situations" can then capture the complexities and diversities of demotic articulations.[42]

In conclusion, positionality influences "our ways of knowing and doing . . . and how we even talk about these issues."[43] Because crisis field research attends to life and death experiences, attending to them on purely a rational level, as Taylor noted, is neither possible nor desirable. Indeed, when people are in survival mode, the articulation of their human experience is existential, emotive and "pure": the lucidities of their anger, frustration, and hopelessness are visceral but so are their joys, hopes, and dreams. The field researcher should be ready to accept these uncluttered articulations from their perspective, not only as a source of data, but as a source of growth as they provide a scholar indelible cues on what it means to be human. The dialectical textures of the informants' world, its contradictions and interrelationships, must be also be detailed with care, with the consciousness of positionality carefully woven into the research process. The main reason why the onus should always be on the crisis field researcher to accommodate and defer to participants in their world is simple: the experiences and wisdom derived from immersion at the crisis site will always be, noted Taylor, a "partial view of the experience, never complete" and "indicative of a particular perspective" that "needs to be recognized for its partiality."[44] Crisis field research thus "checks" one's positionality by allowing the human experience, which in the context of crisis forces people to emphasize their existence, to speak for itself. There is a more humbling and humane reason, however: as an interloper into another people's epic, the crisis field researcher has the discomforting privilege of being able to leave the world of his or her less fortunate participants.

NOTES

1   See Burawoy, Michael. 2000. *Global Ethnography: Forces, Connections, and Imaginations in a Postmodern World.* Berkeley: University of California Press and Burawoy, Michael, Alice Burton, Ann Arnett Ferguson, and Kathryn J. Fox. 1991. *Ethnography Unbound: Power and Resistance in the Modern Metropolis.* Berkeley: University of California Press.

2   See (1) Cook, Ian, "Positionality/Situated Knowledge." In Sibley, David, Peter Jackson, David Atkinson, and Neil Washbourne (eds). *Cultural Geography: A Critical Dictionary of Key Concepts* (I. B. Tauris. 2005); (2) Amit, Vered (ed), *Constructing the Field: Ethnographic Fieldwork in the Contemporary World* (London: Routledge, 2001); (3) Bell, Diane, Pat Caplan and Wazir Jahan Karim (eds), *Gendered Fields: Women, Men & Ethnography* (London: Routledge, 1993); (4) Moss, Pamela (ed), *Placing Autobiography in Geography (Space, Place and Society)* (Syracuse University Press, 2001); (5) Okely,

Judith and Helen Callaway (eds), *Anthropology & Autobiography* (London: Routledge, 1992).

3 See (1) Gill, Hannah E., "Finding a Middle Ground between Extremes: Notes on Researching Transnational Crime and Violence." *Anthropology Matters Journal*, 6, no. 2 (2004): 1–9; (2) Avruch, Kevin, "Notes Toward Ethnographies of Conflict and Violence." *Journal of Contemporary Ethnography*, 20, no. 5 (October 2001): 637–648; (3) Hays-Mitchell, Maureen, "Danger, Fulfillment, and Responsibility in A Violene-Plagued Society." *The Geographical Review*, 91 no. 1–2 (2001): 311–321; (4) and Blee, Kathleen M., "Becoming a Racist: Women in Contemporary Ku Klux Klan and Neo-Nazi Groups." *Gender and Society*, 10, no. 6 (1996) : 680–702.

4 See (1) Gill, "Finding a Middle Ground between Extremes: Notes on Researching Transnational Crime and Violence" and (2) Avruch, "Notes Toward Ethnographies of Conflict and Violence."

5 Gill, "Finding a Middle Ground between Extremes: Notes on Researching Transnational Crime and Violence," 7.

6 Jürgen Habermas, *Legitimation Crisis* (Polity Press, 1988).

7 Amartya Sen, *Poverty and Famines: An Essay on Entitlement and Deprivation* (Oxford University Press, 1981).

8 Ben Crow, "Understanding Famine and Hunger." In Allen, Tim and Alan Thomas (eds). *Poverty and Development in the 1990s* (Oxford University Press, 1992).

9 Burma was renamed Myanmar in 1989 by the military regime. International pressure groups and governments that do not recognize the military regime of Myanmar continue to refer to the country as Burma.

10 Jane granted me permission to employ her real name. However, the Karen individuals to be mentioned in the following pages, Col. San Htay, Hser Kri Paw, and "Signal" are referred to pseudonymously due to their intimate participation in the Karen struggle. These pseudonyms can be cross-referenced to my monograph on the Karen struggle *Revolution as Development: The Karen Self-Determination Struggle against Ethocracy: (1949–2004)* (Boca Raton: Universal Publishers, 2008).

11 Since 1962 there have been three pro-Burman military regimes: the Burma Socialist Program Party (BSPP: 1962–1988), the State Law and Order Restoration Council (SLORC: 1988–1997), and the State Peace and Development Council (SPDC: 1997 to present).

12 The Karen National Liberation Army (KNLA) is the armed wing of the Karen National Union (KNU), the governing body of the Karen State of Kawthoolei.

13 Jonathan Falla, *True Love and Bartholomew: Rebels on the Burmese Border* (Cambridge: Cambridge University Press, 1991).

14 Rodolfo Stavenhagen, "Ethnodevelopment: A neglected Dimension in Development Thinking." In Anthorpe, Raymond and Krahl Andras (eds). *Development Studies: Critique and Renewal* (Leiden: E. J. Brill, 1986); see also Rodolfo Stavenhagen, *Ethnic Conflicts and the Nation-state* (New York: St. Martin's Press, 1996).

15 Many of Stavenhagen's ethnodevelopment views were articulated during his tenure with the United Nations Research Institute for Social Development (UNRISD). The UNRISD is the only UN organization that attends to development issues.

16 A classic example of ethnodevelopment at work was the 1999 United Nation's sponsorship of East Timor independence from Indonesia. Indonesia had invaded the region in 1975, incorporating it into Indonesia proper. Like all forms of colonialism, there was violence and bloodshed in the process, sparking the East Timorese drive for independence. East Timor achieved liberation on May 20, 2002, making it the first new country of the new millennium.

17 San Htay graduated from a university in California, United States of America, before voluntarily returning home to join Karen struggle. He is fluent in English, Thai, Burmese, and Karen.

18 There are many Karen living inside Thailand. Karen Thais, however, have not agitated for independence because the Thai government has traditionally been tolerant of its hill tribes.

19 Many parts of Mae Sot are populated by large populations of Burmese and Karen migrant workers and spies, given the porous border between Thailand and Burma. Pro-KNU and pro-Tatmadaw agents jockey for information daily.

20 On January 31, 1949, after the British granted Burma country independence and departed, the Karen launched their Revolution against the "Union" of Burma amidst the onset of sectarian violence.

21 Thai soldiers know about Karen fighters operating inside their borders. Direct action has not been taken because the Thai government is somewhat sympathetic to the Karen struggle. By "somewhat" I mean that sentiments toward Thai-Karen diplomacy are dependent upon the Thai administration governing the country at the time.

22 During January 2004, the KNU and the Tatmadaw were engaged in historical ceasefire talks. The 2004 talks were significant in that one of the top Tatmadaw generals, Khin Nyunt, had invited Bo Mya to Rangoon, the former capital of Burma, to resolve the conflict. Thai generals were quasi-mediators in the process. Khin Nyunt was purged by Tatmadaw hawks less than a year later and the "gentleman's ceasefire" collapsed. Fighting has resumed at the time of this writing.

23 Refugees on the porous Thai/Burma border often sneak out of camps and cross back into Kawthoolei to assess the conditions of their farms, as well as visit family and contacts. Young Karen refugees are most prone to undertake this activity since many of their parents are active members of the KNU or KNLA, and thus stay inside Kawthoolei.

24 The dry season in Southeast Asia usually ranges between November and April. The monsoon season ranges between April and November.

25 The United Nations, the European Community and the United States have never, during the Karen National Union's (KNU) fifty-eight years of existence, designated or listed the KNU or the KNLA as terrorist organizations.

26 Hser Kri Paw and the multiethnic organization she worked with at the time, the *Free Burma Coalition*, supported "reconciliation at all costs" with the mili-

tary regime. For KNU hawks this line of defeatist thinking for human rights is unacceptable and she was subsequently expelled from the KNU.

27 English educated barrister Ba U Gyi (1905–1950) was the first president of the Karen National Union and launched the Karen Revolution. In August of 1950 Ba U Gyi, along with a high-ranking rebel leader Saw Sankey were tracked down in the jungle by the Burman administration of then prime minister U Nu and assassinated.

28 Most Karen are Buddhist/animists but approximately one-third of the population are Christians, a product of English and American missionary work in Burma during the nineteenth century.

29 The sociologist Max Weber and philosopher Wilhelm Dilthey employed the term to mean understanding and comprehension from within as an antipode to objective and externalized views of subject and social matter.

30 Edward A. Tiryakian, *Sociologism and Existentialism: Two Perspectives on the Individual and Society* (Englewood Cliffs, NJ: Prentice-Hall, Inc., 1962), 115-116.

31 See my works *Revolution as Development: The Karen Self-Determination Struggle against Ethocracy: (1949–2004)*(Boca Raton: Universal Publishers, 2008) and "Revising the Ethnodevelopment Model to Address Karen Self-determination in the Context of Ethnocratic and Military-ruled Burma," in *Ethnic and Racial Studies*, 31, no. 2. (2008): 327–357.

32 The Four Cuts, employed since the 1960s, is a Tatmadaw military strategy based on cutting the food supplies, financial flow, intelligence gather capacity, and ability of the rebels to recruit new soldiers. It is based on the Burman metaphor of "draining the ocean so the fish cannot swim." In practice, it is a notorious scorched earth and forced relocation policy directed mainly against civilians.

33 Hays-Mitchell, "Danger, Fulfillment, and Responsibility in A Violence-Plagued Society" and Blee, "Becoming a Racist: Women in Contemporary Ku Klux Klan and Neo-Nazi Groups."

34 Gill, "Finding a Middle Ground between Extremes: Notes on Researching Transnational Crime and Violence."

35 Gill, "Finding a Middle Ground between Extremes: Notes on Researching Transnational Crime and Violence," 6.

36 Many Karen speak Thai because of their periodic or long-term stay at refugee camps inside Thailand. There is also a small population of Karen in Thailand. Due to the relative tolerance exhibited by the Thai polities toward the Karen throughout Siamese/Thai history, the Karen Thais have not agitated for a separate state. Many Karen also speak rudimentary English since American and British missionaries inculcated English in Karen village schools beginning in the early nineteenth-century. Burmese is spoken when Karen that do not understand regional Sgaw and Pwo dialects communicate.

37 Cook, "Positionality/Situated Knowledge."

38 Avruch, "Notes Toward Ethnographies of Conflict and Violence," 643.

39 I have to thank Dr. Leakhena Nou at California State University, Long Beach, for contributing this phase, now forever ensconced in my development lexicon.

40 Hays-Mitchell, "Danger, Fulfillment, and Responsibility in A Violence-Plagued Society," 315.

41 Carla De Tona, "But What is Interesting is the Story of Why and How Migration Happened," *Forum Qualitative Sozialforschung/Forum: Qualitative Social Research* [On-line Journal], 7, no. 3: Article 13. Available at: http://www.qualitative-research.net/fqs-texte/3-06/06-3-13-e.htm [Date of Access: January 13, 2007]: paragraph 26.

42 Carla De Tona, "But What is Interesting is the Story of Why and How Migration Happened," *Forum Qualitative Sozialforschung/Forum: Qualitative Social Research* [On-line Journal], 7, no. 3: Article 13. Available at: http://www.qualitative-research.net/fqs-texte/3-06/06-3-13-e.htm [Date of Access: January 13, 2007]: paragraph 27.

43 Taylor, Edward, Elizabeth J. Tisdell, and Mary Stone Hanley, "The Role of Positionality in Teaching for Critical Consciousness: Implications for Adult Education," Paper presented at 2000 *Adult Education Research Conference* (AERC). Retrieved Jan 2007. (http://www.edst.educ.ubc.ca/aerc/2000/tayloreetal1-web.htm); 2.

44 Taylor, Edward, Elizabeth J. Tisdell, and Mary Stone Hanley, "The Role of Positionality in Teaching for Critical Consciousness: Implications for Adult Education," Paper presented at 2000 *Adult Education Research Conference* (AERC). Retrieved Jan 2007. (http://www.edst.educ.ubc.ca/aerc/2000/tayloreetal1-web.htm); 4.

CHAPTER FIVE

Building Trust, Enhancing Research: Carrying out Fieldwork in Namibia

By Mónica Ruiz-Casares

"We need elder people to put my girlfriend and myself together, to teach us how we can live, trusting each other." Kavango, boy head of household since age seventeen.

Trust is at the basis of healthy and sustainable relations. Whether the actors on which we depend be individuals or organizations, we quickly learn that not trusting impedes the development of mutually rewarding relationships.[1] On the other hand, acting on trust implies risk and is potentially costly if the actors we trust turn out not to be trustworthy.[2] An object of study across many disciplines such as psychology, sociology, economics and management sciences, trust, we know, may grow over time, yet different tasks require different levels and durations of trust. While unconditional trust remains rare and is often not necessary, distrust can also be appropriate in certain circumstances.[3] Yet, because trust promotes open communication, it is essential to successfully collect data and to ensure the validity, credibility, and believability of our research.[4] Trust is particularly relevant in contexts of uncertainty or ignorance about other people and their intentions,[5] like those that emerge when working with and in different cultures.

This chapter discusses the role of trust in initiating and conducting research with orphans and vulnerable children (OVC) in Namibia, a country previously unknown to me and one in which I was a visible minority. My doctoral experience in Namibia provided numerous opportunities to reflect on the role of trust and power in research relations in a setting rather unique—and often unfamiliar—due to its history and extreme social and economic inequalities, which pose challenges to the development of trust. My doctoral dissertation examined ways in which families and communities can better support child-headed households (CHHs) in Namibia, building upon children's resilience and the strengths of their personal social networks. In general, a CHH is a domestic unit consisting of children "parented" by an elder sibling. I identified unmet needs and existing resources by means of engaging with children heads of household in mapping their social networks (both supportive and negative), assessing children's needs and strengths, and analyzing the contextual characteristics that affect children's options for coping in a country heavily affected by HIV/AIDS. In fieldwork, researchers must engage in relationships of mutual respect and openness if they want to gain a good understanding of the social world of the people they study.[6] However, power asymmetries, unclear expectations, personal biases and assumptions, and other factors can interfere with genuine human encounters and influence the quality of the research. While seeing children as agents in their own lives and valuable contributors to society,[7] I could not ignore that children are a heterogeneous group, locked in a series of interdependent and asymmetrical relationships with adults.[8] Paraphrasing Michelle Fine, doing work of social change in a context that discredits children's voices means that social researchers have to be negotiating how, when, and why to situate and privilege whose voices, and to create communities of friendly critical informants who can help them think through those decisions.[9] Developing these relationships—gaining and retaining trust—requires flexibility, morality, sensitivity to local values and practices, and prolonged local engagement, as I will illustrate throughout this chapter.

TRUST IN RESEARCH: STUDYING THE SOCIAL NETWORKS OF CHILDREN HEADS OF HOUSEHOLD IN NAMIBIA

When I arrived in Namibia in July 2002 hardly did I know that I would end up living there for two full years. I had spent two months in its capital, Windhoek, earlier that year and I was naively optimistic about my timeline. During this first visit, I started to develop partnerships with organizations working with OVC in the country, established affiliation with the University of Namibia, consulted locally to identify who must give permission to my research (i.e., the gatekeepers),[10] and gained first-hand knowledge of the situation of OVC. All of this proved essential. For many months, I had carefully researched the country, enjoyed its music and arts, and read anything containing "Namibia" or "South West Africa" (as this territory has been known since the German occupation in 1884) in its title—from biodiversity in the Kalahari desert to changes in residence patterns among matrilineal groups in the North. I also sought and met Namibians as well as academics and other professionals who had worked there and were now living overseas. Yet, as it usually happens, it was not long before certainty turned into uncertainty and my carefully-drafted plans had to undergo major reconsideration. It would not be the last time either . . .

NAMIBIA: LAND OF THE BRAVE[11]

One of the most sparsely and unevenly populated countries in sub-Saharan Africa, Namibia counts less than two-million inhabitants and 2.1 persons per sq. km, with two-thirds of its population living in rural areas.[12] Like many southern African countries, Namibia has a diverse population, as more than twenty languages and major dialects are spoken in the country.[13] Although human migration to and across this land goes back hundreds of thousands of years, most of the current population descends from groups that arrived in Namibia in the last millennium. As a result of Portugal's arrival in Cape Cross (1486), the European presence in

Namibia followed the guidelines set by Christian missionaries, the British, the Germans (1884), and, finally, South Africans (1915). The Germans confronted the resistance encountered in the Ovaherero and the Nama in 1904–1907 with what historians consider to be the first genocide of the twentieth-century. After World War I, the Peace Treaty of Versailles (1919) transferred the full administration and legislation of former German South West Africa (SWA) to South Africa, which administered it as a League of Nations mandate territory. Since the end of World War II, South Africa has repeatedly opposed requests to place the territory under UN Trusteeship, administering it as one of its provinces and confronting the South-West Africa People's Organization (SWAPO)'s guerilla instead. In the 1960s, South Africa extended to SWA its own system of apartheid, the policy of ethnic and spatial separation. This policy of ethnic fragmentation did not end until Namibia reached independence from South Africa on March 21, 1990. The fragmentation of families due to labor migration, and extreme inequality in access to material resources, water and sanitation, as well as education, set the grounds for one of the major challenges currently facing Namibia—HIV/AIDS.

Namibia is among the most affected countries in the world with HIV/AIDS, with adult national HIV prevalence estimated at 17.8 percent.[14] The country's very young population (40 percent has not reached fifteen years of age) is aggravated by the fact that 13 percent of children have lost their father, 7 percent have lost their mother, and 3 percent have lost both. The three regions in which I gathered data, across Caprivi, Kavango, and Omusati, in Northern Namibia (Fig.1), have higher orphan rates than the national average.[15] Throughout the country, most orphans are absorbed into the extended family system, living primarily with aunts, uncles, and grandparents.[16] However, CHHs started to emerge in the late 1990s. In fact, as poverty, armed conflict, and the AIDS pandemic spread, a number of countries have seen CHHs become more common, less transient, and being headed by younger children.

Figure 1 Namibia: Regions in study

RESEARCH PROJECT: OVERVIEW

The ultimate purpose of my study was to identify ways to enhance family function-ing and children's adjustment through an exploration of children's social networks and existing community resources. Service providers and church-based groups in Namibia had identified the growing occurrence of children living by themselves in some regions, yet no study before had focused on CHHs or their social networks in this country and very little was known about the reasons and conditions of their creation as well as the mechanisms through which these children obtained (and pro-vided) different kinds of support.

This study surfaced the existence of non-orphan CHHs in the regions of Omusati and Kavango, as a way to facilitate school access to children whose parents live in remote rural areas. I found that, while some CHHs emerge due to family unavail-ability or distance, others result from children's own decision in order to keep siblings together, maintain independence, and avoid abuse by relatives. Analysis of children's networks show that most children are not alone, counting on kin and nonkin, adults as well as children, for the provision of different kinds of support. Nonetheless, reci-procity is weak, network composition and patterns of social interactions change in the absence of an adult caregiver, and risk of dependency from outside assistance and abuse (e.g., property grabbing by relatives) are not infrequent. I also identified depressive symptoms in a random sample of school-age children as well as among the heads of household; the latter displayed higher levels of depression and less vari-ability, and almost half of them entertained suicide thoughts although they would not do it. Not only was this information needed for the development of prevention and coping assistance interventions, but the research process itself raised aware-ness of this phenomenon across all sectors of society and provided an opportunity for participating children to reflect on their own resources and how they too can help others.

My study was based on three complementary theories. First, the Ecology of Hu-man Development (EHD), a paradigm that emphasizes the need to examine multiple settings that influence children and families, as well as the interactive relationships between these contexts, and between individuals and their environment within and across time.[17] The second theoretical framework, the stress and coping theory of social support, postulates that support has a stress-buffering effect through either the sup-portive actions of others or the belief that support is available.[18] Finally, the protection and fulfillment of children rights provided a framework for this exploratory analysis of the current situation of OVC in Namibia, and those programs and policies necessary to assist them.

Action and feminist scholarship influenced this study through a commitment to social justice; to me, the project would have failed if, in generating new social re-search knowledge, it had not raised consciousness, challenged oppression, and pro-moted (some) emancipatory change. Some of the ways in which I aimed to do so included (a) the problematization of gender and power relations and structures; (b) a critical reflection on my own identity and an open discussion of ethical dilem-mas; and (c) a personal commitment to participants as a way to foster trust (e.g., though exposing silencing practices, grounding my work on children's everyday lives and concerns, and prioritizing their voices and stories which have long been muted).[19] This was done within the limitations of what was feasible given transportation constraints,[20] large distances, difficult access to remote areas (particularly during the rainy season),[21] available resources,[22] and fluidity and low prevalence of child-headed households in the country. Inviting children to reflect on their own lives not only facilitated a more accurate analysis of their reality, but also raised their awareness of their own resources.[23]

In this study, I used both qualitative and quantitative methods, including individual and focus group interviews, observation, content analysis of fieldnotes and secondary text data, census/demographic survey, depression measure, and network mapping. The interview protocols and depression measures were built and/or adapted in consultation with local experts, piloted and translated to (and back-translated from) three local languages—Oshindonga, Rukwangali, and Silozi. I then used different techniques to promote discussion and ensure the active participation of each child (e.g., card sorting or visual rating). I asked children to reflect on their living conditions, family history, and life changing events; the people who provide them with different types of support (e.g., companionship, emotional support, and instrumental aid) as well as those who make them upset, reciprocity, and measure of depression. Group discussions and community meetings in the initial phase of the study helped me with the local situation analysis and provided visible endorsement from locally respected individuals and organizations. In the latter part of the fieldwork, they assisted me with explanations and interpretation of results while serving as references to test the validity of my analysis.[24] Throughout the research process, trust played a crucial role in gaining access to the setting for data collection and interpretation as well as in the dissemination and utilization of results. I will explore the former in more detail in the next section. As for the latter, my research aimed to contribute to social change, through the creative distribution of findings to a wide audience.[25] Consequently, before leaving Namibia, I shared preliminary results with academics, representatives from the Ministries of Education and Child Welfare, UNICEF, and organizations working with OVC. I was also privileged to be invited to present my findings to a large audience of policy makers, service providers, researchers, and youth from all over the country at the third National Conference on OVC in Windhoek in 2005, as well as to an international audience at the Childhood and AIDS Conference in Paris in 2006. While, unfortunately, I was not able to share the results with all study participants, these presentations served as a way to validate and enrich the interpretation of my findings and give back to a diverse audience at different levels.

NEGOTIATING TRUST IN INTERPERSONAL RELATIONS

Conceptions of Trust

My research would not have been conclusive were it not for the participation of children and their communities. Thus, data collection for my study relied heavily on our reciprocal understanding, respect and trust. Many, often contradictory definitions of trust exist. Some focus on the character or attribute of a person, whereas others underline the relational and/or contextual aspects of trust. In fact, both conceptions of trust are connected as perceived trustworthiness contributes to the development of interpersonal trust, which in turn nurtures integrity, ability, and benevolence, the factors of trustworthiness.[26] Trustworthiness is an essential quality in real-world research situations as it assures potential trusters that the researcher will not betray the trust as a consequence of either bad faith or incompetence,[27] and—I would add—that he/she is committed to research that benefits the target population. In this sense, our efforts are never too many in strengthening our moral values—which prescribe honesty and mutual respect—and our skills in the specific domain in which we hope trust to be given. The same expectation is held by researchers about other participants in the study (e.g., that informant will provide truthful renditions of their experiences). From a more relational perspective, trust develops between two or more actors in a particular situation or relationship, based on the belief that the other(s) either acts upon a moral commitment or genuinely 'encapsulates' or takes our interests at heart.[28] Trust is relational, specific, and dynamic.[29] It develops between individuals in specific situations and grows (and declines) incrementally over time as actors experience each other. This does not mean that, once developed, trust networks can not be mobilized for different purposes, yet it underlines the fact that relationships are constantly negotiated and, along within them, so is trust.

NURTURING (NEW) INTERPERSONAL RELATIONS

The point of departure of a new social encounter can be trust, distrust, or neutrality. Generalized trust—the "default" belief that human beings are trustworthy, provide a basis for initial expectations which are then adjusted through subsequent interactions.[30] Individuals with high levels of generalized trust and social intelligence are more willing to risk as they seek potentially fruitful interactions and are able to make more accurate judgments about the trustworthiness of others.[31] While societies may differ in their tendency to trust,[32] there are also psychological, behavioral, or contextual/cultural factors which may push towards initial distrust in a given situation. Psychologists have shown that trust is essential to secure attachment, and that relationships are satisfying to the extent that they meet basic needs. Notwithstanding the significance of temperament, caregiver responsiveness and social support have proven important influences on attachment quality.[33] Given disruption in the presence of adult caregivers as participating children were mostly heads of household, I expected (some) children to distrust my own dependability or sincere concern with and responsiveness to their needs, and the strength of our relationship. Meanwhile, there were behavioral and contextual factors nurturing my distrust in, for instance, age measurement. Not only was age often conveyed with a hand-gesture (indicating approximate height), but many children did not seem to know their date of birth (as they had not been registered at birth or had lost their identity card) or strategically misreported their age to gain access to public services such as education. As a newly arrived female white researcher in a country with rich ethnic diversity, a fierce history of segregation, and where almost

90 percent of the population is black African in origin, both personal attributes and socio-political representations (including the need to clarify non-endorsement of U.S. foreign policy despite my affiliation with an American university) placed me as an outsider and made learning how to build trust across age, gender, and ethnicity a daily undertaking. Trust is dynamic and requires flexibility, risk-taking and care as the desire to trust and anxiety go hand in hand.[34]

Uncertainty and vulnerability are at the core of the development of trust. In our exploration of the unknown, there is not only a need to suspend certainty and open up to "the other," but cultural differences are also often sources of uncertainty which may generate anxiety that paralyzes us or stimuli that push us to move forward.[35] Trust entails a willingness to accept vulnerability under the expectation of a positive result.[36] During fieldwork, this was repeatedly the case both for me and other participants. The need to accept a certain degree of vulnerability was particularly clear to me when negotiating access to certain communities or solving unexpected problems through an interpreter. In fact, research assistants played a key role as language interpreters and culture brokers.[37] Oftentimes, there was no other option but to have confidence that they had me and the work at heart and would behave in a manner that benefited—or at least did not harm—myself and our work together. Carol Heimer sees trust as a way to handle uncertainty and vulnerability in relationships—uncertainty about other's intentions and competence and vulnerability to their actions.[38] She contends that, by controlling people's behavior, traditional communities tend to focus on reducing uncertainty of interactions, whereas modern/urban societies pay more attention to reducing vulnerability (e.g., through social institutions). While trusting strategies aim to reduce uncertainty, distrusting one's work by reducing vulnerability, is particularly hard due to entrenched power relations.

A generalized sense of interpersonal trust is also damaged in contexts of social unrest, including widespread poverty, power inequalities, and other forms of violence;[39] meanwhile, trust is also needed to sustain unequal relations of exchange.[40] Social and economic inequalities in Namibia are among the highest in the world.[41] The dominance of white ethnic groups (Germans, English, and Afrikaans speaking) and a small elite of black returnees who have direct access to income, education, and health is marked, and are a source of frustration among young people.[42] The times of apartheid and the racial segregation imposed by the Odendaal Commission (1964) are over; active efforts have been made to "de-ethicize" public institutions. Yet, ethnic stereotyping is frequent and racism among post-independence Namibians across all ethnic groups remains a pending issue.[43] Similarly, despite equality rights enshrined in the Namibian Constitution, customary practices that limit equal access of women and children to property and decision-making are still alive.[44] Entrenched hierarchies of power and children's low social status results in the use of physical punishment to discipline children at home and in schools, and the autocratic manner in which decisions concerning children are made by adults.[45] Karen Cook suggests that extreme transparency and fairness is needed in imbalanced power interactions, and stable legal, political, and social institutions can help in managing power differences.[46] Given power inequalities and the normative structures in place (e.g., hierarchy by age and welcoming attitude towards outsiders), children in Namibia are not likely to negotiate; rather, they are used to accepting whatever conditions adults impose on them. Hence, ensuring voluntary participation required an ongoing questioning of children's willingness to participate and, in cases in which there was a possibility of coercion by authority figures (e.g., teachers or NGO workers), asking children again whether they wanted to participate after adults had left. No one opted out.

OTHER TRUST MANAGEMENT STRATEGIES

Trust is fragile. Building it may take time, yet losing it can happen quickly. Although damaged attachment and power differences may beget vulnerability and reluctance to trust, research can start with minimal trust. In fact, managing trust includes both the ability to cope in situations where trust is lacking and to build trust whenever possible.[47] They both entail dealing with risk and vulnerability as well as the complexities and paradoxes inherent in relationships as they develop in context and overtime.

Even if trust does not necessarily increase with relationship length,[48] social interactions provide opportunities for mutual discovery and reciprocation, which in turn beget better data and emancipatory outcomes.[49] Relationships with my four assistants are good examples of how frequency, duration, and diversity of challenges confronted together increase the strength and breadth of trust.[50] After advertising in the three regions in the study, I selected my assistants among several other local candidates through a detailed interview process assessing education level, previous relevant experience, language and interpersonal skills, ethical sensitivity, and availability. They were all dynamic mothers, committed to helping children in their regions. Whereas repeated interactions over time were not feasible or necessary with others, constant and varied interactions with my assistants along with a mutual desire to continue the relationship as well as a commitment to the work we carried out helped develop relations of trust, intimacy, and complicity over time. Efficiency at work, regular debriefing, and emotional support acted as trust-increasing strategies, while distractions, indiscretion, and misunderstandings in translation, decreased trust among us.[51]

I have already discussed the need to deal with power differences and encourage open communication as means to manage risk and engender mutual trust. Other strategies I used to promote trust with children and other participants included: self-disclosing in a thoughtful manner;[52] allowing time to build understanding gradually; taking risks first; treating all individuals respectfully and professionally during each encounter; respecting local mores (e.g., clothing and normative behavior) and using local greetings; honoring my commitments—from showing up punctually for appointments or producing deliverables to maintaining strict discretion and confidentiality; clarifying expectations from the start (e.g., explaining the difference between research and intervention while also committing to disseminating the results to those making policies and programs for OVC); reflecting on my own assumptions and the impact of my current and previous behavior, values, and positions of privilege. Socially responsible research extends these attitudes and behaviors from design and data collection all the way through the interpretation, presentation, and representation of findings because trust and relationships do not end with fieldwork.

Despite the clear benefits of trust in facilitating cooperation and maintaining social order,[53] distrust may not only set the foundation for such trust by allowing people to obtain information about each other and build a relationship history in a relatively safe way[54] but "some distrust can be functional and even healthy in certain circumstances, particularly when there are valid reasons to suspect that another party is not trustworthy."[55] In the context of fieldwork, a careful assessment is not only needed to avoid any exploitation but essential to maintain efficient teams and "weeding out" non-reliable data.[56]

POSITIONALITY

I made earlier reference to the bidirectional and interdependent nature of research relationships, where actors engage in trusting and being trusted. On the one hand, both researcher and participants should gain and be protected from harm. It is in this context that power as an attribute of the actors can help or hinder in the development of trusting, respectful relationships. On the other hand, the degree of the actors' interdependence talks about power as a characteristic of their relationship;[57] from a relational perspective, power cannot be entirely unilateral.[58] In this sense, a question emerges about the level of inter-dependence in my relationships with participants in the study. According to Harding, while some individuals are moved by affection or morals, most people engage in cooperation or behave in a trusting way out of their own self-interest.[59] For my part, I placed high value on participants' accounts and had low access to alternatives, as the number of CHHs was relatively scarce (though growing) and not readily identified. In short, I could not carry the study on my own, requiring the collaboration of children and other participants in the study. As for children, a positive expectation of (material) assistance and perhaps curiosity to talk to strangers or about themselves seemed to lead them to participate.[60] Whatever our individual motives, research could not have occurred without the agreement of each child, each adult, as well as myself and the interpreters I worked with. Failure to engage in reciprocity may beget distrust and impede collaboration with groups as well. This became clear for instance when one khuta or traditional council in Caprivi only agreed to grant us permission to work in their community upon learning that the work was not aimed at benefiting an outside agency. From this perspective, mutual dependency seemed to occur, even if not evident to all parties involved at the time and probably not enough to dissipate any doubts of inequality and lack of trust.

Past research has shown that assessments of trustworthiness are developed cognitively or socially, as actors tend to cooperate with others they know who are similar to them, interact often, or have a good reputation. In this case, empathy plays a mediating role.[61] While reciprocated trustworthy behavior and shared views and goals seem to play a more relevant role later in relationships, observable demographic similarity shapes expectations in brand new interactions.[62] For those of us conducting research in a foreign environment, the challenge is clear because we tend to have limited support networks close-by, may "look different," and/or have not yet been able to establish a reputation as possible exchange partners. Our reputation is unknown as there is little or no previous history of meaningful interaction. In order to overcome the initial lack of trust in situations characterized by incomplete information and uncertainty, a unilateral (low-risk) act of trust is needed to encourage others to trust, followed by gradual and reciprocated exchanges.[63] My active engagement in children's issues facilitated (group) trust through the creation of a sort of "shared identity" within the small community of people working to improve the conditions of OVC in the country.[64] This illustrates how presumptive trust characterizes relationships with strangers. Individuals in this group became key resources and offered valuable endorsements.

While occupying an outsider position entailed a distance to be bridged, it also turned out to be a source of proximity, increasing disclosure through strict respect for privacy and confidentiality. *"I have not talked about it (suicide) with anyone. I know some social workers, but I would not feel comfortable talking to them about it"* told us a boy who had been the head of his household since age sixteen.[65] Gossip is a major concern of children and adults alike. In a country of two-million inhabitants and marked communal life, I often had the impression that I was imposing a "Western" concept of privacy in contexts in which everybody seems to be aware of everyone else's life. Notwithstanding the differing local circumstances and understanding of privacy, I strictly upheld and always required from my assistants that we listen non-judgmentally and keep absolute discretion about participants' identity and all information obtained about them in all contexts, particularly in informal discussions.[66] Given the personal nature of the questions asked, offering strict confidentiality was crucial towards creating a safe environment in which children could disclose sensitive issues such as their suicidal thoughts and abuse by relatives. In fact, trust was the key that transformed the research design into an intervention itself, offering a safe space for reflection and a compassionate ear to children who yearned for it. Furthermore, because breaching confidentiality may irreparably damage trust with the child, we always sought the child's permission before talking on their behalf to someone else who may be able to help them.[67]

Despite significant variations in the understandings of privacy and the attitudes and behaviors which build trust in different contexts, the literature on trust has paid little attention to cross-cultural differences. Nonetheless, variations are to be expected on how trust is defined or negotiated and on how cooperation and trust-like behavior are developed in different cultures. Not only may people in one culture be more inclined to take risks,[68] but risk taking is also indispensable in building trust for some cultures (e.g., Americans), but less so for others (e.g., Japanese).[69] Cook and her colleagues even suggest that in environments of elevated risk and uncertainty such as in societies in transition, trust relations may only be needed for cooperation and social control in the absence of communal norms or social institutions (e.g., law enforcement).[70] This argument introduces the problem of the institutional boundaries of trust, and particularly the role of Institutional Review Boards (IRBs) in the protection of research individuals and relations across cultures. When I arrived in Namibia, I had already obtained ethical approval at Cornell University in the United States of America. In Namibia, I worked in affiliation with the Multidisciplinary Research and Consultancy Centre at the University of Namibia, which (at least at the time) did not have an IRB. There were, however, procedures in place which should precede research implementation, although the criteria used to grant permission were not explicit. I obtained approval from relevant ministries and regional governments as well as school principals and "traditional" authorities (i.e., individual leaders and community councils whose authority is tied to custom) down to the village level. Largely an issue of legal liability, obtaining ethical approval nonetheless obliges researchers to think about the potential impact of their work, and about the protection of those participating. This requires cultural sensitivity and respect, and is better accomplished in dialogue with host country scholars and institutions. During my fieldwork, for instance, mismatch between the ethics review requirements and local cultural norms soon became apparent, raising additional questions about who the IRB really protects—the researcher and university or the participants themselves.[71] For example, contrary to some researchers' practice in Namibia of not remunerating research participants,[72] I felt it fair to compensate children for their time; after discussions with local researchers and practitioners, I settled on giving food and soap to children.[73] Likewise, while obtaining permission from children's guardians (when available) and/or other adults interacting with the child (e.g., teachers), I put emphasis in obtaining the active and "independent" agreement from the child. This challenged the social standing of children, as minors are generally expected to behave as instructed by adults instead of making their own decisions. Additionally, an IRB's role is, in a way, not only to protect individuals and institutions participating in the research endeavor, but also to ensure the stability and prolonged existence of cooperative relations. Given the limitations of IRBs in home institutions to be truly sensitive to culture and the absence of an equivalent local ethics review body, trust in the perceived integrity of the researcher and the involvement of community members gain relevance as mechanisms of control and risk negotiation.

CONCLUSION

Every encounter—both pleasant and unpleasant—with the study population can have a ripple effect throughout the community and greatly affect the individual and/or community's level of response and satisfaction with the researcher(s). Negative encounters or unmet expectations may erode satisfaction with the researcher, block the way into a community, or prompt individuals to withhold valuable information. While a certain doses of distrust may not only be acceptable but also necessary to protect us from exploitation and our data from questionable value, too much distrust can ostracize or even set the researcher at risk. Likewise, positive experiences can positively affect research processes and results. Through ongoing interactions and mutuality of exchange, trust develops gradually, begetting trust in others as the history of the relationship is built. Trust takes different forms and reaches different levels in different relationships, contexts, and times. It is crucial to developing and sustaining effective research teams; working with interpreters and culture-brokers; gaining access to neighborhoods and archival repositories; securing institutional support and cooperation; enhancing the quality of the information obtained; and ensuring prompt utilization of results.

Whether someone trusts for moral, economic, or personal reasons, trust entails a positive expectation about another actor and the willingness to be vulnerable under conditions of interdependence and risk.[74] The development of expectations, and the willingness to take risks and be vulnerable, all essential to the management of trust, are influenced by each actor's personal history and the social context in which they operate. Consequently, even in situations in which actors would benefit from cooperation, disruptions in attachment and social cohesion often impede the development and maintenance of trusting relations. Careful attention to power (a)symmetry and interdependence in research is thus required, capitalizing on the position of the researcher to open private spaces for questioning and to promote context sensitivity and responsiveness in the ethical review process.

Through their academic education, novel researchers are hardly trained in conflict-resolution; complex moral and legal issues surrounding work with specific populations and how they vary from country to country. They are also rarely prepared to deal with the uncertainty, risk, and vulnerability they will face when conducting independent fieldwork. Whereas some of the factors shaping satisfaction and confidence in researchers are beyond the control of the researcher (e.g., social unrest, previous experiences with research, and individual's disposition to trust), others are a direct consequence of researchers' own demeanor. Openness of communication and qualities such as ability, integrity, and benevolence are vital to developing and sustaining trust in relationships. Therefore, it would behoove researchers to pay closer attention to daily interactions and to developing what might be called "bedside manners"—keeping promises, telling the truth, and caring for those who trust us. Whether doing ethnographic research or negotiating access to Census data, taking time to get to know people and engaging in mutuality of exchange usually leads to trust and cooperation . . . and ultimately affects the quality of our work and the longevity of our relationships.

ACKNOWLEDGMENTS

This study was funded by the National Science Foundation (Grant No. 0221244), the American Association of University Women, the Woodrow Wilson Foundation (J&J), and Cornell University through the College of Human Ecology and the Institute for African Development. Thank you to all participants as well as to Cecilia Makindani, Catherine Silume, Josephine Ikosa, and Ehergardis Anghuwo for their assistance in data collection. Cécile Rousseau, Laurie Vasily, and the book editors provided helpful comments to an earlier draft. Map of Namibia courtesy of Santiago Alba Corral. The views expressed are the author's alone.

NOTES

1 Toshio Yamagishi and Midori Yamagishi, "Trust and commitment in the United States and Japan," *Motivation and Emotion* 18, no. 2 (1994): 129–66.

2 Russell Harding, "Conceptions and explanations of trust," in *Trust in society*, ed. K. S. Cook (New York: Russell Sage Foundation, 2001); Messick, David M. and Roderick M Kramer, "Trust as a form of shallow morality," in *Trust in society*, ed. K. S. Cook (New York: Russell Sage Foundation, 2001).

3 Roy J. Lewicki, Edward C. Tomlinson, and Nicole Gillespie. "Models of interpersonal trust development: Theoretical approaches, empirical evidence, and future directions," *Journal of Management* 32, no. 6, (2006): 991–1002.

4 Jane Harrison, Lesley MacGibbon, and Missy Morton, "Regimes of trustworthiness in qualitative research: The rigors of reciprocity," *Qualitative Inquiry* 7, no.3 (2001): 323–345. While the term *trustworthiness* is used by constructivists to assess the "internal validity" of research, I am not discussing here the criteria used by different paradigms to assess the quality of an inquiry. Rather, this discussion focuses on the relationships established between researcher and participants and the role that trust plays in establishing and sustaining cooperation, which ultimately determines the information that is generated (Egon G. Guba and Yvonna S. Lincoln, "Competing paradigms in qualitative research," in *Handbook of qualitative research*, ed. N. K. Denzin and Y. S. Lincoln (Thousand Oaks, Calif.: Sage, 1994).

5 Diego Gambetta, "Can we trust trust?" in *Trust: Making and breaking cooperative relations*, ed. D. Gambetta. (New York: Basil Blackwell, 1988).

6 Ken Wilson, "Thinking About the Ethics of Fieldwork. In *Fieldwork in developing countries*," ed. S. Devereux and J. Hoddinott. (Boulder, CO: Lynne Rienner, 1993).

7 William A. Corsaro, "The Sociology of Childhood," in *Sociology for a New Century*, ed. Bradshaw, J. Misra and V. Roscigno (Thousand Oaks, Calif.: Pine Forge Press, 2005, 2nd ed).

8 Gill Valentine, "Being Seen and Heard? The Ethical Complexities of Working with Children and Young People at Home and at School," *Ethics, Place and Environment* 2, no. 2 (1999): 141–155.

9 Michelle Fine, "Working the Hyphens: Reinventing Self and Other in Qualitative Research," in *Handbook of qualitative research*, ed. N. K. Denzin and Y. S. Lincoln (Thousand Oaks, Calif.: Sage, 1994): 80.

10 This included local laws and cultural expectations requiring the approval of certain government bodies and traditional authorities, as well as immigration and labor permits which had to be requested ahead of time.

11 "Namibia, Land of the Brave" is the national anthem of Namibia composed and written by Axali Doëseb in 1991. The lyrics describe the history of Namibia and its people, their will to survive amid hardship, and their love for their country.

12   Central Bureau of Statistics, 2001 Population and Housing Census. Basic Analysis with Highlights. National Report (Windhoek, Namibia: CBS, National Planning Commission, 2003.). Central Bureau of Statistics, Namibia Household Income & Expenditure Survey 2003/2004. Preliminary Report (Windhoek, Namibia: Central Bureau of Statistics, National Planning Commission, 2006).

13   John Mendelsohn, Alice Jarvis, Carole Roberts, and Tony Robertson, *Atlas of Namibia: A Portrait of the Land and its People.* (Cape Town: David Philip, 2002).

14   Ministry of Health and Social Services, *Report of the 2008 National HIV Sentinel Survey* (Windhoek, Namibia: MOHSS, 2008).

15   MOHSS, and Macro International, *Namibia Demographic and Health Survey 2006–2007* (Windhoek, Namibia and Calverton, MD, USA: Ministry of Health and Social Services [Namibia] and Macro International, 2008). The percentage of children with one or both parents dead reached 31.1 in Caprivi, 18.1 in Kavango, and 22.7 in Omusati.

16   SIAPAC, *A Situation Analysis of Orphan Children in Namibia* (Windhoek, Namibia: MOHSS & UNICEF, 2002).

17   Urie Bronfenbrenner, *The ecology of human development: experiments by nature and design* (Cambridge, MA: Harvard University Press, 1979); Urie Bronfenbrenner, "Environments in developmental perspective: theoretical and operational models," in *Measuring environment across the life span: emerging methods and concepts,* ed. S. L. Friedman and T. D. Wachs (Washington, D.C.: American Psychological Association, 1999); Moncrieff Cochran and J. Brassard, "Child development and personal social networks," *Child Development* 50 (1979): 609–616.

18   Bruce E. Compas, Jennifer K. Connor-Smith, Heidi Saltzman, Alexandra Harding Thomsen, and Martha E. Wadsworth, "Coping with stress during childhood and adolescence: problems, progress, and potential in theory and research," *Psychological Bulletin* 127, no. 1 (2001): 87–127; Benjamin H. Gottlieb, "Coping with chronic stress," ed. D. Meichenbaum (*The Plenum Press Series on Stress and Coping.* New York: Plenum Press, 1997); Richard S. Lazarus and Susan Folkman, *Stress, appraisal, and coping* (New York: Springer, 1984).

19   Cynthia J. Chataway, "Negotiating the Observer-Observed Relationship," in *From subjects to subjectivities: a handbook of interpretive and participatory methods,* ed. D. L. Tolman and M. Brydon-Miller (New York: New York University Press, 2001); Bev Gatenby and Maria Humphries, "Feminist Participatory Action Research: Methodological and Ethical Issues," *Women's Studies International Forum* 23, no.1 (2000): 89–105; John, Gaventa and Andrea Cornwall.. Power and Knowledge," in *Handbook of action research: participative inquiry and practice,* ed. P. Reason and H. Bradbury. (Thousand Oaks, Calif.: Sage, 2001); Daryl Koehn, *Rethinking Feminist Ethics: Care, Trust, and Empathy* (New York: Routledge,1998); Patricia Maguire, "Uneven Ground: feminisms and action research,"in *Handbook of Action Research,* ed. P. Reason and H. Bradbury (London: Sage, 2000); Virginia Olesen, "Early Millennial Feminist Qualitative Research: Challenges and Contours," in *The SAGE handbook of qualitative research,* ed. N. K. Denzin and Y. S. Lincoln (Thousand Oaks, Calif.: Sage, 2005).

20 Namibia has over 5,000km of tarred roads and many more of gravel roads. John Mendelsohn, Alice Jarvis, Carole Roberts, and Tony Robertson, *Atlas of Namibia: A Portrait of the Land and its People*. (Cape Town: David Philip, 2002). While overall well maintained, some require 4x4 vehicles during the rainy season. Additionally, there is virtually no public transportation except in between the major urban centers. Private taxis have to be hired to reach other areas. Similarly, cell phone coverage at the time of the study was restricted to urban areas.

21 The climate is generally dry and hot, although temperatures vary enormously during the day as well as seasonally across the vast country. The average maximums during the hottest months (around the end of the year) are generally above 30 °C, yet in July, the coolest month throughout most of the country, average minimums drop below 10 °C. Namibia receives very little rainfall, which concentrates mainly in the North-eastern regions during the summer months (i.e., December-March), rendering access to certain areas only possible by 4x4, canoe, or helicopter. John Mendelsohn, Alice Jarvis, Carole Roberts, and Tony Robertson, *Atlas of Namibia: A Portrait of the Land and its People*. (Cape Town: David Philip, 2002).

22 A politically stable multiparty democracy since reaching independence in 1990, the Republic of Namibia's economy is closely tied to the South African Rand. Variations in the exchange rates during the fieldwork period were large, with the value of U.S. dollars in Namibian dollars decreasing to half in the first twelve months I lived in Namibia!.

23 Jo Boyden and Judith Ennew, eds. *Children in focus—a manual for participatory research with children* (Stockholm: Grafisk Press, 1997); Jeremy Roche, "Children: rights, participation and citizenship," *Childhood* 6, no. 4 (1999): 475–493.

24 Peter Reason, "Three approaches to participative inquiry," in *Handbook of qualitative research*, ed. N. K. Denzin and Y. S. Lincoln (Thousand Oaks, Calif.: Sage, 1994).

25 Bev Gatenby and Maria Humphries, "Feminist Participatory Action Research: Methodological and Ethical Issues," *Women's Studies International Forum* 23, no.1 (2000): 89–105

26 R. C. Mayer, J. H. Davis, and F. D. Schoorman, "An integrative model of organizational trust," *Academy of Management Review* 20 (1995): 709–734.

27 Margaret Levi and Laura Stoker, "Political trust and trustworthiness," *Annual Review of Political Science* 3 (2000): 475–507.

28 Russell Harding, "Conceptions and explanations of trust,| in *Trust in society*, ed. K. S. Cook (New York: Russell Sage Foundation, 2001).

29 Karen S. Cook, "Networks, norms, and trust: The social psychology of social capital." 2004 Cooley Mead Award address, *Social Psychology Quarterly* 68, no. 1 (2005): 4–14; Carol A. Heimer,. "Solving the problem of trust," in *Trust in society*, ed. K. S. Cook (New York: Russell Sage Foundation, 2001).

30 Mark Lubell, "Familiarity breeds trust: Collective action in a policy domain," *The Journal of Politics* 69, no. 1 (2007): 237–250.

31 Toshio Yamagishi, "Trust as a form of social intelligence," in *Trust in society*, ed. K. S. Cook (New York: Russell Sage Foundation, 2001).

32 Francis Fukuyama, *Trust: Social Virtues and the Creation of Prosperity* (New York: Free Press, 1995).

33 Cindy Hazan and Phillip R. Shaver, "Attachment as an organizational framework for research on close relationships," in *Close relationships. Key readings*, ed. H. T. Reis and C. E. Rusbult (New York: Psychology Press, 2004); Mario Mikulincer,. Attachment working models and the sense of trust: An exploration of interaction goals and affect regulation," in *Close relationships. Key readings*, ed. H. T. Reis and C. E. Rusbult (New York: Psychology Press, 2004).

34 Carol A. Heimer,. "Solving the problem of trust," in *Trust in society*, ed. K. S. Cook (New York: Russell Sage Foundation, 2001).

35 Ellen Corin, "Uncertainty in clinical practice" (paper presented at Working with culture course, McGill University Summer Program in Social and Cultural Psychiatry, May 2007, Montreal, QC, Canada).

36 Behavioral approaches to interpersonal trust development view trust as a rational choice to cooperate based on expectations and observable behavior; trust grows as cooperation is reciprocated. Psychological approaches, however, consider trust to be the result of other factors such as expectations, behavior, and affect. In the psychological traditions, trust grows when positive expectations are confirmed through repeated interactions and knowledge of each other. Uni- and bi-dimensional, as well as transformational psychological approaches exist, based on their understanding of trust-distrust as a single or two independent constructs, or consider the nature of trust to transform as the relationship develops. Roy J. Lewicki, Edward C. Tomlinson, and Nicole Gillespie, "Models of interpersonal trust development: Theoretical approaches, empirical evidence, and future directions," *Journal of Management* 32, no. 6 (2006): 991–1002.

37 According to the last national census, English, the official language of the country, is only the first language to less than 5 percent of the population; half of the country's inhabitants speak Oshiwambo as their home language. Many Namibians speak two or more indigenous languages as well as at least some English, German, or Afrikaans (mostly spoken on farms or in town). While I learnt the greetings and some key expressions in the local languages in the three regions where I worked and took Oshindonga classes at the University of Namibia, the need for interpretation and culture brokerage was essential to approaching participants in their language of preference.

38 Carol A. Heimer, "Solving the problem of trust," in *Trust in society*, ed. K. S. Cook (New York: Russell Sage Foundation, 2001).

39 In this context, Heimer's preference for the term "entruster" over the more commonly used "truster" seems particularly appropriate, as in some circumstances people may be forced to trust someone on whom they depend yet who do not inspire confidence. Carol A. Heimer, "Solving the problem of trust," in *Trust in society*, ed. K. S. Cook (New York: Russell Sage Foundation, 2001).

40 Karen S. Cook, "Networks, norms, and trust: The social psychology of social capital." 2004 Cooley Mead Award address, *Social Psychology Quarterly* 68, no. 1 (2005): 4–14; Karen S. Cook, Russell Harding, and Margaret Levi, *Cooperation without trust?* Vol. IX *Russell Sage Foundation Series on Trust* (New York: Russell Sage Foundation, 2005).

41 UNDP, *Human Development Report 2007/2008. Fighting Climate Change: Human Solidarity in a Divided World* (New York: United Nations Development Program, 2007).

42 Pempelani Mufune, "Youth problems in Namibia," in *Challenges for anthropology in the "African renaissance." A Southern African contribution*, ed. D. LeBeau and R. J. Gordon (Windhoek, Namibia: University of Namibia Press, 2002).

43 Ingolf Diener, "Ethnicity and nation-building: Towards unity respectful of heterogeneity?" in *Contemporary Namibia: The first landmarks of a postapartheid society*, ed. I. Diener and O. Graefe (Windhoek, Namibia: Gamsberg Macmillan, 2001).

44 Heike Becker, "This New Thing That Came with Independence: Gender Aspects of Traditional Authorities and Customary Courts in Northern Namibia." (Paper read at Africa Seminar, Centre for African Studies, at University of Cape Town, October 2, 1996); Scholastika Iipinge, Kathe Hofnie, and Steve Friedman, *The relationship between gender roles and HIV infection in Namibia*. Vol. 8 (Windhoek, Namibia: University of Namibia Press, 2004).

45 Evelien Kamminga, Herero and Owambo Collective Decision-Making Mechanisms and the Implications for Children's Rights Realizations in Namibia (Windhoek, Namibia: UNICEF, 2000).

46 Karen S. Cook, "Networks, norms, and trust: The social psychology of social capital." 2004 Cooley Mead Award address, *Social Psychology Quarterly* 68, no. 1 (2005): 4–14.

47 Siv Vangen and Chris Huxham, "Nurturing collaborative relations: Building trust in interorganizational collaboration," *The Journal of Applied Behavioral Science* 39, no. 1 (2003): 5–31.

48 K. T. Dirks, and D. L. Ferrin, "Trust in leadership: Meta-analytic findings and implications for research and practice," *Journal of Applied Psychology* 87, no. 4 (2002): 611–628.

49 Patti Lather, *Getting Smart: Feminist Research and Pedagogy With/in the Postmodern* (New York: Routledge, 1991).

50 Roy J. Lewicki, D McAllister, and R Bies, "Trust and distrust: New relationships and realities," *Academy of Management Review* 23 (1998): 439–458.

51 Kramer found the recall of trust-increasing and trust-reducing behavior between high- and low-power actors to differ, with the latter recalling more negative actions than the former. This chapter would be enriched by the reflections of other participants in the study, who may have a different perspective on our exchanges. Roderick M. Kramer, "Divergent realities and convergent disappointments in the hierarchic relation: Trust and intuitive auditor

at work," in *Trust in organizations: Frontiers of theory and research*, ed. R. M. Kramer and T. R. Tyler (Thousand Oaks, Calif.: Sage, 1996).

52 Thoughtful self-disclosure is needed to build relationships and generate richer data. Jane Harrison, Lesley MacGibbon, and Missy Morton, "Regimes of trustworthiness in qualitative research: The rigors of reciprocity," *Qualitative Inquiry* 7, no. 3 (2001): 323–345. Finding a balance between corresponding fairly and taking care of myself was not always easy, though. It is important to assess carefully each situation and make sure you do not compromise your safety and wellbeing, particularly when traveling alone.

53 Karen S. Cook, "Networks, norms, and trust: The social psychology of social capital." 2004 Cooley Mead Award address, *Social Psychology Quarterly* 68, no. 1 (2005): 4–14.

54 Carol A. Heimer, "Solving the problem of trust," in *Trust in society*, ed. K. S. Cook (New York: Russell Sage Foundation, 2001).

55 Roy J. Lewicki, D. McAllister, and R. Bies, "Trust and distrust: New relationships and realities," *Academy of Management Review* 23 (1998): 1016.

56 C. W. Langfred, "Too much of a good thing? Negative effects of high trust and individual autonomy in self-managing teams," *Academy of Management Journal* 47 (2004): 385–399.

57 Richard Emerson, "Power-dependence relations," *American Sociological Review* 27, no. 1 (1962): 31–41.

58 Siv Vangen and Chris Huxham, "Nurturing collaborative relations: Building trust in interorganizational collaboration," *The Journal of Applied Behavioral Science* 39, no. 1 (2003): 5–31.

59 While acknowledging that trusting behavior and cooperation are two distinct concepts, I use them interchangeably in this chapter. Karen S. Cook, Russell Harding, and Margaret Levi, *Cooperation without trust?* Vol. IX *Russell Sage Foundation Series on Trust* (New York: Russell Sage Foundation, 2005).

60 It is not clear to what extent children's willingness to be vulnerable and answer "questions that nobody had asked me before," was based on (a) their perception of our trustworthiness (based on my affiliation with a prestigious research institution and their confident expectations and feelings that we would honor trust by keeping confidentiality and disseminating the results as promised); (b) their expectation and need for immediate assistance; or (c) courtesy or a more complex system of social obligations and structures (e.g., if requested to cooperate by an adult in a position of authority such as a school principal or religious authority).

61 Karen S. Cook, "Networks, norms, and trust: The social psychology of social capital." 2004 Cooley Mead Award address, *Social Psychology Quarterly* 68, no. 1 (2005): 4–14; Messick, David M and Roderick M Kramer, "Trust as a form of shallow morality," in *Trust in society*, ed. K. S. Cook (New York: Russell Sage Foundation, 2001).

62 Daniel Z. Levin, Ellen M. Whitener, and Rob Cross, "Perceived trustworthiness of knowledge sources: The moderating impact of relationship length," *Journal of Applied Psychology* 91, no. 5 (2006): 1163–1171.

63 Karen S. Cook, Russell Harding, and Margaret Levi, *Cooperation without trust?* Vol. IX *Russell Sage Foundation Series on Trust* (New York: Russell Sage Foundation, 2005).

64 Messick, David M. and Roderick M. Kramer, "Trust as a form of shallow morality," in *Trust in society*, ed. K. S. Cook (New York: Russell Sage Foundation, 2001).

65 A highly Christianized country, suicide is considered taboo in Namibia and hardly discussed by family members.

66 Children were interviewed separately and privately although in public spaces or within the sight of others. We interrupted the interview and recording any time that people came close by and continued only when they had left.

67 Priscilla Alderson, *Listening to Children: Children, Ethics and Social Research* (Illford, Essex: Bernardo's, 1995). This decision was compounded by another complex moral dilemma, namely, whether the research was justified at all given the impossibility of providing immediate follow up activities as there were hardly any resources available in these regions (e.g., social workers, psychologists, etc). I decided to carry on with the study on the belief that participation in the study would benefit children and communities both directly and indirectly, by raising awareness of children's resources and needs and informing policy and programming with data which did not exist elsewhere.

68 Nancy R. Buchan, Rachel T. Croson, and Robyn M. Dawes, "Swift neighbors and persistent strangers: A cross-cultural investigation of trust and reciprocity in social exchange," *American Journal of Sociology* 108, no. 1 (2002): 168–206.

69 Karen S. Cook, Russell Harding, and Margaret Levi, *Cooperation without trust?* Vol. IX *Russell Sage Foundation Series on Trust* (New York: Russell Sage Foundation, 2005).

70 Karen S. Cook, "Networks, norms, and trust: The social psychology of social capital." 2004 Cooley Mead Award address, *Social Psychology Quarterly* 68, no. 1 (2005): 4–14; Karen S. Cook, Russell Harding, and Margaret Levi, *Cooperation without trust?* Vol. IX *Russell Sage Foundation Series on Trust* (New York: Russell Sage Foundation, 2005).

71 Susan Tilley and Louise Gormley, "Canadian university ethics review: Cultural complications translating principles into practice," *Qualitative Inquiry* 13, no. 3 (2007): 368–387.

72 Local academics explained this position was aimed at facilitating access to researchers with limited resources.

73 Gift giving, particularly when not reciprocated, may generate patronage rather than equalize relationships. Ken Wilson, "Thinking About the Ethics of Fieldwork," in *Fieldwork in developing countries*, ed. S. Devereux and J. Hoddinott (Boulder, CO: Lynne Rienner, 1993). Hence, it is important that researchers observe and learn from members of the community the local principles of gift—what to give to whom and when.

74 Roy J. Lewicki, D. McAllister, and R. Bies, "Trust and distrust: New relationships and realities," *Academy of Management Review* 23 (1998): 1016.

CHAPTER SIX

Cross Cultural Research: Implications for Data Collection

By KRISTEN CONWAY-GÓMEZ

INTRODUCTION

Preservation of biodiversity in fragile environments has concerned researchers and many others the world over[1] and is reflected in the environmental policies adopted by numerous countries.[2] Specifically, acknowledging the importance of biodiversity has defined a research agenda that aims to identify endangered species and increase our understanding how human behavior threatens particular animal populations. Critical dimensions of this larger research agenda include studies that address the ways in which particular communities in lowland tropical regions exploit the environment for their livelihood by harvesting animals for sale in local and regional markets.[3] My dissertation focused on the harvest for consumption of two species of Amazonian turtles—the yellow-spotted river turtle (Podocnemis unifilis) and the giant South American river turtle (P. expansa)—in rural lowland tropical communities in the Bolivian Amazon and the potential effects of market activity and wealth on people's consumption patterns. Humans throughout the Amazon basin have included Podocnemis river turtles in their diets since at least the sixteenth-century.[4] Centuries of harvest and consumption (of adults and eggs) have led to the decline of many Podocnemis species throughout their ranges[5] and has left remaining populations of P. unifilis and P. expansa turtles seriously reduced. Today, these turtles remain important wildlife resources for ribereño (floodplain) communities in and near at least one national park in the Bolivian Amazon for subsistence and market consumption.

In this chapter, I reflect upon the experience of data collection in a cross-cultural setting. I address research preparation and how unexpected events during fieldwork, an essential geographic activity, can impact the outcome of research; the influence of language on the fieldwork experience; and my perspective on being a North American woman working in the field on a topic usually considered a part of the male domain. The singular guarantee of fieldwork is that it will lead to unexpected developments, no matter how extensive the planning involved, and that these developments will inevitably impact the course of one's research and analyses. In my experience, honest communication with informants, flexibility in one's schedule, objectivity in approach, and creativity with data collection are among the best means to increase the effectiveness of data collection.

GETTING STARTED–HOW THE PROCESS EVOLVED

My decision to work in Bolivia was the result of academic as much as personal choices. Academically, I wanted to expand my experience in Latin America beyond Central America (Costa Rica, Honduras and Panama), where I had studied and conducted research as an undergraduate and master's student. I was interested in studying a human-wildlife interaction in a tropical lowland ecosystem with which I was familiar. The Amazon Basin was a logical choice of study site. I was already fluent in Spanish, which narrowed my field down further. Examining research conducted in Spanish speaking nations suggested that there was much yet to be done in Bolivia and Ecuador. Thus I leaned towards these two countries. This is where the personal choices interceded. While an undergraduate, I had three Bolivian friends who spoke very highly of their country, which had piqued my interest in seeking a Bolivian study site. A graduate school colleague who had just returned from fieldwork in Bolivia suggested that I look at the management plan for the national park in which she had worked, and where there was an increasing interest in the human use of river turtles. Reading the management plan sealed the deal for me—I had found a research topic that suited my academic need for a human-environment topic and personal interest in Bolivia.

When embarking upon a research project, one critical element for success is passion for the topic. This is particularly true for someone considering international fieldwork. Take time up front to explore possibilities, be willing to go down paths that you might not have initially considered, for it is possible, even likely, that through such an exercise, you will come upon a topic and location that suit you and about which you are passionate. You will need both passion and dedication to negotiate the myriad of steps involved in preparing for and conducting international research.

Any research project involves acquiring permissions and meeting requirements—institutional review board [IRB] for human subjects, funding, logistical arrangements and local acceptance, among others. The specifics will depend upon location and project, but one will need to identify contacts and earn both their confidence and support to get a project running. To start my research project, I began by developing a proposal in conjunction with classes that I was taking. My coursework forced me to articulate specific questions and identify their theoretical basis, which was important as I sought institutional support at my university, from the relevant international institutions, from the local communities and various funding sources. Some procedures are clearly outlined, such as IRB approval, which requires forms be filled out and a review to be undertaken. Other processes are not so clear cut. In my case, I needed to identify local institutions and individuals whose support I would need to conduct my research. I began this process by contacting people whose names were suggested by some of my professors. This was a snowballing process as I learned which institutions and individuals were involved in my future research site. I made a three-week preliminary site visit in 1999, when I sat down face to face with people with whom I had been in phone, email and letter contact over the previous year. Through these interactions, I became aware of their exact expectations and familiarized myself with the steps I would need to follow to satisfy their requirements. This involved writing letters asking for formal permission to work in the park and local communities I identified with the help of the park director, agreeing to train Bolivian students while conducting my field research, and presenting my projects to communities for their final permission and approval.

While developing a proposal, seeking permissions and addressing the necessary logistics, I was taking classes to fulfill requirements for a PhD in geography with a concentration in natural resource conservation. Due to the specialized nature of a doctorate, my classes were in some way directly or indirectly related to my proposed project. Classes directly related to my field work included: wildlife ecology; research design; tropical wildlife use; geography of Amazonia; geography of South America; turtle conservation issues; and Portuguese. Classes indirectly related to my field work but important for my training as a geographer included: introduction to GIS; remote sensing; contemporary geographic thought; development in Latin America; and quantitative methods. Undergraduate students will have broader requirements, but will find that these classes will help develop critical skills, which is important for researchers. In addition to formal coursework, I practiced my Spanish with native speakers and added some Portuguese to my linguistic proficiency, since my work was to be located on the Brazilian frontier. After two years of coursework and other preparation, I was ready to leave for the field in May 2000 and planned on being overseas for a year. I was finally ready to start investigating the research questions I had developed based on my understanding of the cultural and physical characteristics of eastern lowland Bolivia.

Although I left for the field as well-prepared as I could be, I was still faced with unanticipated surprises. I left with assumptions and expectations that I would be living in rustic conditions: Bolivia is often perceived as the poorest nation in South America, with reduced access to many conveniences to which I am accustomed at home—not the least of which is technologically related, since there is no electricity in the communities in which I had chosen to work. Yet Bolivia enjoys many characteristics in its physical and cultural geography that make it a particularly attractive or interesting country: it is one of the two landlocked countries in South America; is characterized as having the highest indigenous population in South America—upwards of 50 percent; has diverse climatic zones that range from tropical lowland to Andean altiplano; has been affected by a colonial presence that has impacted the culture and views of its people; and, in spite of a turbulent political history, it is today largely a peaceful nation.

In addition to reading about the cultural and physical environment of Bolivia, my preparation included raising my own consciousness about frontier zones, since I would be living and working in one. This helped ready me for fieldwork in a frontier setting that overlaps with a national park, which, as part of its mission, protects endangered wildlife from overconsumption by local people—thereby offering a myriad of complicating factors. Background information on the park and multinational legislative guidelines restricting the quantity of turtle and egg harvest that make these illicit products was important in the design of my interview questions and also helped me modify them once I arrived and discovered needs for adjustment—as all fieldworkers do at some point during their fieldwork.

THE RESEARCH QUESTIONS

To better understand the dynamics of the human-environment relationship and the implications for biodiversity represented by the use of river turtles for human consumption, I quantified turtle abundance and human socioeconomic characteristics on the Chico and Grande Rivers.[6] My research targeted three locations: Palo Verde—a smaller and comparatively more subsistence-oriented settlement, Chacarilla—a larger, wealthier, and more market-oriented settlement, and Las Petas—a former human settlement that was abandoned in 1996. I decided to focus on these three sites to examine whether turtle abundance differs depending on proximity of human communities and whether different socioeconomic characteristics affect turtle consumption. To examine turtle abundance, I counted basking turtles 20km upstream and downstream from two human-inhabited communities and along a 40km transect at the abandoned human community site to obtain turtle abundance data. I then tested for differences in turtle abundance between sites. The tests revealed that significantly higher numbers of turtles were seen at the abandoned sight in comparison with the two human-inhabited sites—a difference that may be a result of hunting pressure.

One of the key elements of change in the Amazon basin has been the international market, which has directly affected social groups and their use of wildlife, including Podocnemis turtles. Recognizing and understanding the social, political and economic contexts within which systems of production and consumption are nested[7] is one way of understanding complex social systems. These areas of inquiry are relevant to the natural and social systems in which Podocnemis turtle use in the Amazon basin is embedded. Current accounts in eastern lowland Bolivia indicate that there are markets for Podocnemis sp. meat, eggs and oil.[8] Interviews I conducted in three Bolivian floodplain (ribereño) communities in August 1999 on the Chico and Grande Rivers confirmed these phenomena. It is the intersection of these dynamic ecological, social and economic systems that I addressed in my research.

For the people in Palo Verde, Las Petas and Chacarilla, Bolivia, sale and trade of Podocnemis sp. is part of everyday life. For many households, harvest and trade of turtles are vital components of family subsistence and livelihoods. Harvest of turtle meat and eggs for sale and trade in local markets was the most common response, thirty-four out of thirty-six responses, to the question "If you believe there are fewer turtles today than ten years ago, why?" that I asked in a preliminary study.[9]

Peoples' responses to my questions indicated that both species of Podocnemis turtles found in this area continued to play roles in local and regional systems, which led me to ask additional questions: Does a human presence have a measurable influence on turtle abundance? Is there a difference in turtle size, which can serve as a proxy to indicate hunting pressure, at different distances from human communities? What, if any, is the role of household wealth on turtle consumption? Are there measurable socioeconomic characteristics that may indicate consumptive use of turtles? These questions were addressed in the five hypotheses[10] tested in my dissertation.

To answer these questions, I used a framework that drew upon ecological and social theories to address this natural resource use issue. To assess the status of the turtle resource, I used wildlife ecology methods to measure turtle abundance and size class in relation to human communities. To elucidate socioeconomic factors that drive wildlife resource use, I borrowed elements from microeconomic theory to discern potential influences of household wealth and market integration on turtle use. For this, I measured socioeconomic characteristics (including wealth, years of education, income source, time dedicated to hunting turtles, and trips out of the community) and tested their effects on consumptive use of turtles—both subsistence and market.[11] Finally, based on the data collected and analyzed, I suggested a pre-plan that might serve as a starting point for development of a participatory conservation program.

Since the communities I studied lie in the zone of influence of a protected area, the results have implications for protected area management. The design of a management plan would benefit from consideration of the impacts of hunting and the driving forces behind it—such as access to cash, years of education and household wealth. Development of a conservation and management plan in this lowland tropical setting must include active participation of community members and support about the relevance of my data to such a plan. Ideally, such a plan would inform community-based wildlife conservation elsewhere in Amazonia. To this end, I returned my data to the communities where I collected it. Since analyzing the data and producing the dissertation were decidedly not participatory, returning the information to the communities was my attempt to help residents see concrete results in terms of the impacts on turtles since the time they shared their opinions with me, answered my questions, and supported my research. I sincerely hope that possessing this information will lead to their ownership of it and to the eventual development of a community-based management plan.

BRIEF DESCRIPTION OF FINDINGS AND ASSUMPTIONS

The combined data regarding turtle abundance and human socioeconomic conditions gathered in my study have implications for the effects of increased access to cash income on wildlife resources and community-based conservation and management of species important in subsistence (less cash-based systems) and market economies (cash-based systems). I expected, based on theory and deductive reasoning, that the people living closer to market (Chacarilleñas) would exhibit higher preferences for cash because they were more likely to be frequent participants in a cash economy, compared to people living farther from market and who were less likely to participate in a cash economy (residents of Palo Verde) and therefore would consume more turtles. The insights I gained during conversations with local people suggested that local phenomena including household wealth, subsistence-based livelihoods and indigenous origins are more appropriate explanations of turtle consumption. Among the socioeconomic factors that Godoy and others[12] found important in explaining wildlife consumption were income and education, which I also considered. In addition, I collected data on many other socioeconomic factors that I felt might have bearing on turtle consumption, since once I left the field, I knew that I would not have access to this type of information again.

One consideration I felt important was road access to cities. If roads to cities on the Bolivian side are improved, it is likely that residents in these communities will have more ready access to cash-generating employment and in turn, cash-requiring goods. My findings suggest that turtle abundance is negatively related to hunting pressure, as I anticipated. Hunting pressure appears to be related to access to cash—people hunt to get more cash or, because they have ready access to goods acquired only with cash, they have a greater motivation to hunt. I also found that poorer households are more involved in turtle harvest and sale, which was a surprise. Palo Verde, the more subsistence-based and less cash-oriented community, whose population has indigenous origins, reports more turtle consumption—both as a non-cash acquired food and as a cash-generating food product. Increased access to cash, which is one likely result of road improvement and ensuing integration into market economies, may actually reduce turtle consumption, potentially positively affecting turtle abundance and conservation efforts. Contrarily, if the road is not improved and no growth in market access experienced, the alternative scenario is the status quo, in which turtle abundance is likely to continue declining. There was a greater preference for cash in Chacarilla compared to Palo Verde, which was likely driven by the greater amount of river transit and contact with outside forces that make more goods available and ultimately raises people's desired buying power. The stronger outside influence observed in Chacarilla is the likely result of greater influx of people and goods associated with river transit on the Grande River vs. the Chico River. Ultimately, my fieldwork helped me to better understand the importance and quantity of turtle consumption in eastern Bolivia, but I cannot yet explain with confidence the directionality of the cash-market access-turtle relationship—this is the basis for future investigation.

THE CONTEXT MATTERS

My academic preparation and preliminary fieldwork were important in preparing me, but no amount of preparation can substitute for experience. My status as an outsider asking about this sensitive topic in a setting where there is confusion and disagreement about what constitutes legal turtle use likely affected the ways in which people perceived me as a researcher. Furthermore, as the first woman to arrive in the communities asking questions about activities that were primarily performed by men—fishing for turtles—I was viewed as peculiar. My unconventional position undoubtedly affected the data that I collected. While I was honestly interested in assessing turtle abundance in relationship to human communities and ascertaining socioeconomic drivers in the consumption of turtle, community members were weary and suspicious of my intentions and efforts over the course of the year that I conducted research.

It is not surprising that in this rich cultural, legislative and economic setting, some amount of skepticism about me, the researcher, was present on the part of residents. But a field setting does not have to be complex in these ways to pose challenges to data collection. No matter the challenges, one needs to make efforts to remain objective and maintain an appropriately naïve approach to interviews and interactions in the field. To do so, I consciously tried to avoid inserting my own assumptions about turtle use into my data collection. I strove to speak as little as possible while urging my interviewees to do most of the talking, allowing them to lead me along the path to understand the situation. For my part, I had also assumed that any biases in the data collected were consistent across samples.[13] To gain the confidence of my informants, I spent time with people in non-data collection activities. I participated in rice harvest, fishing activities, cooking and clothes washing to better familiarize myself with the local schedule and culture, deepen my own understanding of the local daily life and gain the community's respect and trust.

Price[14] reflects upon her experiences in the field, noting that one can spend a fair amount of time becoming less of a stranger. Participating in the daily work activities of informants is one way of de-emphasizing one's outsider status. This doesn't always directly result in data collection, but it nevertheless is a critical component of fieldwork. Establishing strong relationships takes time in any context; fieldwork is not an exception in this regard. From my perspective and experience, time invested in developing relationships specifically with women has provided me with access to situations and people that I would never have secured on my own. The cultural contexts in which I have worked have been gendered in terms of activities and duties. As a woman, I have felt more comfortable in some situations due to the presence of other women. In some of the field settings I have been in, there simply was no way around the fact that I was an obvious outsider—due to my being taller, whiter and my speaking with an accent. Having a common characteristic such as sex provided a starting point for relationships with informants. Local women acted on my behalf as gatekeepers and as protectors in critical situations, facilitating my access to situations I would not have otherwise had the opportunity to observe or participate in. For example, women rather than men told me where to avoid potential gunshots in Honduras. In all of the locations in which I conducted field work, it was most often women rather than men who invited me to participate in activities. In many cases, women gave me detailed information about their spouses' and partners' turtle-related activities in Bolivia that the men had not been sharing with me. This information provided much needed insight into my research questions.

Additional ways to better understand the research setting include taking time to acquaint oneself with the local idiom and adjusting to the daily rhythms. In comparison with the United States, Latin America moves at a slower pace. You are likely to become frustrated and encounter resistance on the part of locals if you try too hard to move at your pace rather than theirs. Adjusting to the local culture involves adjusting not simply to the language, but also to the schedule. It is worthwhile to take the time to observe and understand the pace of life and make efforts to fit into it. As with local dialects, being aware of the local schedule and operating within its parameters as much as possible is beneficial for one's research. It amounts to understanding the context in which one is working and on which one depends.

Sharing and helping are also important in the context of fieldwork, especially because informants generously give of their time to help researchers advance their own goals, which usually is of little benefit to them. Although they supported it, my project had not been initiated by local people, which meant that there was less of a direct benefit to them. I faced competing academic requirements and the desire to offer some return to my informants' time and effort. What I did to attempt to satisfy the latter was to return, to each household in both communities, a copy of my data in the form of a two-page summary in Spanish with graphs. I also made explicit that I would be willing to answer any questions they may have about the results or its interpretation. As a foreign researcher coming into a place that is not mine to claim, I have an obligation to return concrete data to the people who live there and who my research and what I took away possible.

During the course of my year in the field, I was made aware, to varying degrees and at different times, that my data collection was affected by my standing as an outsider. This became quite apparent to me during a conversation I had with a woman who had taken me into her confidence. The level of trust we had achieved allowed her to illuminate a significant factor affecting the data I collected, unbeknownst to me. Luisa disclosed the fact that the bus manager in Chacarilla was not accepting shipments of turtles nor of turtle eggs while I was conducting research. This temporary prohibition of turtle shipments was the manager's attempt to make the community appear "environmentally sound." By so doing, he would not have to lie to me about the numbers of turtles or eggs shipped out on the bus, nor would there be evidence in the bus records about such cargo going out of Chacarilla, to which I might request access. People would also have fewer incidents to tell me about. Luisa also shared with me that she and others had smuggled turtles on the bus as unregistered cargo despite the bus manager's refusal to accept them. This refusal of turtles as registered cargo not only highlighted for me the types of restrictions that could be imposed on their use, it also emphasized that people's responses to my inquiries about the number of times households sent turtles or eggs out on the bus were likely affected. The trustworthiness of my informants' responses, the numbers they reported and whether or not their responses were consistent across households is, however, conjecture. In both communities, I am certain that some people were uncomfortable sharing this information because they were aware that turtles and their eggs are illicit products.

My way of dealing with these unexpected revelations that compromised my research results was to find an excuse to be nearby and watch the weekly loading of buses while discreetly observing the cargo. These observations provided me with clear evidence that turtles did in fact go out on the bus from both Palo Verde and Chacarilla. Visual observation allowed me to verify turtle consumption in a less threatening manner, and to compare my findings with what people had told me about their consumption of turtles. This type of triangulation of data collection is a good policy to observe. When one is working with memory recall and sensitive research issues, triangulation becomes an important tool to reveal the validity of the information collected. In this case, observation helped me obtain a clearer picture of turtle consumption without having to push my informants to divulge information they were not comfortable sharing. I continued to ask questions about turtles and eggs being sent on the bus, but no longer felt compelled to press for numbers. The verification of consumption through observation added a qualitative element to my analyses. I was satisfied with the information I was able to acquire in this way; it provided me the confirmation I needed to confidently state that there exists non-subsistence turtle consumption in both communities.

Another geographer who works in Latin America, Eric Perramond, has shared stories from his field work, which include reactions to sensitive socio-political situations such as this one. Perramond[15] reconstructs a field experience, describing his use of multiple methods of analysis (oral histories, ethnographic interviews, personal conversations and pile sorting) that led to the development of his dissertation. Through this process, Perramond realized the difficulties and complexities of entering a situation "in the middle," which most fieldwork entails, because "rarely does anyone arrive at the true "beginning" of any event, process, or story."[16] Triangulation of methods, including casual chats, is one way of correcting this arrival "in the middle" of a situation. Casual conversations have provided me with some of the most valuable insights into the situations I was investigating. These casual conversations have also provided me with the incentive to continue my work, often in directions that I had not previously considered, and with greater insight. For example, in my Bolivian fieldwork, I was asking people how many turtles and turtle eggs they were sending out on the bus each month. Based on comments made by an informant as well as my own retrospective reflection, I have since realized that these questions were not completely adequate. I was asking people how many turtles were being sent out on the bus to the two cities, Chacarilla and Palo Verde, to which buses traveled to and from. I did not ask about other locations that could have been potential destinations or about other means of transportation, such as private or work vehicles, for example. A second appropriate line of questioning would have dealt with assessing how many as well as whether or not turtles were being sent to the St. Francis mine, which lies just south of Chacarilla, in private vehicles. If enough turtles were sent there, it would represent a significant sink for turtles that I had not considered in my research design, but one that would help explain the hunting pressure on the turtles and their cultural value. I did not inquire enquire any further because I discovered this flow of turtles in the tenth month of a twelve month field season while talking with a mine employee I

met in Chacarilla. At that point, it was impossible to get more than just this anecdotal account of the potential turtle consumption at that site.

What this anecdotal information did provide me was insight into a potential
additional source of pressure on the turtles and a question to be included in future
research. This is potentially important in terms of turtle consumption because the
demand for turtle meat at the mine is likely due in part to the Catholic Church
having declared turtle meat a white meat, which is relevant to the majority of residents in that area who are practicing Catholics. Additionally, the mines are an
employment source for residents of Chacarilla who naturally take their cultural
values of eating turtle with them when they leave their communities. While I was
not able to get to the mine to confirm shipments of turtles, a Canadian manager
working there reported seeing two turtles in the kitchen. Although he could not
identify whether they were river turtles, I presume that they indeed were based
on his description of being laid on their backs for immobilization. This type of
immobilization is only effective for Podocnemis turtles due to their wide shallow carapaces that prevent them from rolling over, unlike the land tortoises found
in this area (the South American yellow-footed tortoise Geochelone denticulata
and the South American red-footed tortoise G. carbonaria), which can turn themselves over and are thus immobilized by being tied up. What this indicated to me
was that the turtles being eaten at the mine were likely river turtles, and thus consisted in an additional source of turtle consumption in the area. Although I never
witnessed it, I was also told that truckloads of turtles were sent up to the mine,
especially during the week preceding Easter. These turtles were sold to workers
there, many of whom are from the communities (five households in Chacarilla
reported mining as their primary source of income). My conversation with the
mine worker illustrates the value of casual conversation to supplement interviews
and other data collection techniques. This case also illustrates the importance of
triangulation of methods and of reflection on fieldwork while in progress.

POSITIONALITY OF RESEARCHERS–WHO ARE WE? WHO ARE THEY?

When working in the field, it is easy to enter a research setting without being
mindful of who one is in relation to those one relies on or interacts in their daily
context. Personally, I have to work on consciously placing myself in the social context of the field setting and remind myself that there are histories and previous
experiences that perhaps unconsciously influence people's perceptions of me as
a researcher. Considering one's positionality is important in terms of opening a
dialogue that does not reinforce uneven power relations or further stereotypes
of other cultures as less than one's own. Sundberg states that "increased attention
to the nexus of power and knowledge and in particular, to how the researcher's
geographic location, social status, race, and gender fundamentally shape the questions asked, the data collected, and the interpretation of the data. Dialogue about
these issues in our teaching and writing not only will better prepare students for
fieldwork, but also has the potential to foster research that subverts rather than re-

produces power inequalities."[17] This is particularly important for researchers coming from nations that have historically acted as colonial powers, as was my case coming from the United States to conduct research in Bolivia. I try to be sensitive to my background as a female American and to the associations it may engender. I have made efforts to avoid furthering an imperialistic relationship by sending back summaries of my analyses in the native language and photographs of people I have taken to the communities where I have collected data. I feel this is important for the sake of respecting the people involved in my research. Without their input, I would not have a story to tell. Giving back the research results and a summary of the project are simple reciprocities. Yet they foster good relations between foreign nations, respect of other cultures, allow for positive impressions of other cultures.

Talking about such underlying issues of positionality is also crucial to strengthen the efforts of future generations of fieldworkers towards ending uneven power relations. As scholars, we can do so by sharing stories with our students as we interact both formally and informally with them before they head out to the field to conduct their own research, or to spark their interest in conducting fieldwork. Speaking frankly of my experiences, including mistakes I have made and how I have corrected them when possible, is a valuable learning experience for my students as well as for myself. I have sometimes gained additional insight as a result of reflecting upon my experiences in a classroom setting. I have shared with my students stories about opportunities to use my foreign status as a means of obtaining information from males in patriarchal cultural settings where this would not generally be an option for a native woman, as she might risk social and/or physical repercussions. Such examples not only offer insight into the fieldwork experience, but also foster students' global awareness and teach them to be sensitive to or critical of behaviors they believe to be normative or take for granted in their home nation. Part of preparing students for fieldwork consists of raising their awareness of other ways of life and regulations that as researchers, it will not be their place to evaluate or judge, but rather to abide by and learn not to disrupt.

During my fieldwork in Bolivia, I was interestingly accused of spying on the communities for the benefit of the national park itself. Two different people in Chacarilla with whom I had worked closely over the course of my time in the field told me, upon my return from a brief trip to the city, that rumors were circulating about my working for the park. They said that I was being accused of gathering information about the community, and that such information would be used to purchase the community's land for US$2,000. My initial reaction was one of disbelief, followed by sadness that people whose confidence and trust I had worked so hard to gain would believe such a betrayal possible. In the end, the incident became a source of great humor for me and many others. But, first and foremost, it became a learning opportunity for me.

In the community of Chacarilla, I had not insisted on a community meeting before beginning my year of fieldwork, as I had for preliminary work, once the mayor told me that it was not necessary. In Palo Verde, by contrast, I held community meetings before both periods of fieldwork. When the spy accusation surfaced, it was the people in Chacarilla who suspected me, not those in Palo Verde. The lesson learned was simply that one should insist on a community meeting before beginning any fieldwork in a given community. Ultimately, I believe that because I had publicly communicated to residents of Palo Verde the goal of my work, and individually to the residents of Chacarilla over the preceding eight months, and because I had sought to remain a neutral albeit foreign woman working on turtles, this accusation was eventually diffused as untrue in both communities. My data collection was not unaffected by this accusation, however. Based on recommendations from several community members in Chacarilla and Palo Verde, I stopped carrying around my global positioning system (GPS) unit since it might be perceived as corroborating evidence to the rumors. I was therefore not able to collect the waypoints for Chacarilla, which meant I was not able to collect waypoints to directly map it in a geographic information system for analysis. But this was a small sacrifice to make in comparison to the potential detriment the accusion might have caused—bodily harm was suggested by some to be a potential consequence of confirmation of my spy status, and I had heard stories of people losing their lives over motorcycles and cattle (which are not worth more than US$2,000 each). I preferred not to test my luck and to come out of the field alive, with slightly less data than planned, rather than risk some form of an altercation. Ultimately the sacrifice of data collection was minimal in the face of what I believed to be legitimate threats. People remained willing to talk with me about turtle consumption, but I judged the collection of data not explicitly related to turtle abundance or consumption to be unwise. In an area where the annual income for a majority may be in the neighborhood of US$1,000 to US$1,500, the sum of US$2,000 is quite a large one. In the context of my field work setting, this sum represented a significant enough amount of money to encourage someone to take a risk.

Interestingly, my classification as a spy provided grounds for some of the more insightful conversations with community members in regards to their use and consumption of turtle. Becoming part of local gossip opened up avenues for conversation about turtles, because it seemed to have made me more of a local, or at the least opened avenues of conversation that we had not traveled down before the label emerged. Because I listened to the accusation and did not do more than consistently and calmly state that it was not true, I think it made people more willing to talk with me about the accusation as well as about turtle-related (and other) topics, particularly in Chacarilla. When they saw that I responded reasonably when questioned and that my data collection remained consistent—I did not change my style of interaction or data collection, except for eliminating the use of the GPS unit—they felt that they had the evidence they needed to refute the accusation. In these conversations, which took place in people's living rooms and porches at their and my own initiation, we candidly covered topics ranging from peoples' dependence on the turtles and their eggs, history of this use, what the future holds if nothing changes, and what conservation of turtles means for the people and the resource. This experience provided an opening to deal with the turtle issue in a way that felt more honest and potentially productive to me. I sensed that people were more willing to let down their guard once I had been "exposed" as a multidimensional character, or at least someone who had something at stake—my identity related to the turtles—they could relate to. For me, this story had a happy ending. I felt my data collection benefited as a result of the increased willingness of most individuals to talk with me about their use of turtles and their thoughts about the turtle resource. We also talked more in depth about community politics as people offered their candid opinions of community leaders and governance, which shed light for me on the socio-political system within which turtles are embedded. In subsequent visits to both Chacarilla and Palo Verde, I have enjoyed warm welcomes and we have laughed at jokes about my spy status. I plan to continue data collection in both communities and have been told that I will be welcomed back.

For me, these conversations were a segue way into the culture in which I was working—they offered me further insight into the culture I was studying as well as the questions I was asking. In terms of approach to fieldwork in distinct cultural settings, Bernard offers advice based on his decades of experience in the field by stating that the focus should be on "developing good research questions, good hypotheses, and strong measurements for testing those hypotheses," while letting one's "biases influence choice of topic, not measurements."[18] As Bernard further notes, although we all have biases that in some way influence our research, what we owe to the public, including fellow researchers and our students, is to be honest about these biases in our writing. So, when we focus solely on conveying the results of our analyses, we miss out on opportunities to share the experiences associated with unearthing data with our students and colleagues. Research focuses in many cases on the presentation of results and analyses while experiential/empirical stories are left out. By leaving out our personal experience, we forego the potential to assist our students and fellow researchers who go out to the field, and do not give credit to our informants who have given of their valuable time to assist us in learning from their lives and contexts.

CONCLUSION

Tuan observes that the humanist scholar "needs to have a firm grasp of the socioeconomic and intellectual conditions that promote the savoring of life."[19] Possessing such a disposition towards reflection helps individuals "appraise the meaning of what they have undergone," which increases the quality of life.[20] I believe that engaging in reflection also increases the quality of our research, scholarship and teaching. My research experience in Bolivia provided me with many opportunities to reflect upon the process of fieldwork as I was collecting data on the abundance of turtles and patterns associated with their consumption by ribereños in two communities. While I learned a great deal about socioeconomic characteristics that contribute to turtle consumption, I also learned about myself as a fieldworker. First and most importantly for me, I demonstrated to myself that I can successfully complete fieldwork, which is, at times, a grueling job. I also learned that I am able to effectively deal with difficult interpersonal communication and relationships that accompany fieldwork in a cross-cultural setting. I have realized the value of reflection while working in the field and the importance of listening to these reflections so as to adjust my data collection while in progress. These considerations made a difference for me as a researcher in the field, and I hope that they will be of some benefit to you, as you embark upon fieldwork yourself.

NOTES

1   E. O. Wilson, *The Diversity of Life* (Cambridge, Mass.: Harvard University Press, 1988).
2   World Resources Institute, United Nations Environment Programme, and The World Conservation Union, *National Biodiversity Planning: Guidelines Based on Early Experiences around the World* (Baltimore: World Resources Institute, 1995).
3   Ricardo Godoy, *Indians, Markets, and Rainforests: Theory, Methods, Analysis* (New York: Columbia University Press, 2001), C. A. Peres and I. R. Lake, "Extent of Nontimber Resource Extraction in Tropical Forests: Accessibility to Game Vertebrates by Hunters in the Amazon Basin," *Conservation Biology* 17, no. 2 (2003), David S. Wilkie et al., "Role of Prices and Wealth in Consumer Demand for Bushmeat in Gabon, Central Africa," *Conservation Biology* 19, no. 1 (2005).
4   P. Marcoy, *Travels in South America: From the Pacific Ocean to the Atlantic Ocean* (New York: Scribner, Armstrong and Co., 1875).
5   Ibid, R. Spruce, ed., *Notes of a Botanist on the Amazon and Andes* (London: Macmillan and Company, Ltd., 1908), N. J. H. Smith, "Aquatic Turtles of Amazonia: An Endangered Resource," *Biological Conservation* 16, no. 3 (1979), Z. Castro de León, "Geografía Histórica De La Tortuga Del Orinoco" (Universidad Central de Venezuela, Facultad de Humanidades y Educación, Escuela de Historia, 1986), P. C. H. Pritchard and P. Trebbau, *The Turtles of Venezuela* (Oxford, Ohio: Society for the Study of Amphibians and Reptiles, 1984), A. D. Johns, "Continuing Problems for Amazon River Turtles," *Oryx* 21, no. 1 (1987), P. Ergueta and C. de Morales, Libro Rojo De Los Vertebrados De Bolivia (Gland, Switzerland: International Union for the Conservation of Nature, 1996), J. Ojasti, *Wildlife Utilization in Latin America: Current Situation and Prospects for Sustainable Management* (FAO, 1996).
6   I use pseudonyms for all rivers, places and people's names throughout.
7   (e.g., A. Bebbington, R. Peet, and M. Watts, in *Movements, Modernizations, and Markets: Indigenous Organizations and Agrarian Strategies in Ecuador* (London: Routledge, 1996).
8   J. Caballero Guerrero, "Comparacion De Cuatro Tratamientos De Manejo Para La Proteccion De La Peta De Agua (Podocnemis Unifilis), Troschel 1840, Y Estimación De La Supervivencia De Las Crias En Las Playas Del Río Itenéz" (Universidad Autonoma "Gabriel Rene Moreno," 1996), Ministerio de Desarollo Sostenible y Medio Ambiente, *Plan De Manejo Parque Nacional Noel*

Kempff Mercado (Santa Cruz, Bolivia: Fundación Amigos de la Naturaleza and The Nature Conservancy, 1996).

9   I asked this question to people who had answered "fewer" to the question "How does the number of turtles today compare with ten years ago?"

10   Hypotheses: H1: turtles will be less abundant closer to human communities. H2: there will be more turtles at Las Petas (less hunting pressure) than at Chacarilla (more hunting pressure). H3: turtles will be smaller closer to human communities than farther away. H4: there is greater market consumption of turtle protein in Chacarilla than Palo Verde and greater subsistence consumption of turtle protein in Palo Verde than in Chacarilla. H5 there is a negative correlation between wealth and turtle protein sale/trade such that as personal wealth increases, the consumption of turtle protein decreases.

11   Subsistence use of turtles was defined as consumption within or between households as gifts and not as payment for services. Market consumption was defined as when turtles were captured and used as cash-producing items.

12   Godoy, *Indians, Markets, and Rainforests: Theory, Methods, Analysis*, Ricardo Godoy, "The Effects of Rural Education on the Use of the Tropical Rain Forest by the Sumu Indians of Nicaragua: Possible Pathways, Qualitative Finds and Policy Options," *Human Organization* 53, no. 3 (1994), Ricardo Godoy, Nicholas Brokaw, and David Wilkie, "The Effect of Income on the Extraction of Non-Timber Tropical Forest Products: Model, Hypotheses, and Preliminary Findings from the Sumu Indians of Nicaragua," *Human Ecology* 23, no. 1 (1995), Ricardo Godoy et al., "Of Trade and Cognition: Markets and the Loss of Folk Knowledge among the Tawahka Indians of the Honduran Rain Forest," *Journal of Anthropological Research* 54, no. 26 (1998).

13   H. R. Bernard, *Research Methods in Anthropology: Qualitative and Quantitative Approaches*, Second ed. (Walnut Creek, California: Altamira Press, 1995), 158–64.

14   Marie D. Price, "The Kindness of Strangers," *The Geographical Review* 91, no. 1–2 (2001).

15   Eric P. Perramond, "Oral Histories and Partial Truths in Mexico," *The Geographical Review* 91, no. 1–2 (2001).

16   Ibid.: 156.

17   J. Sundberg, "Masculinist Epistemologies and the Politics of Fieldwork in Latin Americanist Geography," *Professional Geographer* 55, no. 2 (2003): 180.

18   H. Russell Bernard, email communication, April 9, 2007 2007.

19   Yi-Fu Tuan, "Life as a Fieldtrip," *The Geographical Review* 91, no. 1–2 (2001): 45.

20   Ibid.

PART III

Encumbrances

CHAPTER SEVEN

"You can't bring a child in here, this is a place where people come to do serious research work!": Negotiating Lone Motherhood and Fieldworker Identities

BY CECILY JONES

Anthropologists and geographers working within feminist ethnographical research methodologies have drawn attention to what previously amounted to a seemingly conspiratorial silence surrounding the presence of family members—spouses, partners and children—who accompany researchers on overseas fieldwork. As Frohlick argues, the dominant model of the overseas fieldworker is that of the intrepid, unaccompanied male or female, who enters "the field" free to pursue research unencumbered by the demands and anxieties of familial responsibilities.[1] Yet, as Cupples and Kindon point out, researchers are rarely alone in the field; yet to admit the presence of family members is somehow to bring professional integrity and identity into question. Although ethnographic researchers have for decades been accompanied by family members or friends on overseas fieldwork, scholarly conventions demand the erasure of the visible presence of these "others" from the final published research account.[2] This report generally reflects the research process as a seamless and disembodied experience, uncomplicated and unsullied by the presence of anyone other than the researcher. Even the standard acknowledgments in published fieldwork accounts, which thank family and friends for their support during research, fail to covey their multiple implications within the process. As Frohlick writes:

> Since when are our children and spouses and friends not a part of our field sites in some manner, if only to complicate how we negotiate our research time and place? Perhaps this is much more of a concern for graduate students and new researchers than it is for established scholars. Yet, it still strikes me as somewhat taboo to acknowledge the presence of our families, in other words to blur and even violate the boundaries of our field sites with visible traces of our personal lives and relationship, however important these relationships and biographies are in enabling us to understand the phenomenon we are studying.[3]

Recently reading my doctoral thesis in preparation for publication, I realized that I too was a collaborator in the reproduction of these exclusionary practices. Beyond a salutary mention in my acknowledgments, nowhere in over three hundred pages of text had I made a single mention of my daughter's presence on my field-work journeys. Yet in my notes, written on an almost nightly basis in the field, my daughter's lively presence spilled over onto every page, captured, for instance in my observations of her enchanted response to the sight of a humming bird hovering over a hibiscus, or her amazement one morning when confronted by the sight of a green monkey, casually sitting on the wall. My journal entries recording these magical moments in my daughter's life, were, however, interspersed heavily with more serious concerns arising from her presence on fieldwork. I also wrote about my frustrations over the difficulties encountered in enrolling Ruth into a school and the subsequent impact this had on the time available to pursue my research, my ongoing difficulties of finding childcare, my worries about her initial isolation from other children, my guilt at having taken an afternoon away from my research to watch her first ever performance in a "Bajan" school play, and my anxieties over removing her from the familiar environment of home to one often marked by relative discomfort. At the age of thirteen, my daughter's needs and wants dominated my thoughts daily as I grappled with the ever-present challenges of performing my responsibilities as her mother, alongside my often frustrated efforts to fulfil my student-researcher role and successfully complete my fieldwork.

Once back at home, I had ruthlessly excised all the messy, complicating, and *unprofessional* evidence of my daughter's presence from my notes. In so doing, I had concealed the uncomfortable blurring of personal and professional boundaries that pervades the fieldwork experiences of the accompanied researcher. This was not a decision of my own making, but rather recommended unexpectedly by my dissertation committee upon submission of the first draft of my methodology chapter. While I believe that acknowledgment of her presence and the ensuing implications remained fundamental to my account, as a graduate student, I did not feel sufficiently empowered to challenge the decisions of senior scholars. At the same time, more personal concerns shaped my acquiescence. In an era in which single motherhood, especially black single motherhood stills carried a residual stigma, I felt loath to draw undue attention to my status, especially within an institution that remains defined by white middle class standards.

The uneasy acknowledgement of my daughter's erasure from my finished thesis provoked another uncomfortable revelation. I had, I thought, presented a suitably reflexive and scholarly account of the methodological challenges posed by archival research, yet I had totally elided any discussion of the practical difficulties that arose from the conflicts between my dual roles as mother and research student. In essence, I had presented a very neat, but ultimately *partial* account of my fieldwork experience. Hence, while the finished thesis represented a significant contribution to multidisciplinary scholarship, it did not offer much of benefit to graduate parents whose research would take them and their children into the field. Ethnographers are continuing to challenge the model of the solitary overseas fieldworker, and their spirited discussions have done much to illustrate how overseas fieldwork accompanied by family may lend methodological, theoretical and epistemological insight to the research processes. However, most of this body of work has narrated the fieldwork experiences of experienced researchers rather than that of graduate students who, as parents, face diverse challenges.

Graduate students with parental responsibilities have few resources on which to draw as they prepare for their fieldwork. Little attention has been given to helping future overseas researchers accompanied by family members negotiate the often difficult pre-departure practicalities and formalities. Handbooks dispensed to overseas-bound research students still assume the single status of such students, and the particular needs of student parents are unacknowledged. Fieldwork guidance rarely discusses specific practical, financial, and emotional challenges that graduate researchers will inevitably encounter in their dual roles as parent and research student. Consequently, many are ill-informed and unprepared for the numerous, complex and often time-consuming pre-departure arrangements that have to be made before they can even enter the field.

This chapter is not intended as a "how-to" guide; instead, in reflecting on some of the problems, practicalities and challenges encountered prior to and during my fieldwork, I hope to signal some considerations for parent researchers. I discuss some of the problems of securing adequate funding, finding affordable and secure accommodation, schooling and childcare, negotiating sexual politics, dealing with isolation and with frustrating encounters with local bureaucracies, the importance of organizing time to conduct the research. These represent just a few of the challenges with which I struggled in the course of my own overseas fieldwork.

In what follows, I also want to reaffirm feminist critiques of the traditionalist representations of fieldwork and the field as a masculinized space. Within this space, male researchers are abstracted from familial relationships, free to engage in the pursuit of knowledge construction and production, without the disruptive presence of a spouse, partner or children. Such an image of fieldwork reproduces the field as the embodiment of public/private divide, as one from which children and partners are banished in order for the solitary researcher to produce legitimate knowledge of the social world. Clearly, the presence of loved ones within the fieldwork process abruptly disrupts the neat but ultimately untenable theoretical dichotomous categories of private and public.

Feminist researchers have insisted that researchers engage in critical, honest reflexive introspection of the ways in which their positionality informs social research. Much of the feminist inspired debate on positionality concerns the ways in which our multiple identities inform the power relationships between researcher and the researched. However, as Cupples and Kindon argue, there remains the important imperative that we critically reflect on how being accompanied on fieldwork impacts our positionality.[4] Frohlick also notes that while ethnographers have stressed the significance of positionality on the research process in the field, "less has been written about how, prior to entering the field, these positions affect the nature of the field sites we choose or how they actually play out in the field."[5] Throughout the months of pre-departure planning, for instance, no decision I faced could be made without factoring my daughter into the equation. Either before or during my visit in the field, few problems that I encountered were not intimately related to my identity and role as a mother.

In this chapter, I am concerned with how my multiple subject positionality, as an unmarried single mother, as a transnational western-based, black graduate research student, gave definition to the nature of my fieldwork experience. I am also concerned with its significance in shaping my choice of research topic, the complications it introduced in approaching fieldwork, and the fieldwork process itself. Moreover, my transnational identity as Barbadian/Black British inevitably situated me as an "insider/outsider," informing my identities as a researcher and as a mother in complex ways. Most often though, my positionality as a mother defined my fieldwork experience. It determined and limited my research topic, fieldwork possibilities, and experiences. I do not claim that these experiences are representative of graduate parents' in general, for their experiences will be defined by their country of location, their financial status, the levels of institutional support available to them, any previous overseas experience, and other variables.

RESEARCH AND FIELDWORK AIMS

I am a historical sociologist. My research interests are multidisciplinary, traversing the terrains of history, women and gender studies. My doctoral thesis sought to explore the complex interweaving of race, gender, social class and sexuality in defining the contours of white women's lives in the colonial and antebellum slave-holding societies of Barbados and North Carolina. I argued that despite their gendered subordination, white women's social positioning as members of the dominant racial group afforded themselves privileges and opportunities denied to non-whites, whether enslaved or free. In conceptualizing white women as active agents, rather than as mere victims of patriarchal authority, I sought to disrupt prevailing gendered discourses of white women's marginality to the development of colonial societies. Among the research questions I posed were: How did the institution of African slavery penetrate and shape the social worlds of white women in the Americas? What socio-economic roles did white women play in these societies? What forms of power, if any, did white women exercise? How did the nexus of class, gender and class relations structure their material experiences? What strategies did white women deploy in managing their subjugated female status? How was whiteness maintained, reproduced, and what became of women who transgressed the norms of white society?

Pursuing these research questions raised vital methodological challenges. As is acknowledged, until the 1970s, women remained largely excluded from historical scholarship, and this was equally true for historiographies of Barbados and North Carolina. Feminist challenges to traditional masculinist historical inquiry encouraged the emergence of women's and gender history within academia, and heralded a substantive body of scholarship that reflected women's diverse historical roles within American society. I was able to draw on this scholarship to provide a framework for the North Carolina aspects of my study. Preparatory research in the UK had uncovered the existence of an abundance of North Carolinian women's own literary products including journals, correspondence, and their plantation accounts, and it was relatively easy to discover the location of the valuable sources in southern archives. However, this preliminary research also revealed the near-absence of similar sources for white Barbadian women, so that in going to Barbados, I faced the very real possibility that I might not uncover more than a few source documents of any value. After some reflection, I determined that while it might prove impossible to find personal testimonies of Barbadian women, I could at least gain a window into their material realities by analyzing other available historical sources such as newspapers, wills, property deeds, parish records, and court records. Although these sources were not produced by women themselves, they potentially offered important perspectives on white Barbadian women's lives. It was for this reason that I determined to conduct archival research in Barbados. My initial plan was to spend three months there followed by a similar duration in North Carolina.

During my doctoral studies, I spent a total of eight months conducting archival research in Barbados and five in North Carolina, though the narrative that follows is based primarily on my experience in Barbados. When I began my studies, I was aware that a period of overseas research was a distinct possibility, and I looked forward to this "rite of passage" for a number of reasons. I had been born in Barbados, but at aged six, was sent to join my parents in the United Kingdom, where they had emigrated soon after my birth. I did not return to Barbados again until my early twenties, which came as the fulfillment of a long-held dream. Yet I had always been conscious that brief visits to Barbados as a tourist left me unable to derive any more than a superficial understanding of the place that I stubbornly insisted on calling "home." The prospect of a prolonged stay in Barbados, while also introducing my daughter to her Caribbean heritage was thus deeply exciting for both of us. Of course, other more scholarly motivations also informed my wanting to conduct fieldwork in Barbados. Though my research was specifically historical in nature, I felt it important that, as an outsider, I gain an appreciation of the legacies of centuries of slavery and colonialism on the contemporary socio-political, cultural, and economic landscapes of the society.

Petley, writing reflexively on his experiences as a white British graduate student conducting archival research in Jamaica, prompts our understanding that as westerners conducting research within post/colonial societies, we become inevitably implicated in the reproduction of exploitative inequalities between the global north and south.[6] Petley reminds us that overseas research does not occur within a political vacuum, and that our decisions to conduct research within the societies of the global south inherently involves our entanglement within exploitative consumption practices. These practices benefit our individual scholarly careers, thereby perpetuating the privileges that follow from our positionality as western-based scholars. Petley argues that a sensitive "grounding" in the contemporary realities of the societies we seek to understand may not only give authority and validity to the "outsider" scholarship, but may also be transformative. Petley draws on the critical perspective of bell hooks who argues that white who shift their locations may develop different perspectives on how they view the world.[7] Petley suggests that "by living in the region whilst conducting research, reflective scholars can hardly avoid gaining an insight into the past and present impact of colonisation and racial terror in the region. By facilitating recognition of past and present inequalities and by confronting researchers with their own involvement in these systems, the research process might therefore be seen as an experience that can help, in hook's words, to 'decolonise our minds and our imaginations.'"[8] While Petley speaks to white western-based researchers, his argument does have resonance for non-white western based transnational researchers such as myself, for whom the Caribbean represents not merely a fieldwork site, but also an ancestral home and heritage. In going to Barbados, I would occupy an uneasy and problematic "insider" status; yet my location within the global north meant that I would potentially also be able to draw on the privileges afforded to "outsider" researchers.

SHOULD I STAY OR SHOULD I GO? PRACTICAL CONSIDERATIONS

That I would actually be able to undertake fieldwork, even for a limited duration, was never a foregone conclusion. As a self-financing student on a low income, the costs of such a project were extremely prohibitive. I was already working long hours as a teaching assistant, and my income barely enabled me to cover graduate school, housing and childcare costs, and would certainly not stretch to cover one airline ticket, let alone two! Providentially, in my second year of graduate school, I was awarded a full studentship, which enabled me to transfer to full-time registration. Most importantly, it also included a nominal dependant's allowance, which eased my precarious financial situation, though not sufficiently to cover my projected fieldwork costs.

My near-impoverished state was not the only obstacle before me. As a student, I had long understood and accepted that my mothering role would inevitably compete with the equally challenging demands of my student identity, but the prospects of overseas fieldwork brought that conflict into even sharper relief. Foremost was my desire to maintain stability in Ruth's life. Since the age of three, Ruth had led a relatively peripatetic existence as I moved from city to city, pursuing higher education and employment. I felt guilt-ridden at the prospect of introducing yet more upheaval into her life—she had only recently settled into a new school, made new friends, and was doing well academically. Briefly, I mulled over the possibility of making a couple of short research trips alone. This proved impossible, not least because I had no close relatives with whom Ruth could live in my absence, but also because neither of us relished the prospect of even a short separation. For a while, I prevaricated, half-hoping that despite the lure of the Caribbean and North Carolina, the fruit of my research in UK archives would be sufficient to enable me to complete my thesis without having to go overseas.

It was actually a relief to me that the paucity of UK archival sources forced my decision to go overseas. And any lingering reservations were soon dispelled by events in my daughter's own life. Ruth, who had been schooled in predominantly all white environments, was now beginning to verbalize ambivalence and confusion about her racialized identity. I thought—rightly, as it later materialized—that a period of immersion in her Caribbean heritage, living within a predominantly black environment would strengthen her self-identity as a young black woman. Researchers are rarely entirely explicit about the reasons for choosing particular fieldwork sites, as objective standards of research require that we deny anything other than a scholarly interest. While this may sometimes be the case, researchers often choose field sites based on personal desires.

In retrospect, my concerns over taking my daughter into the field paled besides the practical aspects of planning our fieldwork trip. Overseas fieldwork research requires an inordinate amount of forward planning, organizing and sound financial preparation. As I discovered, the process is made even more difficult for parents faced with limited budgets and the general absence of practical advice and guidance. Financial preparation is an important part of the field-work planning process, and accompanied parent-students should not underestimate the huge financial costs. Outgoings include expenditure on passports, health and travel insurance, visas, domestic and local travel, immunizations, new school uniforms, books and equipment, climate appropriate clothing and footwear, childcare costs, extra-curricula activities, and healthcare and medicines. University sponsored research visits often cover students and faculty only, so parent students must ensure that they take out additional health insurance for accompanying children and spouses. While these costs vary depending on where the fieldwork takes place, they nevertheless represent additional financial burdens for graduate parents, most of whom are often barely surviving on low-incomes. Fortunately, a number of charitable trusts offer financial support to students with children; competition for these awards is fierce, and the size of grants generally small. The application processes are often time-consuming, but a successful application may be well worth the time and effort expended.

I encountered financial difficulties from the outset as enquiries to my funding body revealed that while my overseas fieldwork allowance covered my personal travel and accommodation costs, I would not receive financial support for Ruth. In several frustrating but fruitless telephone calls to my sponsors, I pointed out the futility of providing me with an overseas budget without providing for my dependent child. While generally sympathetic, the bureaucracy was unmoving. An irate bureaucrat went so far as to question the need for Ruth to accompany me. Could she not remain in London with other family members? I still cannot explain the sense of shame I felt when forced to confess that I had been raised in a children's home, and had no family to turn to. Without adequate funds, how was I going to afford the equipment that we would both require?

Fortunately, my thesis supervisor had previously worked with student-parents experiencing financial hardship, and was able to direct me to a number of charitable educational trusts. I submitted numerous applications, despaired over the many rejections letters, and had almost decided to abandon both fieldwork and the half-completed dissertation when two trusts responded positively. They generously agreed to sponsor Ruth's travel and accommodation costs in addition to my department's limited sponsorship.

It goes without saying that comprehensive pre-departure preparation is critical to the overall success of the fieldwork project. Parent-students accompanied by children have to be prepared for every eventuality. Ruth and I were going to

be away for many months, visiting two different countries, and for each I needed
to be forearmed with as much information as possible. The practical issues first
involved my own research objectives: did I have the necessary skills and training?
How would I negotiate access to archives and other depositories in Barbados and
North Carolina? What official paperwork would I need to facilitate my access to
these sources? What arrangements would I need to put in place for ongoing supervision while away? Ruth's presence introduced many more practical issues: How
would I go about finding safe affordable accommodation for us both? What childcare options would be available? How would she be able to continue her schooling? As Starrs discovered when he undertook fieldwork in Spain accompanied by
his wife and two young daughters,

> With family along, fieldwork is no longer just about the researcher and a cluster
> of cherished contacts - documents and archives, people and places, organiza-
> tions and outlooks. Suddenly logistics become far more complex. From securing
> a room for the night to entertaining kids while conducting interviews . . . noth-
> ing with family is as simple as toughing out privations that we would routinely
> subject ourselves to, solo.[9]

Yet parent researchers are often left without support as they organize the
daunting business of transplanting their entire families to sometimes completely unknown countries. To my despair, in all the months of planning that
followed, I was forced to negotiate various bureaucratic mazes alone. At times,
even the most seemingly mundane matters seemed to take on gigantic proportions—just how much baggage did we need to pack for a six month overseas
visit? And of course airport baggage allowances remain the same whether one
is headed for a two week vacation or an extended overseas visit. Deciding what
was necessary and what could safely be left behind at home became an exercise
in military planning. And last, but not least, there were the various household
pets to consider: what were we to do about Basil, our five year old mongrel,
who had been a member of our family since he was five weeks old (he eventually went to stay with friends) and with my daughter's collection of gerbils,
guinea-pigs and tropical fish (they eventually went to live with new-owners)?
And what would happen to our rented home in our absence? Unable to afford
the costs of maintaining our home while we were away, I reluctantly decided
that the only viable solution was to terminate our lease. This would mean that
on our return, we would have no place to live; we would, in effect, be homeless.
Still, this was a worry that I could not dwell long on, as the matter of Ruth's
education demanded more immediate attention.

From the start, I was overtly conscious that, in my drive to further my education, I would be disrupting my daughter's own schooling. I planned to enroll her in
schools in Barbados and North Carolina, but worried about how she would cope
with these transitions. Would she make many friends? How would she handle a
different curriculum and a stricter school ethos? In some ways, these questions
were informed by my own western cultural thinking about what constituted good
mothering—and my actions in removing her from a familiar environment to pur-

sue my own interests certainly seemed to go against it. My ambivalence about juggling the dual roles of mother and student was often underscored by faculty. Since my undergraduate days, I had become used to professors who questioned my ability to successfully combine both roles, vocalizing their beliefs that campuses were no place for children and their scorn for selfish mothers like myself, who insisted on achieving an education rather than attending to their parenting responsibilities. I was fully aware that my decision to be accompanied by Ruth could be construed as the selfish actions of an irresponsible mother willing to disrupt her daughter's life and possibly expose her to risks. I was consumed by self-doubts about my ability to be a good mother, which was further exacerbated by the fact that I was—apparently selfishly—raising my daughter outside the sanctity of a nuclear family. As the single, unmarried mother of a young child who had no contact with her father, I had already transgressed culturally prevalent understandings of proper motherhood. Yet, contrary to the many veiled criticisms, I felt strongly that I would have been a bad mother had I chosen to leave my daughter behind in the care of friends for such an extended period of time.

I shared my concerns about the implications of Ruth's extended absence from school with her teachers, whose understanding helped reassure that my daughter would most likely find schooling in Barbados and North Carolina a stimulating experience. We discussed ways of ensuring that she would not fall behind her classmates on our return. I also agreed that the inevitable disruption could be minimized if we delayed our departure to coincide with the summer vacation.

Securing accommodation in two separate foreign research sites probably represented my greatest pre-departure challenge. On my previous visits to Barbados as a single person, my needs were relatively simple as I could easily find a room in a cheap hotel, or a night's accommodation on a friend's spare couch. But being accompanied meant I could not take such a casual approach. I was fortunate that in North Carolina, the university to which I had gained visiting student affiliation was enormously supportive—organizing our visas, arranging transport from the airport, and finding a house for us to sublet in a friendly neighborhood. Finding accommodation in Barbados, however, proved rather challenging. Despite previous visits, my knowledge of the island's geography was limited. I had no idea which neighborhoods were safe and could not assess the location or quality of schools, frequency of public transport, distances to local stores, libraries, the university or archives. As the time for our departure drew near, I considered booking us into a guest house as an interim measure until we had become more familiar with the island and the local rental market. Then, with just a week to go, I was contacted by the owner of a guest house who, by some means, had heard of my search, and feeling enormously thankful to have resolved the matter of our housing, gratefully arranged to rent a small apartment from him, a decision that I would soon have real cause to regret.

INTREPIDLY INTO THE FIELD WE GO . . .

Ruth and I arrived in Barbados for what I had planned would be a three month visit. Almost immediately, my carefully laid plans began to unravel as we experienced a series of events that we could not have foreseen. These were to impact the progress of my fieldwork so much that I was forced to extend our stay by another four months. Our accommodation turned out to be a tiny squalid, dilapidated room, which we shared with an army of huge cockroaches. The shower barely worked, there was neither air-conditioning nor a fan, electrical fittings sparked dangerously when switched on, and the locks on the doors were broken. It was located away from any regular transport routes, and some distance from amenities, the university and archives. More seriously, our landlord, whom at first we thought to be a genial, amiable old man, proved to be lecherous and sexually intimidating, often turning up at our door unannounced. His increasingly bold questions about my marital status, lewd remarks, and a supposedly joking offer to reduce my rent in exchange for sleeping with him, left me fearful for myself and for my daughter's safety.

As many researchers have noted, the sexuality of women travelers—whether accompanied by spouses or partners—is likely to be subjected to scrutiny by those she encounters, in ways that may become problematic. For instance, it is often assumed that western women are "easy sexual targets" (in Barbados, the levels of western, female sex tourism would seem to support such a view) and women researchers often attract unwanted sexual attentions. So intimidated had I become by my landlord's unwelcome sexual intrusions that I felt myself and my daughter to be in danger, with no-one to turn to for help or support. After two weeks of living in fear, I found another apartment. Literally under cover of night, we fled even though we had paid a full month's rent in advance. But this frightening start to my fieldwork trip did have its positive outcomes. Our new home was a self-contained apartment in a family home, and our landlord and his wife were warm people who soon made us feel a part of their family, often including us in family meals, introducing us to new friends, taking us on shopping trips, and showing us around the island. Throughout the months that Ruth and I lived with them, I was frequently grateful for their generosity and support.

I had planned our arrival to coincide with the long summer vacation, and we had both presumed that there would be many organized summer activities for school children so that Ruth could make new friends and I could begin my fieldwork. Contrary to our expectations, however, there were very few and what limited provision existed was reserved solely for children already registered at certain schools. I could not afford to employ full-time childcare for Ruth, and I did not feel that I could leave her home alone in an unfamiliar environment while I pursued my fieldwork. One day, desperate to begin my research, I turned up at the archives, daughter in tow, hoping that my promise that she would be on her best behavior would persuade staff to tolerate her presence. It was to no avail as the archivist sternly reprimanded me, "You can't bring a child in here, this is a place where people come to do serious research work!" Ruth and I were summarily evicted! Fortunately my landlady, recognizing my plight, came up with a nanny-share solution. For three hours on three mornings a week, I could share her nanny, Delia, an arrangement that I gratefully accepted, though I could barely afford the expense.

Even with Ruth's childcare partially resolved, I was still not in a position to begin archival research. Because of time constraints, I thought that my time would be more wisely spent on library based research. The local library was well-stocked with secondary sources—books, journals, and Caribbeana—that were not easily accessible in the UK, and while as a nonresident I did have not have borrowing rights, I was still able to make notes or voluminous photocopies from them. Microfiched holdings of eighteenth century Barbadian newspapers were also an important source, for they often cast light on socio-economic, political and cultural aspects of colonial society and helped give background context to my research. This library-based phase of my research also had the additional benefit that I could take Ruth with me when I did not have a nanny. While I worked, she would read, catch up on school-work, or write postcards to her friends and teachers back home. I tried to make sure that we always had some "family time" each afternoon and we would take time off to explore Barbados.

As the summer vacation drew to a close, I turned my attention to finding a suitable school for Ruth, only to encounter sundry bureaucratic problems that delayed her enrolment for almost two months. In order to register Ruth for a school, as I discovered, the Ministry of Education first required sight of original transcripts from her London school, a process that would take weeks. My pleas that she be allowed to enroll temporarily until the required transcripts arrived failed to move the officials, who reminded me that Ruth's status as a non-national meant that the Ministry was under no obligation to provide her with schooling. Even assertions of my Bajan heritage and citizenship failed to move officials, understandably to me now, for I had contributed nothing to their developing economy, yet still believed myself entitled to access their already strained educational resources. Though Bardadian born, officials regarded me as a westerner, and assumed that as such, I would be wealthy enough to afford private education. Even without the missing transcripts, our enquiries to individual head-teachers proved fruitless. There was simply no room for my daughter at any nearby school, and the only schools prepared to accept her were either private fee-paying or were located some distance away, which would require long hours of traveling daily on overcrowded buses.

Weeks went by, Ruth was still not enrolled in a school, and I became extremely anxious that she was missing out on her education. Ruth was herself isolated, restless, homesick and began to act up, often throwing in my face that I had taken her away from her friends. Her nanny had returned to university, I had not been able to find another regular babysitter, we were both frustrated at the situation, and my own research had virtually come to a stand-still. Certainly, all the problems we had experienced had been detrimental to my progress, and I had little substantive work to show for the two months we had already been in Barbados. I was seriously considering abandoning what seemed to me a disastrous period of fieldwork and returning home, when, with the assistance of an acquaintance, I was eventually able to enroll Ruth in a small independent fee-paying church school. Though my agnosticism caused some initial misgivings over educating my daughter within a religious school whose compulsory uniform I could scarcely afford, I seized upon this solution, even though it meant abandoning my principal stance against private education. But at least it meant that I could complete my fieldwork and not have to return home in defeat.

PROMISES AND PITFALLS OF ARCHIVAL RESEARCH

As a historical sociologist researching the intersections of gender, social class and race in colonial slave societies, archival research held both promises and problems. Historians consider a nation's archives to be the memory and conscience of a society, through its preservation of public and private records of the nation's past. Hence, archival research represents the main research method of historical scholarship, and involves the analysis of an extensive range of documents produced by a given society. In addressing my research questions, I drew on a diversity of historical documents sourced from the Barbados archives, including parish records, property and land deeds, household inventories, court records, government proceedings and legislation, records of births, baptisms, marriages, deaths, maps and rare books, plantation records, private correspondence and journals. Analyzing and interpreting these varied documents enabled critical understanding of the patriarchal attitudes towards women, and illuminated many aspects of women's lives in colonial Barbados. They revealed, for instance, the extent of women's investment in property, both real estate and human, their complex relationship with white males and enslaved and free African peoples, the strategies deployed by women to secure autonomy over their lives, and the efforts of the poor relief board to regulate the socio-sexual freedoms of poor white women. Few of these documents were produced by women, but my apprehension that I would return to the UK with little to show for my time in Barbados was unrealized.

While I was relieved to uncover such an abundance of historical documents, archival research was not without its difficulties. Archival research is generally labor and time-intensive requiring both application and perseverance. While there is no charge to researchers using the archives, and students generally only need to show proof of status and/or university affiliation, access is not always easy; opening hours may be limited, irregular or inconsistent, and dependent upon the weather. Ruth had hardly settled in school when the archives were suddenly closed for a period of two weeks for reasons that never became clear to me, before re-opening for a week or so, and then closing again for the Christmas vacation. Subsequently, I had to fit my childcare arrangements around their weekday opening hours of 9:30-4:30p.m., which still left me with very few hours in which to work, given the lengthy travel time to and from the archives (roughly two hours each way) and my need to be home by 3:30p.m., when Ruth arrived from school. Time spent in the archives became a precious commodity, and I often experienced a resigned sense of frustration at the wasted hours. For instance, the time taken from requesting a document to actually receiving it could range from an hour to an entire day—especially when there were many other researchers present, and the archivists were busy meeting the various requisition demands. At other times, I would request a document, only to be informed after hours of patient waiting that it is available only to approved researchers or senior scholars, and that as a graduate student, I fell into neither category. I would then have to cajole a member of the university staff to persuade the archivists to allow me access. Befriending some of the archivists, which took me a couple of months, solved such problems.

I had gone to the archives confident that I was trained in archival skills, but my experience revealed just how under-prepared I was. Having only a cursory idea of the nature of materials held on deposit, I expended considerable time determining just what documents would be of relevance. Finding aids were not always up-to-date, which made the process of locating some documents difficult. I was, at times, frustrated in my search when documents that were cited as being among the archives' collection could not be found; they had either been lost, removed to another location for repairs, or, because of concerns over their fragility, were no longer available for research purposes. There were also other frustrations to be contended with. I would start to read a will or a land deed, only to find that it was incomplete so faded by the passage of time that it could not be deciphered, or that it contained nothing of value to my research. Many archived documents are in a poor state, partially eaten by insects, damaged by sunlight or rainwater, and are therefore difficult to read. I had not received training in paleography—the study of old handwriting—and this laguna had serious implications. Many of the documents I read were centuries old, originating between the fifteenth and eighteenth centuries, and appeared to me either illegible or unintelligible, or both. Not only did I struggle to understand handwriting on old stained, torn and faded documents, but I also had to learn to understand legal terminology. It could take me days to correctly decipher the meaning of a single document. Once I became familiar with the language of various legal documents, my reading progressed relatively rapidly. Another factor that determined the pace of my research was that the documents that I had been working on had to be returned to storage at the end of the day. Each morning, when I arrived, I would have to repeat the same laborious process of completing a request slip and then wait—impatiently—for the documents to be delivered to me. If another researcher had managed to get to the archives ahead of me and had requested the same document, I would have to wait an unknown period of time, sometimes several days, to access the same document. When this occured, I would have to determine what documents I could next analyze, and then hope that whatever I decided on and requested would be made available to me on the same day.

Most archives do not permit photocopying of old and rare documents, and so they have to be transcribed by hand, a lengthy time consuming process. I had planned to read and transcribe volumes of documents over the course of three months, but it soon became clear that time constraints would not permit this. In efforts to get around this problem, I decided to use some of my limited funds to engage the services of a research assistant. Despite briefing her on the nature of my research, I discovered that she had been less than scrupulous in transcribing documents, and had omitted potentially valuable information relevant to my study. I then had to retrace her steps, recovering all the missing information, which further eroded my precious time. I had very little time in the archives to critically reflect on the data that I was collecting, and took a broad approach that involved collecting any materials that seemed even marginally significant—only to find later on that it was irrelevant to my needs. On our arrival in Barbados, I had begun to keep a daily journal, and while I had initially intended it solely as a memoir of our stay, in time it became more of a fieldwork aide. Each evening, with Ruth asleep in bed, I would assess the day's progress, identify further sources that I needed to consult, and map out my next steps. I used this quiet time also to reflect on the material I had consulted, to consider its relevance to my research, and to begin the preliminary analysis of the transcribed documents. I had agreed with my dissertation supervisors that I would send them weekly progress reports (necessitating time-consuming searches for an internet café), and the extensive notes that I recorded in my journal were extremely helpful for this purpose. My journal, which eventually ran to several volumes by the end of my fieldwork, became the means through which I could impose an element of order in my research.

RACE/ING FIELDWORK: NEGOTIATING TRANSNATIONAL IDENTITY IN THE FIELD

Although motherhood was a critical component in determining the nature of my overseas research fieldwork, my positioned identity as a transnational researcher was equally important in shaping my experience. Much feminist research has addressed the methodological problems of conducting research in "other" communities to which they do not have membership. Throughout the corpus of this reflexive work, there rests however an assumption of the researcher's whiteness, and it is therefore the white researchers' negotiations of racialized politics that dominates the literature on race and fieldwork research. Relatively little attention has been given to the complex racial dynamics introduced when western-based transnational non-white researchers conduct fieldwork research in predominantly non-white societies.

I had assumed that as a Barbadian/African Caribbean woman conducting research in Barbados, I would encounter few of the problems described by white researchers conducting overseas fieldwork.[10] To some extent, this was certainly the case, but in many instances, the problems I encountered were different from, and in some instances, *greater* than those described by white researchers. While white researchers may struggle with the difficulty of being outsiders in a different culture, my own challenges revolved around my coming to terms with my status as an outsider within a society that I considered home. I was *of* Barbados, but not *Barbadian* and this subtle distinction was to have recurrent implications throughout my fieldwork. Certainly it was a critical factor in shaping my relationship with the various official authorities that I encountered. As was often pointed out, my problems in finding a school place for Ruth would have been much reduced had I found acceptance as a Bajan. Although I subjectively identified myself as Barbadian, it soon became clear to me that I was not accepted as a "Bajan." My walk, my clothing, my hairstyle, the ashy gray tone of my skin, and above all perhaps, my English accent served to mark me out as "other." Try as I might, years of living in the UK left me incapable of articulating the Bajan dialect, and locals took delight in poking gentle fun at my "funny" British accent. Ruth, however, quickly grasped the intricacies of the local dialect and would chatter away quite comfortably with children and adults alike-a fact that amused locals who would laughingly point out that she was much more Bajan than me. To my considerable embarrassment, my difference was often revealed in other ways: I did not always understand local norms or aspects of cultural behavior, and sometimes unwittingly breeched local conventions. Often I would be walking along, deep in thought, and not notice that a passerby had wished me the customary greeting of "good-day," and would fail to return the courtesy, earning me a reprimand for my poor manners. When Ruth inadvertently breeched similar conventions, I was criticized for being a bad mother; for a good Bajan mother would have instilled good manners into her "girl child." And if at school, Ruth dared to "backtalk" a teacher, I would be summoned before the Head and invariably given a dressing down for my disciplinary failures. Often these criticisms appeared to be a veiled attack on the laxity of "English" parenting, and as a British mother, I was tarred by association with English people "dem." Many Bajans perceive Black British as "crazy," a perception derived from the disproportionately large number of blacks detained in British psychiatric institutions. This perception of British Blacks as crazy worked for and against me . . . it excused my oddities—walking out without a parasol in the heat of mid-day sun, or when, after having waited in some office for hours, my patience was exhausted and I would loudly demand to see the manager. Always, I was defined by my difference, by my "Englishness," an identity that I wore with irony, for in the UK, Englishess was, and remains, inherently associated with whiteness.

Not only did my perceived Englishness situate me as an outsider in my own homeland, but my racialized blackness raised other problems that bore more directly on my research. I arrived in Barbados in the midst of tense public political debates surrounding colonial slavery and its legacy of racism—a subject that remains uncomfortable for many Barbadians, black and white. So the topic of my research was often viewed with suspicion and I with distrust. From white and black alike I was asked: Why did I want to study slavery? What did I, an outsider, know about slavery? White Barbadians questioned: Why was I interested in studying white women? Was my purpose just to reveal white people as brutal perpetrators of oppression? Was I just trying to expose old wounds? Could black people objectively study white people? And from Black Barbadians: Why was I interested in white history? Was I attempting to excuse white women's roles as pro-slavery agents? Didn't I feel a sense of responsibility to engage in the ongoing work of recovering the marginalized history of enslaved Africans? Such questions were not always easily answered, and equally my answers only grudgingly accepted, but in their probing, I was forced to become more reflexive than I might otherwise have been about my positionality as a black researcher engaged in research on "race" and whiteness.

CONCLUDING REFLECTIONS

Researchers who have worked overseas accompanied by their children often highlight the positive benefits that the presence of their child/ren lent to the research project. Cupples for instance, discusses how the presence of her children on her ethnographic fieldwork in Nicaragua served to facilitate a sense of rapport between herself and the mothers who formed the subjects of her research. Cupples also stresses the benefits that an extended period of time away from their New Zealand home had on her children—their heightened consciousness of global inequalities, their recognition of their own privileges as they encountered poverty stricken Nicaraguan children, and their acquisition of new language skills.[11] In my own case, I remain ambivalent about the benefits in so far as they impacted my own research. Archival research is very much a solitary endeavor, and while my daughter's presence determined the *pace* of my work, it in no way affected my research outcomes. At times, Ruth's presence did help to facilitate interpersonal relationships. My landlord and his family, for instance, felt protective of me as a single mother, kept a watchful eye over us, looked after my daughter at times when I had no childcare, and introduced us to other families with young children, thereby helping to dispel the sense of isolation that we sometimes experienced. Though they did not understand why I chose to remain unmarried, and sometimes insisted on introducing me to "suitable" local young men, they nevertheless expressed admiration for my determination to not let my status as a single mother deter me from pursuing an my educational goals. Often, passersby would strike up conversations with my daughter on overhearing her "strange" accent; and several lasting friendships started in this way. And when Ruth finally began school, hardly a week passed without an invitation to visit her new friend's families, thus broadening our social circle. Ruth, for her part, came to appreciate her Caribbean heritage, and attending a predominantly black school helped strengthen her sense of pride in her racial identity. She developed a much better understanding of my work and grew interested also in Barbadian history. There were times when she grew frustrated at the stricter school ethos, (we both had difficulties over the fact that schools still used corporal punishment), and she never got over having to attend Saturday morning bible classes, but she did enjoy the practical agricultural lessons which would not have been part of her curriculum at home. And as she admitted, she also came to appreciate just how much better resourced schools were back at home, where she was used, for instance, to having regular access to computers and to not having to share books. And best of all, she made numerous new friends, many of whom she remains in contact with.

Ultimately, I found accompanied fieldwork to be a challenging experience, as I attempted, often unsuccessfully, to balance the demands of motherhood with those of my research responsibilities. There were periods when the lack of childcare severely interrupted my fieldwork, leaving me anxious about my ability to complete the project within the original time period. This of course led to further anxieties and self-doubts—perhaps my lack of progress stemmed from my own ineptitude, or perhaps I just simply was not organizing my time properly. And of course, explaining to my supervisors at home, why, after three months I had collected so little data and would be extending my time in Barbados, left me feeling that I had somehow failed as a researcher. While I never regretted my daughter's presence, I could not at times refrain from experiencing moments of envy when

I encountered other fieldwork researchers who were free to pursue their research activities without the additional responsibilities of a young child. Of course, such moments left me feeling guilt-ridden, and I would remind myself of my great fortune in having my daughter's company. Being accompanied by family on overseas research inevitably complicates the fieldwork process, especially as it so clearly blurs personal and professional identities and boundaries. Although Ruth and I may have disrupted the traditional masculinist model of fieldwork, ultimately, the challenges that we encountered served to reinforce in my eyes the unhappy disjuncture between motherhood and scholarly career.

NOTES

1   Frohlick, Susan E., "'You Brought Your Baby to Base Camp?': Families and Field Sites," *Great Lakes Geographer*, 9, no. 1 (2002): 49–58.
2   Cupples, Julia and Sarah Kindon, "Far from Being 'Home Alone:' The Dynamics of Accompanied Fieldwork." *Singapore Journal of Tropical Geography*, 24, no. 2 (2003): 211–28.
3   Frohlick, "'You Brought Your Baby to Base Camp?'" 52.
4   Cupples and Kindon, "Far from Being 'Home Alone,'" 212.
5   Frohlick, "'You Brought Your Baby to Base Camp?'" 49.
6   Petley, Christer. "Flying Away and Grounds for Concern: Mobility, Location and Ethical Discomfort in Researching Caribbean History from the UK." in *Beyond the Blood, the Beach and the Banana: New Directions in Caribbean Studies* edited by Sandra Courtman (Kingston, Jamaica: Ian Randle Press, 2004), 15–23.
7   Cited in Petley, "Flying Away," 20. See hooks, bell, "Representing Whiteness in the Black Imagination." in *Cultural Studies*, edited by Lawrence Grossberg, Carey Nelson and Paul Treicher, (London, Routledge, 1992), 338–46.
8   Petley, "Flying Away," 20.
9   Starrs, Paul F., Carlin F. Starrs, Genoa I. Starrs, Lynn Huntsinger, "Fieldwork . . . with Family." *Geographical Review*, 91, no. 1/2 (Jan. - Apr. 2001): 74–87.
10 See for instance, Abbott, Dina. "Disrupting the 'Whiteness' of fieldwork in Geography." *Singapore Journal of Tropical Geography* 27, no. 3 (2006): 326–41; Cukor-Avila, Patricia and Guy Bailey. "The Effects of the Race of the Interviewer on Sociolinguistic Fieldwork," *Journal of Sociolinguistics* 5, no. 2 (2001): 254–270; Mullings, B. "Insider or Outsider, Both or Neither: Some Dilemmas of Interviewing in a Cross-Cultural Setting," *Geoforum* 30, no. 4 (1999): 337–50; Sidaway, James D. "In Other Worlds: On the Politics of 'First World' Geographers in the 'Third World'" *Area* 24, (1992): 403–408.
11 Cupples and Kindon, "Far From Being 'Home Alone'" 65.

CHAPTER EIGHT

Serendipitous Treasures: Rethinking Archival Research in the Twenty-First Century

By Rebecca Sammel

When I received a Fulbright grant as a doctoral student to study early imprints in the Alsatian region of France, I was thrilled. A medievalist by training, I was researching the Stultiferae Naves, or "Ship of Fools" texts in the genre of late-medieval and early modern social satire.[1] The library of Sélestat houses a collection of these early imprints from the private library of the early-modern humanist and philologist Beatus Rhenanus, who lived and taught there. Rhenanus' close friend, the more famous humanist Erasmus of Rotterdam, wrote an encomium (still housed in the library's collection) praising "noble Sélestat" and the intellectual spirit so "fecund and generous" of this city famous for its Latin School and scholarly community.[2]

Technically, a scholar of the European Middle Ages studies the lengthy period that begins, in a hotly debated point of nomenclature and chronology, with the crumbling of Roman authority in Western Europe. The traditional "end" of the Middle Ages as the Italian Renaissance is just as hotly debated, but scholars continue to find continuities in both directions of the alleged beginning and ending. The "Renaissance" is as full of medieval continuities as the Middle Ages are full of intellectual innovations. The archives themselves respect no such tidy chronological categories created by historians; one can find a monastery's grocery bill embedded with a classical Roman text such as Virgil, with a fourteenth-century sermon warning that God's wrath is manifested in the current plague. By contrast, Sélestat's collection represents a slightly more homogeneous body of early sixteenth-century humanistic texts, a unique archival resource, and a revealing emblem of early-modern Alsatian humanism.

Alsace was a major center of humanistic endeavor in early modern Europe primarily because one of the first printing presses began operation in Strasbourg in the mid-1400s. For my project, as I first envisioned it, the challenge of studying these early imprints, called incunabula,[3] lay in their production as embedded in the locus of the printing press. I was interested in how the process of printing necessarily involved editing and mutations of the text in its transmittal to moveable type. The limitations of that medium informed the content, as had scribal abbreviation styles in medieval manuscripts. The crux of the project lay in my interest in how hermeneutical problems of the early printed text might be suggestively informed by those of the handwritten text. It seemed, in some passages, that a printer operator used something we would call a "macro" on a modern computer, or typesetting shortcuts to save ink and paper. I intended to study such early "macros" more closely to search for repetitions and variants, to discern whether it was perhaps a mechanical pattern built into the machines' movable type, or the individual operator's whim in setting the machine. In other words, compared to the medieval scribe using his own abbreviation system, how much editorial control did the printer-operator have in manipulating the text? What motivations—perhaps didactic, ideological, or purely economical—might have informed how he used the machine?

The incunabulum of St. Augustine's *De Civitate Dei* housed in Sélestat's collection expresses perfectly such a crux among these early imprints.[4] The text features gothic characters, printed in 1468 on the legendary press at Strasbourg. Its delicate craftsmanship resembles a manuscript written by a particularly meticulous scribe, and its abbreviations are the common ones codified in paleographical handbooks. Hence, given the superior efficiency and control wielded by the printer operator as opposed to the scribe, why does this early imprint resemble so closely a handwritten text? Why would the printer operator choose to replicate precisely the codifications and abbreviations of a monastic copyist? I thought I might approach the resolution of this problem in my perusal of the Sélestat archives.

Once I arrived in France and began my study, however, I realized that the dual literary and mechanical focus of my project required that I examine the printing machines themselves. Much as a paleographer as a scholar of old writing deciphers scribal handwriting and the scribal production of manuscripts, I needed to study the typographical processes of the presses themselves. My dual research vector of both process and product would attempt to elucidate the relationship between technology and artifact, as well as the "editorializing" function of the press itself as wielded by the operator.

Yet I had no idea which specific machines had been used for these texts, whether they were still intact, where they were housed, or whether I might be granted access to them. I lacked the specifically-tailored letters of introduction that would undoubtedly be required. Different facilities and a highly technical and specific vocabulary presented an intriguing challenge, but also a practical obstacle to a graduate student just beginning her dissertation. Nor did I have the time or funding to extend my stay in Europe, or even travel outside of Alsace; my budget and schedule accounted for every day, every meal, and every franc (in pre-euro France). Eventually, I was compelled to redefine the project entirely. And it was the practical concerns, i.e., getting my work done on the limited funding, that determined the project's ultimate content, for deciphering the technicalities of the printing process and its impact on content demanded more than my time, budget, and preparations allowed. Studying the printers was in fact a separate project whose extra time and expense would be fatal to my original project. I had not planned for such substantive changes to my project's scope. How does a researcher cope with such a potentially catastrophic situation? I was forced to change my project in medias res. How to preserve the integrity of my project's original conception when the pressures and limitations of time and budget threatened to annihilate it?

Resigning myself to studying only the texts collected in the Sélestat archives, and limiting my project to that scope, I began the steady work of poring through the archives. There, in the Sélestat library, I began to discern a pattern in the collection itself that became my project's new focus. I focused my work on not just the texts themselves, but also on the group of humanists, students and scholars alike, who had gathered in that historic city—because of the proximity of the famous printing press—to generate such work. It was a serendipitous detour that took my research in a direction that I could complete in practical terms, but that also related in a more germane way to my larger research interests, into communities of scholars that gathered in the vicinity of a printing press, as in Strasbourg. If I had not run into that roadblock blocking me from studying the actual presses, I would have missed the suggestive threads I glimpsed in the archives themselves, the threads of a close, even self-referential community. This scholarly group, gathered around Erasmus, Beatus Rhenanus, and the Strasbourg press, discussed, taught, and commented on each other's writings on various issues of late-medieval rhetorical inquiry. My research now involved continuities in lines of inquiry within the textual collections that create a defining identity, much as the bright, verbose, twelfth-century theologians gathered around Peter Abelard at Paris are now seen as a scholarly community called "The Scholastic Philosophers."

The practical concerns of budget and time hence dictated the scope and even content of my project, yet the seeming limitation of being able to study only at the one archive proved to be not an obstacle but a springboard. My discoveries within those archives could have occurred only in the presence of the archives themselves.

Professor Timothy Burke aptly expresses this serendipitous pleasure of archival research (assuming, of course, the absence of prohibitive budgetary and time constraints):

> I like it best when the materials are relatively unorganized . . . where I'm just on a fishing expedition, uncertain of what I want or what I might find. That kind of research is always an important cautionary reminder of what can happen when you enter an archive with overly narrow tunnel vision: you tend to ignore what is typical or representative about an entire class of documents in favor of your specific predefined needs.[5]

The discovery of a linking theme within the archives transformed rather than annihilated my project. My practical concerns for surviving on a budget were, then, just as essential as my scholarly and linguistic background. Funding for humanistic research being the precious commodity it is, with fierce competition for sparse funds, the contemporary researcher must prepare for archival research abroad not just with letters of introduction, but with some clear-sighted preparedness for inevitable changes in the project itself, changes driven by budgetary or time limitations. I was compelled to forego the study of the machines themselves, as my budget and preparation would not allow that research vector. Yet what I found in the archives proved rich enough to sustain the transformed project I ultimately completed.

META-RESEARCH: DECIPHERING CATALOGUES

In 1992, the Internet had not yet revolutionized library cataloguing systems, but as anyone who has studied at the Bodleian knows, most of the old catalogues are handwritten, storied troves of precious notations and personal observances recorded in the wispy hands of generations of librarians and archivists, usually respected scholars themselves. Such entries, with their idiosyncratic, even eccentric choices on what textual features to record for the reader, warrant a study in itself. For my project, it was a study, certainly, for another day and a larger budget.

The most fruitful part of archival research, in my experience, has resulted from approaching such handwritten catalogues as cultural productions in themselves, just as important as the artifact itself. Descriptions of artifacts/machines in the archives themselves are often written by archivists, curators, or specialists in paleography or archaeology, and therefore have a limited scope that cannot reveal points upon which one's own research depends. One may see new directions for research that will require more funding and time. The vocabulary of the organizing terminology can be mystifying: for example, the English bibliographic terms for manuscripts are often different from those used by a nineteenth-century archivist whose spidery handwriting with pen-and-ink contains mysterious, sometimes indecipherable terms and especially, abbreviations. My work required linguistic research in archival and cataloguing languages and abbreviations used in handwritten catalogues such as those housed in the Bodleian Library.

An irresistible aspect of such eclectic collections of miscellaneous texts catalogued by unknown hands, ink-stained and dog-eared by centuries of readers, is the silently codified privilege hidden in archival collections. What was deemed worthy of collection, and why? According to Shwartz and Cook, "until very recently, archivists obliged by extolling their own professional myth of impartiality, neutrality, and objectivity. Yet archives are established by the powerful to protect or enhance their position in society. Through archives, the past is controlled. Certain stories are privileged and others marginalized."[6] Writings by women are few, and we all know why: women were kept uneducated, the better to cook, clean, serve, and breed. The power imbalance is not caused by, but is reflected in, the omissive silences of the archives: the rare author who was not a monastic male was usually known for being suspected of heresy or other unorthodoxies; Margery of Kempe or Hildegard of Bingen come to mind. Even Sappho of Lesbos, the great poetess of Greek antiquity, unanimously admired by her contemporaries, is mostly lost to us because of Christian archivists' appropriation of editorial privilege in destroying her work. It stands to the great disgrace of early Christian and medieval Christian archivists that we have no surviving independent texts of Sappho's work. Its occasionally homoerotic subject matter deemed scandalous, her poetry was destroyed by those in charge of copying and maintaining archival collections in what we now view as the grossest of crimes against humanistic accomplishment. Her work was so fervently admired that several male poets (whose work did survive) of classical antiquity copied out her poems in collections of their own, so that at least three of her poems remain in their entirety. In the case of Sappho, the archival omission was not passive, but active; her work was not simply omitted, but actively sought out and destroyed. Homoerotic material written by males survived, intact and in abundance; the gender-based power inequity was tragically enforced in the archives.

This chapter can only mention a few of these enforced silences and omissions of the archives, but the phenomenon of archival silence is instructive for any scholar who approaches collected texts. Joan M. Schwartz and Terry Cook argue that archivists have traditionally perpetuated a "professional myth of impartiality, neutrality, and objectivity" that continues to require scrutiny and interrogation. It is the users of the archives who can best perform such interrogation, by cross-checking within collections and consulting contemporaneous collections, preferably housed elsewhere, for clues to textual material omitted or removed. Archivists do wield, as Schwartz and Cook assert, "enormous power over memory and identity."[7] In the case of female writers of antiquity and the European Middle Ages, that power is hegemonic; only the student who approaches the archives can challenge it by exposing omissions and silences, and thereby its false neutrality.

It is perhaps true that the historian is trained by the academy to make better use of archival materials than is the literary scholar. Burke notes that "[many] scholarly disciplines are involved in going to libraries and databases for their evidence, but historians, at least potentially, have the greatest range of experience in working with heterogeneous documents and materials, and the greatest potential creativity in the ways they make use of those materials."[8] Researchers in other humanities disciplines might find fertile ground in the catalogues themselves, finding items that might have been omitted by an electronic search engine searching only for keywords or phrases. What I found in the Sélestat holdings was the sensory richness of looking through handwritten catalogues, using my eyes and hands instead of my computer's browser. That inimitable privilege of being in the presence of the texts and catalogs, and glimpsing the thought processes behind the original text collectors themselves, and their marginal marks and comments, may be what is lost in the era of electronic searches, for all their global harvesting power. I had forgotten, perusing digital databases, the very questions that had drawn me to the Middle Ages in the first place: "how did people think back then?" and "why did they see things the way they did?"

That richness of discovery, however rare or ephemeral, results only from inquiry within material texts rather than their digital, virtual representations. And that sort of discovery supports my view that graduate students need training in archival research; i.e., in the physical, tangible, material objects housed in the archives. The process of discovery is so random and serendipitous that it cannot be predicted by impressions gleaned by searching online catalogs and databases of holdings. However, archival research focused on medieval texts does eliminate one challenge of cross-cultural research, the issue of positionality. It is true that archives have generally been considered apolitical and passive methods of research. One of the reasons, especially when studying medieval and late-medieval texts, is that cultural nuances disappear under the lingua franca of the Latin language. In the texts I studied, it is often impossible to tell where an author wrote or lived, because they wrote in Latin, the language of the learned. In fact, many were called "wandering scholars" because they wandered looking for patrons, and Latin eliminated any language barrier. Although I am not an expert paleographer, in my experience, the archives do not tend to reveal cross-cultural nuances.

Burke's article on the very issue of examining tangible material might seem a eulogy for the lost art of searching through physical documents rather than the invisible, ephemeral mass of digital data. And at least one university is paying attention to possible consequences and benefits of this shift to all-electronic data. The University of the Arts London, a major educational institution of arts and design, has founded a new Photography Archive Research Center that will support investigation of the idea and meaning of the term "archive." The Centre is interested in inquiries into "ways in which the meanings and values of images and objects can be determined by the systems within which they are collected and displayed." This sort of inquiry recognizes that archives are themselves cultural productions, defined and constrained by the cultural values that create them.

MY BACKGROUND AND THE ALSACE PROJECT

Extensive study of Latin in my undergraduate and graduate work made research in the Romance languages relatively straightforward. My knowledge of French was adequate, aided immeasurably by my familiarity with the Latin roots of its semantic and grammatical structures. Likewise, bibliographical vocabulary in texts edited by Romance-language-scholars holds few mysteries for the student of Latin paleography, and I had ready my dog-eared Cappelli handbook[9] of scribal styles and abbreviations, still a starting point for students of both Latin and Romance paleography. I arrived in France full of confidence and excitement, armed with several letters of introduction from other scholars. I had studied manuscripts in Oxford University's illustrious Bodleian Library, and felt no qualms about engaging in the same work in France. I imagined that the only problem facing me was that of finding lodging both inexpensive and comfortable enough to sustain me as long as possible. As a world traveler, I was accustomed to being creative and flexible in solving practical problems. On a chilly night in Wales, unable to find lodging, I hiked out to a castle to sleep in the shelter of its wall; finding myself locked out of a French hostel after curfew, I climbed over its spiked iron gate, eased in at a window, and slept in a deserted wing; I had drunk pepper tea with Himalayan villagers in Pokhara, sipped kava from a dirty gourd in Fiji, and smoked a foul-smelling substance with Papua New Guineans in Ukarumpa. Language or lodgings had never been barriers before; what could possibly present a problem in the familiar territory of France? Yet I discovered that I needed another specialized technical vocabulary for the processes and technologies that produced the items I wanted to study. Stymied by the language barrier of my workable-but-non-specialized French, I quickly struggled to ask for what I required, lacking the technological vocabulary and jargon. Struggling to communicate with archivists and librarians, I starting feeling like an outsider as I never had in my world travels.

ACCESS AND BUREAUCRATIC OBSTACLES

Every library I visited had a team of administrative team that presented a formidable, one might even say Byzantine, barrier of sometimes nonsensical-seeming requirements to the hopeful researcher. Access restrictions to collections are not always made clear until one arrives at the library, and usually require extensive documentation of one's scholarly status. One must present credentials and documents that can be difficult or time-consuming to produce; they should in fact be understood and prepared before one arrives. My letters of introduction were rarely enough; staff often wanted to see the actual documents, my certificates and diplomas themselves. One university required my high-school diploma, and no amount of reasoning that my numerous academic degrees superseded that particular document availed. One staff member would not be satisfied with Master's degrees or the PhD; only the high-school diploma would do. I had to ask a friend to go through my boxes in storage to look for my high-school diploma, and when she couldn't find it, she forged one on a $1.29 blank "Certificate of Merit" bought at a stationery store, and faxed it to the university. It worked. My PhD carried no weight with this staff; my high school diploma did. Sometimes the rigidity of the requirement depended on the staff member: documentation requirements sternly delineated for me by the person Monday morning might be contradicted by the person there on Wednesday. I learned to ask the full name of any staff member I spoke with about access restrictions.

In another institution, my PhD diploma itself was required, as well as an established address in France. Fortunately, I had friends in Paris and gave their addresses, but I certainly had no established address of my own. What made these bureaucratic interactions difficult was my lack of specialized administrative French. Any traveler abroad should master the specific vocabulary for these rules and requirements, and formulate a list of what I'll call linguistic equivalencies: what is the term for specific documents "letter of introduction" or "certificate" in the language of the place where you will do research? Often these terms include a possessive form of the noun (the institution) that confers them. The most efficient way to ascertain these terms is to speak to a scholar from that country before you leave home. Academic email lists within your specialty can be a good resource for this sort of information.

The best resource was having specific names of contacts from both institutions at home and in the country of research. At one facility, my friendship with a scholar who had previously studied there disposed the staff to receive me warmly. And of course, anywhere I went, the lessons my parents taught me about politeness, friendliness, respect for the staff, and gratitude for their help served me in good stead. Credibility is enhanced if your letters of introduction include easy modes of contact such as email or telephone numbers that the staff can call.

It was essential to arrive financially prepared for the expenses of an unforeseen delay in meeting requirements of the institutions where you plan to work. My work was delayed a full week while I waited for faxes and mail deliveries of documentation. To this end, bring extra money, or some way of obtaining it electronically and quickly.

BUDGET RESTRICTIONS: STAYING FLEXIBLE

While in Alsace, I soon realized that my precious grant money would cover only a little of a longer stay's expense. The slow and painstaking research I needed to perform required more travel, access to more libraries, and a highly specialized and technical vocabulary that I lacked. Suddenly, the practical concerns of my research threatened to undermine the project. How could I, on my limited budget and compressed schedule, attempt to cross the boundary from outsider to insider? What resources were available to me?

I intended to stay in comfortable, though not luxurious, hotels while conducting my research. However, at every turn, I faced bureaucratic obstacles that took time to resolve and thus ate away at my funds. I needed to find ways to stretch my budget. Although the following solution will not work for everyone, I gave up hotel lodging and resorted to camping outside the towns where I needed to conduct my research. Camping is not for the faint of heart; its challenges include dealing with the vagaries of weather, finding a way to bathe, keeping business clothing clean, securing valuables while at the library, and eating well without refrigeration. Its advantages include new friendships with other travelers, and impressive savings that can allow other luxuries.

The first lesson I learned in my world travels is that when on a budget, eating in restaurants must be given up, no matter how tempting. Sometimes I gave up even my morning *cafe crème* at a café on my way to the library. Instead of eating at restaurants, I made time in my schedule to stop at the market every day to buy small quantities of fresh food just for that day, since I had no refrigerator.

Reluctant to leave camera and other valuables in my tent while working at the library, I used storage lockers at various places, including the library itself. Sometimes the staff was willing to keep things behind the counter for me, since cameras weren't usually allowed in the manuscript archives anyway. On questions of personal security while camping, I made sure to ask as many local people as possible about the security of the campsite, and the incidence and types of crime in the area.

I always depended upon the most valuable resources: the townspeople. The people in cafés and restaurants were sometimes more gregarious and interested in my work than the staff at the libraries. Sitting down for a coffee, I would chat with the people standing at the café bar, and ask for their opinions and advice. Local proprietors became my best resource: the person behind the bar often knew the history of the region and the careers of its archaeological and archival holdings. Being scrupulously polite and friendly is of course a requirement that I hardly need mention; respectful persistence also helps. Local people drawn into a conversation often knew staff or where artifacts were stored, if not what was required to access them. For example, when I wanted to look at some manuscripts in the Trinity College library in Dublin, I found the staff inexplicably reluctant to allow me access. Finally I learned from the proprietor of a pub that those manuscripts contained medieval writings that were considered obscene, and that those venerable archivists looked askance at anyone desiring to see them.

KNOWING THE RULES OF THE COLLECTIONS

Particularly essential when researching abroad is taking care to follow the institution's rules. If your research involves looking at tangible artifacts that are delicate or protected, ensure that you abide by the institution's rules, yet receive fair access to see everything to which your credentials entitle you. Here again, a specialized technical vocabulary might be required. If gloves are required for handling manuscripts, if no writing implements are allowed, if masks are required, be sure you know the expressions for these requirements and can recognize them when uttered by the staff. Otherwise the staff might think you are flouting the rules when you simply don't understand them.

KEEPING THE SCOPE OF THE PROJECT FLEXIBLE: META-RESEARCH

Since I wasn't able to access all the collections I had hoped to study, and because by the same token I encountered other items I hadn't known of, I revised my project's scope while doing the actual research abroad. If the project's scope has room for revision and/or expansion, it can benefit from access to unforeseen artifacts even if its original direction must change. You may not be able to see one artifact/collection, but might be able to see others that are useful in other ways. Take advantage of the serendipitous treasures that your "meta-research" may yield: scrutinize the cataloguing strategies employed to glean the cultural information hidden there. What documents, for example, have restricted-access? Which documents are stored behind the librarian's desk, available only upon request of the librarians, with letters verifying one's scholarly credentials, and what political or cultural rationale justifies their restriction there? In the Library of Trinity College, Dublin, I sought access to manuscripts containing material that Victorian librarians considered bawdily scandalous; they were still stored there in the late twentieth-century, and the librarians pursed their lips and retreated for a private conversation when I asked for them. These omissions and restrictions are imposed, or inherited by people who control the very essence of these treasure-houses of knowledge, yet their strictures remain unquestioned, invisible, and seemingly invincible. It would behoove the scholarly community to research upon those people themselves—the administrators who restrict the knowledge from scholars—as cultural artifacts themselves, and yet a powerfully oppressive force upon humanistic endeavor.

RETHINKING ARCHIVAL RESEARCH

Writing many decades before electronics revolutionized archival and reference systems, C.S. Lewis observed in *The Discarded Image* that of all modern inventions, the medieval scholar would have most admired the card index file.[10] The gentle wit of his remark comprehends the spirit of high medieval culture, that peculiarly medieval urge to impose order and harmony on chaos. The medieval love of encyclopedic techniques, of organizing and codifying information, the medieval imagination that embraced the beautifully logical and inaccurate geocentric model of the Ptolemaic cosmos, would have embraced the order of the index file. The intellectual riches of a library, visibly ordered in an index file and available at the brush of a finger, would indeed have appealed to a medieval scribe. I suggest to researchers sifting through electronic databases that the full offerings of a text, or the collection that houses it, may not be fully apparent until one can examine the original archives and catalogs themselves. As scholars of the humanities, we stand on the shoulders of giants, as Bernard of Chartres allegedly wrote;[11] we may see further than our predecessors, but only with the fuller view their labors extend to us.

A SUGGESTED BIBLIOGRAPHY FOR ARCHIVAL RESEARCH

Archivum: International Review on Archives 1 (195–1). [Annual journal.]

Bade, Josse. *Stultiferae Naves* [Ships of Fools]. Critical edition by Charles Béné. Translated into French and annotated by Odette Sauvage, in Publications de l' Université des langues et letters de Grenoble, 1979.

Brooks, Philip. *Research in Archives: The Use of Unpublished Primary Sources.* Chicago: University of Chicago Press, 1969.

Chartier, Roger. "Libraries without Walls." *Representations* 42 (Spring 1993): 38–52.

Collison, Robert Lewis. *Published Library Catalogues: An Introduction to their Contents and Use.* London: Mansell, 1973.

Iredale, David. *Enjoying Archives: What They Are, Where to Find Them, How to Use Them.* Newton Abbot, Devon: David and Charles, 1973.

Reiman, Donald H. *The Study of Modern Manuscripts: Public, Confidential, and Private.* Baltimore: Johns Hopkins University Press, 1993.

Scholars and Research Libraries in the Twenty-First Century. ACLS Occasional Papers 14. New York: American Council of Learned Societies, 1990.

Smith, Eldred. *The Librarian, the Scholar, and the Future of the Research Library. Contributions in Librarianship and Information Science* 66. New York: Greenwood Press, 1990.

Thorpe, James Ernest. *The Use of Manuscripts in Literary Research: Problems of Access and Literary Property Rights,* 2nd edition. New York: Modern Language Association of America, 1979.

NOTES

1   The popular medieval genre portrays sinful humanity as adrift on a "ship of fools" captained by imbeciles and headed to eschatological shipwreck.

2   [Nobile Selestadiu, tua quis pomeria primus/Signans, tam dextris condidit auspiciis. Unde tibi Genius tam felix tamque benignus.] Erasmus of Rotterdam, Encomium Selestadii Carmine Elegiaco per Erasmum Roterodamum. Printed at Basel, August 1515.

3   Latin plural noun (neuter), a term used figuratively to signify "cradle texts," printed after the invention of printing in Europe and generally before the 16th century.

4   Saint Augustine, De Civitate Dei. B.H.S., K 1 267.

5   Timothy J. Burke, "Easily Distracted: Culture, Politics, Academia, and other Shiny Objects," in http://weblogs.swarthmore.edu/burke (accessed June 2008).

6   Joan M. Schwartz and Terry Cook, "Archives, Records, and Power: The Making of Modern Memory." *Archival Science* 2, nos. 1–2 (2002): 1–19.

7   Schwartz and Cook, "Archives, Records and Power," 1.

8   Burke, "Easily Distracted."

9   Cappelli, Adriano. Lexicon abbreviaturarum: Dizionario di abbreviature latine ed italiane. 6th ed. (Milan: Ulrico Hoepli, 1979).

10 C.S. Lewis, *The Discarded Image* (Cambridge [U.K.]: Cambridge University Press, 1964), 37.

11 John of Salisbury makes the famous attribution in his twelfth-century treatise on logic and philosophy *Metalogicon*.

CHAPTER NINE

Negotiating the Politics of Conducting Research on Widows in India

By Shweta Majumdar Adur

INTRODUCTION

I was born, brought up and educated in New Delhi, India. I finished my Master's in Sociology before moving to the United States to start a second Master's degree and eventually continued on to earn my PhD In India, I am considered an upper-caste, upper middle-class, urban, educated, Bengali-Hindu woman. As the daughter of Liberal Arts professors, I was raised with progressive ideals and feminist principles. Neither of my parents cared too much for organized religion. They believed, and had me believe, that God exists in everyone and everywhere and that sectarianism is bred out of ignorant dogmatism. As a non-western feminist constantly negotiating the racialized assumptions of being the "proverbial Third World Other" in the American academic context, I found myself particularly drawn to postcolonial feminism during my studies. While in India I am simply a feminist, I see myself leaning towards hyphenation in the United States as a non-western or a postcolonial feminist.

It is perhaps this particular leaning that makes me aware of the representation of the non-western world in Euro-American tabloids. The research study I decided to pursue was first inspired by the press coverage that followed Deepa Mehta's "Water," a film based on the lives of widows in pre-independent India. It starts out with the story of a girl widowed upon the death of her elderly husband and presents the evils of child marriage and the precarious existence of widows at that time in India. Though the film is set in pre-independent India, it generated ample controversy in present-day India. Hindu fundamentalists attacked Mehta for showing the underbelly of Indian tradition and culture and called the film anti-Hindu.[1] A mob encouraged by the RSS (Rashtriya Swayamsevak Sangh), an ultraconservative and fundamentalist political faction, destroyed Mehta's movie sets in Varanasi in the Indian state of Uttar Pradesh. After the incident, even the local authorities allegedly told Mehta that they could no longer guarantee her safety were she to continue shooting the film. She was forced to cancel its production. Mehta resumed the shooting of the film under an assumed name after a four-year gap and made major changes in the film cast. The film eventually had to be completed in Sri Lanka. These events renewed international concern for the "misery of Hindu widows" as reputable newspapers formulated it, capturing the western imagination once again.

In the years following the release of the film, I found myself reading about the "Hindu tradition" and the "Hindu Widow" as Widows of Varanasi and Vrindavan were constantly on the news. Headlines such as "Shunned from Society, Widows flock to City to die" (CNN)[2] or the "India's Neglected Widows" (BBC),[3] "Dignity Urged for Hindu Widows (Chicago Sun-Times);[4] "Married to a Barbaric Custom" (The New York Post)[5] became commonplace. One such article reads, specifically: "*Ostracized by society, thousands of India's widows flock to the holy city of Vrindavan waiting to die. They are found on side streets, hunched over with walking canes, their heads shaved and their pain etched by hundreds of deep wrinkles in their faces*" (CNN, 2001).[6] Touted as "ascetic/religious" widows, the widows of Vrindavan and Varanasi somehow became the stereotypical ahistorical face of the "Hindu widows"—even though the standardized and hypermasculinist version of the "Hindu religion" that the conservative faction preaches is not the same as the spiritual leaning of the widows they ostensibly defended. Theirs were heartrending stories of abandonment and misery that spoke about the ills of the Hindu tradition. In each picture, the widows of Vrindavan appeared in their white saris with pain etched on their weathered faces. Their stories were meant to incite horror and/or pity. As an urban, middle-class, Hindu woman, I too was appalled. Yet I also realized their portrayal was a gross violation of human rights and constituted a gendered form of violence that ran the risk of being oversimplified as a "problem of a backward culture." But as someone who had grown up in urban and progressive India, I also knew that this wasn't merely a violation based on cultural and religious practices, but rather one derived from previous socio-economic marginalization that widowhood had merely accentuated. As a result, I decided to conduct some research to expose the hardships that widows faced in Vrindavan, a project which was facilitated by a grant from the Human Rights Institute at the University of Connecticut. Who else would be better positioned than I was to conduct this type of research? I was after all from India, spoke the languages and was aware of the importance of cultural sensitivity. In reality, my naïve assumptions brought me much closer to the status of an outsider as I was forced to realize once in the field.

Not until my trip to Vrindavan did I become aware that the news stories never once spoke of these widows' resilience and courage or conveyed the hope that also marked them. By representing them as objectified hopeless and hapless victims of faith or tradition the news articles perpetuate violence against these women by assuming their lack of agency. Their words, stories and emotions rarely find a place in the annals of what was little more than well-intentioned journalistic voyeurism. Never once did any of these articles mention that, in reality, the women in Vrindavan constitute a minority compared to the total number of widows in India. Practices of widowhood actually vary drastically across India and within Hinduism as well, through different ages. Undoubtedly, these nuances are rarely discussed in the news pieces due to a shortage of space and time. India is a nation of multiple religions, languages, ethnic groups with a significant degree of cultural syncretism and pluralism, making it a very heterogeneous nation. Speaking of "the Hindu Widow" is instantly an oxymoron as widowhood in India varies drastically across region and religion while many practices have also changed over time.

In this chapter, I reflect on my experiences of conducting fieldwork for the purpose of this particular study.[7] After providing a short overview of widowhood in India, I focus on two specific issues: first how to negotiate cross-cultural fieldwork experiences through an institutional lens, which allows me to discuss how to secure funding, ensure one's safety, choose a research site and comply with the Institutional Review Boards. Second, I revisit the insider-outsider debate to engage in a critical, reflexive introspection and assess the ways in which my positionality and multiple identities actually informed this research project, its results, as well as my relationship with the interviewees.

WIDOWHOOD IN INDIA

In her authoritative text on widowhood, Martha Alter Chen incisively summarizes the immortalized images of the Indian widow that have dominated the national and the international imagination by stating: "the plight of the Indian widow—or, more specifically, the Hindu widow has long captured the attention of Indians and foreigners alike. Three images in particular—the child widow, the ascetic widow, and the widow who burns on her husband's funeral pyre—evoke pity, awe and horror."[8] Uma Chakravarti[9] calls widowhood a "social death" while Dr. Mohini Giri[10] in turn refers to widows as the "Living Dead"; Martha Alter Chen[11] herself argues that the life of a widow is one of perpetual mourning. It is true that patrilineal inheritance and patrilocal residence make widowhood a particularly precarious experience for women, especially for women without alternative means of sustenance and income.[12] Although rituals and practices associated with widowhood vary across religious sects, regions and caste standing, the marginalization faced by widows today is often traced back to the fundamentals of Brahmanic patriarchy, which results in upper-caste widows suffering from most restrictions. Upon the demise of their husband, upper-caste Hindu widows are expected to renounce all worldly desires and live a life of ascetic self-denial based on imposed stringent dietary, ritual fasting and dress restrictions.[13] However, lower caste women do not have the same restriction and widow remarriage is permitted. Similarly, tribal widows have considerably more rights than women within the caste system, as they can inherit property in addition to being able remarriage.

It is not known exactly when women or widows began to arrive in Vrindavan in large numbers since the journey from Bengal was not only long but was especially onerous for women in those days. Typically in most regions women upon widowhood continued to stay at their affinal homes as an auxiliary member of the extended household with little freedom and say, engaged in disproportionate amounts of housework. We do know that affluent and propertied Bengali widows often chose this pilgrim town as their last refuge. Indeed, death and last rites performed in Vrindavan were believed to be means of attaining "Moksha" or salvation.

Some widows left in search of salvation, yearning to break free from the constraints of domestic life. Others moved there because they had been refused support by their families; without supportive institutional structures and alternative means of sustenance, mendicancy provided a meager income. A study conducted on the widows of Vrindavan revealed that, "many of them had renounced domestic life voluntarily and felt a strong apathy against it. Some of them go back every year to their families, but are eager to come back to Vrindaban where even while they suffer from many privations, the superincumbent pressure of domestic life is absent."[14] Sending widows away to the pilgrim sites of Varanasi and Vrindavan is not part of the Hindu tradition, but is rather a tradition borne out of the socio-economic contingencies of colonization[15] practiced predominantly by Bengalis.[16] The ancient pilgrim route between Bengal and Varanasi/Vrindavan is the chief reason why there are more Bengali-speaking widows in Vrindavan even though Vrindavan in Uttar Pradesh is far from Bengal. The widows of Vrindavan are mostly Vaishnavites, that is followers of Lord Krishna, which is a particular sect of Hinduism. Vrindavan is mythically associated with Lord Krishna's childhood and youth and was developed in the sixteenth-century as a pilgrim center, which supported by generous endowments, served as alternative structures of support for the socio-economically vulnerable.[17] Clearly the widows of Vrindavan or even of Varanasi were from a particular sect and a particular region of India, yet class, caste, age, marital and familial status would have created variations among them. Regardless, the assumption perpetuated in the news, that these women were overwhelmingly abandoned, is erroneous. This evidence should, however, not be mistaken as validation that this "voluntary" migration offered a life of ease. Widows' accounts of neglect and marginalization remain irrefutable.

In post-independence India, the changing times and the advancement of literacy, provision of legal protection and welfare measures have resulted in some far-reaching changes in the status of widows. Remarriage or divorce no longer shocks the conscience of most Hindus. Restrictions on diet and dress are no longer enforced with force. Today, the onerous burden of widowhood falls disproportionately on the least privileged sections of the society. For the widows of Vrindavan, the experience of widowhood amplifies the experiences of socio-economic marginalization that preceded widowhood. A study published by the Guild of Study[18] found that the overwhelming majority of women in these spaces were illiterate thereby precluding chances of finding alternative forms of income. Sexual and economic exploitation have, in fact, been reported as rampant among widows of Vrindavan. The international attention and the tireless work of some NGOs, such as Guild of Service started by activist Dr. Mohini Giri, has resulted in the construction of some old-age homes or widow homes that have improved some of the adverse living conditions.

NEGOTIATING CROSS-CULTURAL RESEARCH: INSTITUTIONAL BARRIERS

By the time the idea of this project had crossed my mind, I had already begun working on my dissertation proposal. This one was therefore destined to be a side project. International fieldwork has its own costs but when fieldwork is intended to gather data for a non-dissertation related project, the cost increases incrementally. Although securing funding is a researcher's first concern, fewer opportunities are available for graduate student research not aimed at writing a doctoral dissertation. The grant I was awarded from the Human Rights Institute at the University of Connecticut was enough to cover a portion of the airfare for one trip, some material costs and travel to and from Vrindavan. I, however, had to make two trips to India, first to establish relevant contacts and decide on a research site, second to conduct the actual interviews, most of which were to be limited to widows living in a home in Vrindavan. At the same time, I intended to speak to local activists to gain a better understanding of the contemporary challenges faced by the widows' rights movement in India. The interviews with the activists were to be conducted in English interspersed with Hindi while the interviews with the widows were to be conducted in Bengali.

Besides financial concerns, time also became a pressing issue: as a full-time graduate student working on a dissertation and teaching as a part-time instructor, my time in India had to be secondary to my academic calendar in the United States. This played a large role in my decision to restrict my study to one geographic site: I chose Vrindavan simply because to its spatial proximity to Delhi where I had some family. I figured that it was a way of ensuring that I would have some local support, which turned out to be only partially true. While I was able to enjoy the comforts of home while doing archival research in Delhi and secure safe transportation to Vrindavan, I was also constantly pressed for time. I found myself struggling to explain to family and friends, whom I had not seen in two years, why I could not hang out and had to work continually. I often annoyed my mother by refusing to fulfill certain social obligations, such as visiting extended family, because I had to go to work. And I honestly found it challenging to concentrate amidst the hustle-bustle of home. I was too easily distracted by the competing demands of research and of the desire to spend time with people I had missed so much while in the United States.

Beyond these circumstantial or contextual difficulties, negotiating with the Institutional Review Board about the parameters of data collection became probably the toughest unanticipated hurdle that I came across while conducting this type of cross-country research. The Institutional Review Board (hereafter, IRB) is an ethics committee that has been formally designated to approve, monitor, and review biomedical and behavioral research involving humans with the aim to protect the rights and welfare of the research participants. Most universities in the United States have an in-house IRB that oversees the research conducted by faculty and students alike. What I disclose in the following pages must not be mistaken for an argument in favor of abolitioning the IRB process, far from it. We have all witnessed the harm that can be done during a research study if the researcher is not held accountable—who would want a Tuskegee[19] to repeat itself! However, I also think it is equally important to check and balance the IRB requirements, especially if they threaten to jeopardize the research project itself. IRB's lack of familiarity with given international contexts can make it onerous if not impossible to apply or translate its formal rules, regulations and requirements. There is, for example, no equivalent research ethics body in India. It is therefore extremely difficult to explain what the IRB does and what good it can do for research participants outside of its jurisdiction.

When I proposed my research project, the first thing that the IRB mentioned is that I should think of ways to protect participant widows from emotional and psychological harm. It was suggested that questions about the participants' life history may trigger a strong emotional response and upset the participants. In order to protect their rights, I was gently told that providing participants' access with a counselor or on-site therapist would be highly recommended. Though well-intentioned, my interlocutor most likely had no idea of the impossible challenge this could pose for a researcher. Seeking professional help through therapy is still a relatively new concept in India; few people have recourse to such services. As a result, this stipulation severely restricted my access to a field site. In the end, I was forced to limit my research to a widow home run by an NGO as only such an institute offered counseling services onsite. I came to realize that I would have no way of interviewing women who I might meet in temples or on the streets. This introduced an inevitable bias in my research as the women living in the home run by the NGO were relatively better off than women encountered on the streets or living in boarding homes. The IRB regulations forced to come to terms with the fact I would be unable to document these women's voices.

In another instance, I remember the frustration I felt when examining the requirements to secure an informed consent from all study participants. Such a measure may well be impossible to materialize in certain contexts. Signing a piece of paper is a big deal and signing one about which an individual has no clue about is an even bigger deal! When working on other projects, I have often met activists and educated individuals who refused to "sign" any paperwork. In the past, one of these activists had said to me, "why do you need me to sign this, I said I was willing to be speak with you . . . why do you need me to sign this? Do you not trust me?" hence questioning my trustworthiness as a researcher. As this example makes clear, the pressure to sign paperwork before the interview process even begins can inadvertently tarnish the researcher's rapport with the interviewees. One can explain at great length that no one will have access to the consent forms except the IRB and the investigators. But how can anyone who is not aware of the workings of IRB trust a nameless and faceless institution with a signature that directly and culpably links the participants to the interview? In my case, I was worried that the widows—most of whom were illiterate—would be frightened if I even ventured into the bureaucratic details of IRB. Explaining the need for IRB regulations latently communicates that there might be a need to be protected from me; the underlying message is again that I am possibly untrustworthy and that interviewees should exercise caution.

During my first negotiation with the IRB, I attempted to explain why I would not be able to use the consent form as I anticipated that the majority of my research participants were likely to be illiterate. It was a small mercy that I was allowed to use "Information Sheets" which required that I read out the parameters

of the study to the interviewee and have them agree explicitly to the conditions before embarking on the interviewing process. The IRB did require that I translate all
the forms into two languages, English and Bengali, to which I agreed. Once these
translations were completed, I figured that the issue had been resolved satisfactorily. But once in the field, I realized that it was far from the case. Every time I sat
down with an interviewee and started reading aloud the conditions of the research
study, the interviewee was either annoyed or perplexed as to why I am wasting her
time. As a sixty-five year old lady said to me with great aggravation, "I said I would
do the interview so why don't you just get started with what you have to ask?"
Another older woman remarked with equal frustration: "of course I know you
will not pay me for this, why are you telling me this if I haven't asked for money?"
I found myself feeling increasingly embarrassed when constantly reiterating, "no
compensation will be given for participating in this study" as this specific clause is
probably one of the most culturally inappropriate. Even at the expense of reifying
East-West differences, I feel the need to stress that the whole notion of "compensation" and instant reciprocity is a very Euro-American concept which does not
apply in India where there exists an extra-material dimension to relations separate
from the expectation of financial compensation. The women who agreed to being interviewed did not expect anything in return for their time or effort. Most of
them agreed to speak with me out of goodwill to "assist" me with my research. My
repeating "there is no money to be made here" was interpreted as rude enough to
undermine their goodwill and generosity.

NEGOTIATING POSITIONALITY: REVISITING THE INSIDER-
OUTSIDER DEBATE

The researcher-informant relationship brings into play dynamics of race, gender,
class, nation, and age and this research study was no different. The Insider versus
Outsider debate—whether it is more effective to conduct fieldwork as an insider or
outsider to the communities one chooses to study—has generated lively exchange
among scholars. At the onset of my research, my "insider" status was far more
salient than my "outsider" position. By most measuring standards—language,
awareness of cultural sensitivity, region, and gender—I was considered an insider.
After all, I wasn't a white western feminist who was engaging in fieldwork to learn
about poor third world women. I was, however, an "outsider" in so far as my class
background, educational credentials, and age were concerned.

Yet the eventualities of the field forced me to revisit the insider-outsider tension
and I found myself leaning increasingly towards Nancy Naples' position. Nancy
Naples argues that insiderness-outsiderness do not correspond to fixed attributes,
but undergo instead a dynamic reconstitution in the field. In her own words, "the
bipolar construction of insider/outsider sets up a false separation that neglects
that interactive process through which "insiderness" and "outsiderness" are constructed."[20] Or as Judith Lorber famously pointed out herself, "feminist researchers
start with the assumption that the content and dividing lines for genders, sexes,
and sexualities are fluid, intertwined, and crosscut by other major social statuses;

Thus, there are no "opposites."[21] In other words, positionality may consist of different poles that constantly inform each other rather than create a clear opposition.

As an urban, upper middle-class, upper-caste, Hindu, Bengali, Indian woman studying in the United States, I had taken great care to hiding my class background. To meet my interviewees, I wore the traditional north-Indian attire of salwar-kameez and a well worn-out pair of slippers. Despite my efforts, I was offered a chair to sit on during our first encounter while the women sat on the floor. I was the researcher and the outsider. Offering a chair especially when chairs are in short supply is a mark of both hospitality and respect, but it can also imply social distance. I politely refused and took a seat next to the women on the floor. The mere gesture of sitting on the floor broke the ice as I had communicated, nonverbally, my desire to disregard boundaries of class. In their women-only space, my gender definitely acted as an advantage by granting me access to the everyday life of the widow home. I could visit the women in their own rooms and walk around freely in the premises. My Bengali-Hindu identity also served as a welcome bridge as many women could judge from my last name that I, too, was a Bengali. During several occasions, I was asked to reveal my ancestral roots—the village or district that my family hailed from. Many were curious about my marital status; one woman even told me that I should be married at my age and that too much education would bring no good to me. Although I had anticipated these reactions, what I had not foreseen was that the unfolding dynamics of "age" and "language" in the field would trump my other statuses.

I had walked into the field with the assurance that I was a native Bengali speaker but soon realized that some of these women spoke a dialect of Baangla that is most frequently spoken in present-day Bangladesh. This dialect is quite different in many respects from the "modern Bengali" that I expected them to speak. This difference despite an apparent commonality of languages often marked me as the "other." Some women wanted to know, for example, whether I was a "baangal" (from East Bengal/present-day Bangladesh) or a "ghoti" (from West Bengal). I found myself being drawn into jocular alliances as some women who came from the same region as my ancestors would playfully warn other women of dire circumstances if they did not cooperate with me. In addition to having to negotiate this somewhat precarious terrain, I had to be keenly aware of the power relations and differentials that are encoded in language. Without a trained ear, many of these linguistic nuances may be lost in the field. For example, in the English lexicon, "you" is used to address a person regardless of their age, sex, credentials, etc. whereas in Bengali, there are different ways of saying "you"—"tui" is used for someone who is younger while "tumi" and "aapni" are used to formally refer to someone elder than onself. Unspoken yet coded in the language are expectations of deference and respect. While I was automatically referred to as "tui," I had to be careful to refer to the interviewees as "tumi" or "aapni" consistently as the majority of the interviewees were above the age of sixty. In India, calling people who are elder to you by their first names or even Mrs. So-and-so is a social faux pas as it communicates downright disrespect. Indians tend to use kinship terms to address neighbors and strangers. For example, it is rather common to call your neighbor an "aunty," a stranger who might just be a shopkeeper or a cab driver as "bhai/dada" (brother or elder brother), or your father's friend or neighbor a "Kaku" (which means father's younger brother) or a "Jethu" (father's elder brother) depending on the friends age, or to call your mother's friend a "Mashi" (meaning your mother's sister). Similar kin terms are used all over India to address those not related by blood. As one woman put it fondly, I was like a "naathni" (grand-daughter) to them and I eventually resorted to calling all of the women "dida"—which means grandmother in Bengali.

Seniority is a significant axis of power and, in my research setting, my educational and urban identities became secondary to my age and gender. In some respects, the great age difference between myself and the participants acted as an advantage while in others it became a palpable disadvantage. One of its first benefits was that my presence in the home of these women was never perceived as a threat since I was able to blend into their everyday routine. The women in the widow home wanted to tell me stories of their lives and of "the old days"; they wanted me to sit and listen as they sang religious hymns; they wanted me to eat with them. I was an eager participant in all of these activities. What is more, they were far more forgiving of my ostensible lack of knowledge about several traditions and customs that a perceived "insider" would automatically be liable to know. I found out that despite the commonality of language, region, religion, and gender, I had little knowledge of their lives, which was often more religious and less urban than my own while growing up. During our conversations, they would make passing references to certain rituals and customs without explaining them as they automatically assumed that I knew of them. Yet, I had grown up in an urban, progressive, liberal family with parents who were not overtly religious and hence knew little about the nuanced traditions and rituals of Hinduism and much less about the Vaishnava sect. The fact that Hinduism is a polytheistic religion, according to which, depending on one's household, one follows certain Gods or Goddesses and not others, further complicated the issue. When I'd ask them to explain the widowhood rituals in more detail, they would chide me and ask, "did your mother never tell you all this?" Yet they would dismissively forgive me for being "*aajkal kar mey aar ki hobe*"(literally, a "girl of today's generation, what else would you expect"), which implied that the "modern" generation has little regard for the rich traditions and cultures of the past. One of the women blatantly stated, "I understand you mother taught you nothing, but did your grandmother also not do her job?" To these mild accusations, I responded that I barely knew my grandmothers as my maternal grandmother had died before I was born while my paternal grandmother had been a distant entity in our lives. Nevertheless, they would painstakingly explain the ritual to me in great detail in a manner that, I suspect, went well beyond the informant-researcher model. Instead I could see their desire to teach and groom me. In many ways this dynamic reversed the powerful/researcher versus powerless/informant model. In their eyes, I was not a "modern-distant researcher" who was gathering information in order to publish. I was instead a "curious and ignorant child" who needed to be enlightened. Contrary to what several field researchers have noted, I was never marked or treated with contempt for being an "armchair anthropologist" or an "ivory tower intellectual." Although I was never told "how would you know what it is like to be in our shoes?" I also doubt that these women would have taken the time to explain cultural subtleties in such great detail, had the interviewer been from a different region or country. Though I was still an "outsider-looking-in," I was treated like an "insider who had lost her way on the outside," which came in very handy to better understand these women's lifestyle and values

This relational model also came with some major drawbacks as I constantly struggled to be taken seriously. Much to my amazement, I found myself internalizing the unspoken codes of etiquette by deferring to their seniority instead of remaining polite while drawing conclusions as an active and objective researcher. I found myself doubting the questions that I had confidently jotted down on my interview schedule while sitting in the comfort of my office in the United States. In the field, I was suddenly stumbling and improvising as I went along, unsure of the direction to take. For example, some of my original inquiries focused on the type, frequency, extent and intensity of the violence committed against widows in Vrindavan. Sitting down for interviews, I suddenly questioned the appropriateness or efficacy of the questions because it seemed culturally unviable for someone in my age group to ask these types of question of someone the age of my interviewees. Sometimes when I did muster the courage to inquire, the answers were vague and shrugged away as "matters beyond my comprehension." I realized that it had been culturally naïve of me to assume that these women would ever admit to having been violated to someone of their "granddaughter's age." I constantly had to improvise and resorted to asking them the same questions in more general terms, inquiring instead if there is a lot of violence towards widows who live there and if so, what kind of violence, for example. I asked if they knew of anyone who has had to face violence. Being forced to depersonalize the questions I posed during the course of my fieldwork made me realize that power flows between the researcher and the participants, which can sometimes put the researcher in a position of relative powerlessness.

CONCLUDING REFLECTIONS

Review boards are seldom sensitized to the problems of conducting international research especially in contexts where there are no prior examples. In addition, adopting the status of insider is a position that must be navigated with utmost awareness and caution. Though my gender and linguistic commonality made me an insider in this particular case, I was also an outsider due to my age, class and educational background. Although the researcher's age is rarely interrogated in field research, I now realize it is my age that had the most significant impact on my research outcome. On the one hand, it is my young age, relative to my interviewees, that allowed participating widows to treat me like a "naïve/uninitiated insider" who needed to be made aware of exalted traditions. Their attitude and explanations in turn helped me understand their social position and the difficulties they encountered on a much more intimate level, thus helping me transcend the status of the urban-educated-outsider. On the other hand, it is this very intimacy, and the requisite etiquette mandated by our age differential that also made it difficult for me to enact the role of the dispassionate, objective researcher. Ultimately, treating research as a truly self-reflexive process may be the only way to ensure that one's research outcomes remain true to the testimony of one's study participants.

NOTES

1   Elisabeth Bumiller, "Film Ignites the Wrath of Hindu Fundamental-
    ists," *New York Times*, May 3, 2006, http://www.nytimes.com/2006/05/03/
    movies/03wate.html (accessed October 5, 2010).
2   Arwa Damon, "Shunned from Society, Widows Flock to City to Die," *CNN*,
    July 5, 2007, http://articles.cnn.com/2007-07-05/world/damon.india.wid-
    ows_1_widows-vrindavan-india?_s=PM:WORLD (accessed March 16,
    2009).
3   Jill McGivering, "India's Neglected Widows," *BBC South Asia*, February 2,
    2002, http://news.bbc.co.uk/2/hi/south_asia/1795564.stm (accessed October
    5, 2010).
4   Rahul Bedi, "Dignity urged for Hindu Widows," *Chicago Sun-Times*, Decem-
    ber 14, 1998.
5   Kyle Smith, "Married to Barbaric Custom" New *York Post*, April 28, 2006.
6   Arwa Damon, Shunned from Society.
7   I wish to acknowledge the NGO—Guild of Service, based in New Delhi for
    facilitating the study. I also wish to extend my special thanks to Dr. Mohini
    Giri and Ms. Meera Khanna for their support and advice.
8   Martha Alter Chen, ed. *Widows in India: Social Neglect and Public Action.*
    (New Delhi: Sage Publications, 1998).
9   Uma Chakravarti, *Rewriting History: The Life and Times of Pandita Ramabai*
    (New Delhi: Kali for Women, 1998).
10 Mohini Giri, ed. *Living Death: Trauma of Widowhood in India.* (New Delhi:
    Gyan Publishing House, 2002).
11 Martha Alter Chen, ed. *Widows in India: Social Neglect and Public Action.*
    (New Delhi: Sage Publications, 1998).
12 There are exceptions to the rule of patrilineality and patrilocality, for example,
    traditionally in the Nayar society of Southern India, inheritance was in the
    matriline only and brothers often left their property to the sister's children.
13 Widows were expected to wear monochromatic colors—typically white (in
    Northern parts of India) or saffron (in Southern India). In some parts, the
    heads are shorn and ornaments taken away to make the widows unattractive
    and undesirable.
14 ——. "The Hidden Violence of Faith: The Widows of Vrindaban," *Social Sci-
    entist* 29, no. 1/2 (Jan–Feb 2001): 75–83.

15 Swati Ghosh, "Bengali Widows of Varanasi." *Economic and Political Weekly* 35, no. 14 (April 2000): 1151–1153.

16 Those belonging to the pre-partition state of Bengal which includes India as well as present-day Bangladesh

17 Malini Bhattacharya, *In Radha's Name: Widows and Other women in Brindaban* (New Delhi: Tulika Books, 2008).

18 Guild of Service supported by the National Commission for Women, *Status of Widows in Vrindavan and Varanasi: A Comparative Stud,* 2002 http://www.griefandrenewal.com/widows_study.htm (accessed July 15, 2010).

19 The Tuskegee syphilis experiment, known as the Tuskegee syphilis study was a clinical study conducted between 1932 and 1972 in Tuskegee, Alabama, by the U.S. Public Health Service. Investigators recruited 399 impoverished African-American sharecroppers with syphilis for research related to the natural progression of the untreated disease. In return for participation, the participants were given free meals, free medical exams and free burial insurance. They were never told they had syphilis, nor were they ever treated for it despite the fact by late 1940s Penicillin had been validated as an effective cure of the disease. The Tuskegee Syphilis Study led to the 1979 Belmont Report and the establishment of the Office for Human Research Protections (OHRP). It also led to federal regulation requiring Institutional Review Boards for protection of human subjects in studies involving human subjects. The Office for Human Research Protections (OHRP) manages this responsibility within the U.S. Department of Health and Human Services (HHS).

20 Nancy A. Naples, "The Outsider Phenomenon." in *Feminist Perspectives on Social Research.* ed. Sharlene Nagy Hesse-Biber and Michelle L. Yaiser (New York: Oxford University Press, 2004): 373–381

21 Judith Lorber, "Shifting Paradigms and Challenging Categories," *Social Problems* 53, no. 4 (November 2006): 448–453.

PART IV

Crossroads

CHAPTER TEN

Performative Approaches to Interdisciplinary and Cross-Cultural Research

By Virginie Magnat

Can we still speak about "conducting research abroad" today, when investigating transnational cultural practices that increasingly reflect the processes of transmission, exchange, resistance, appropriation, and transformation pertaining to globalization? Recent developments in performance ethnography, rooted in postcolonial theory and significantly informed by the Indigenous critique of dominant Euro-American and methodologies, are not only challenging conventional approaches to conducting, writing and disseminating research, but are also provocatively redefining the terms "research" and "abroad."

In mainstream cultural anthropology, for example, researchers have traditionally been members of the Euro-American academy while the researched belonged to the so-called developing and underdeveloped areas of the world typically encompassed by the term "abroad." However, studying cultural processes from a transnational perspective and within a global context requires that Western and non-Western researchers collaborate to develop new research paradigms and new methodologies prioritizing plurivocality, accountability, and an ethics of positionality that must be constantly renegotiated.

The recently published *Handbook of Critical and Indigenous Methodologies*, co-edited by American scholars Norman K. Denzin and Yvonna S. Lincoln in collaboration with Maori scholar Linda Tuhiwai Smith, is a case in point. By examining how new critical and Indigenous scholarship informs research, policy, politics, and social justice, this handbook foregrounds the hybrid methodologies that have emerged from recent interdisciplinary and cross-cultural perspectives. Such approaches, which combine dialogical, reflexive, feminist, Indigenous and performative methodologies, are precisely designed to decolonize dominant research models and destabilize notions such as "participant observation," "fieldwork," and "conducting research abroad."

My commitment to developing interdisciplinary and cross-cultural research methodologies is rooted in an experience of the transnational that preceded current scholarly debates on globalization. In 1982, I was fortunate to receive a two-year full scholarship to study at the Lester B. Pearson United World College of the

Pacific, a non-profit, nondenominational institution promoting international understanding through education. As a member of this "global village" which hosted two hundred students from sixty-five countries in the coastal forest of Vancouver Island, I became aware of the infinite potentialities that arise when people with different cultural legacies strive to achieve what phenomenologist J. N. Mohanty defines as "mutual communication."

In his essay "The Other Culture," Mohanty posits phenomenology as a philosophical attempt to "know knowing," or to "understand understanding," and goes on to ask how one can know another culture. He contends that no culture can be totally different from one's own since all human beings have a body. Indeed, we all apprehend the world through bodily, experiential processes, and while lived experience differs from one individual to the next, it is always embodied. Mohanty describes the foreign as that which is produced by the oppositions familiar/strange and sameness/different, and remarks that such oppositions already exist within one's home-world. Subcultures, for example, are defined in opposition to dominant societal practices while belonging to the same larger cultural group. Moreover, members of a certain subculture might find the practices of another subculture "strange" simply because they are unfamiliar. Therefore, the binaries familiar/strange and sameness/different cannot be said to exclusively define the foreign.

In order to bypass binary thinking, Mohanty proposes a dialogical model of cross-cultural research that hinges upon "mutual communication" between cultures. He states that if A, B, and C come from three different cultures, they will necessarily interpret one another's experiences in ways that will make notions of what is familiar relative. He observes that this complex triangular relationship "obliterates the priority accorded to one's home language (culture, world)"[1] since it requires that A, B, and C engage in an on-going dialogical process in which no single perspective may be privileged. He concludes by observing that "it is not simply one-sidedly knowing the other, but "mutual" communication which removes "strangeness." The idea of one world for all is constituted through such communication and may serve as *a norm* for critiquing one's home-world."[2]

At Pearson College, such a dialogical process not only enlivened classroom discussions, but also fueled monthly "village meetings," shaped personal relations, and underscored the live performance events through which students shared their cultural traditions by teaching them to each other. "How can there be peace without people understanding each other, and how can this be if they don't know each other?" asked Lester B. Pearson during his 1957 Nobel Peace Prize acceptance speech. In this speech, Pearson refers to "cooperative coexistence," thereby suggesting that knowledge and understanding must be reciprocal. This sense of reciprocity significantly informed the curriculum at Pearson College, which combined the International Baccalaureate academic program with a wide range of social services and cultural activities. The idea of "one world for all" hence became a very concrete reality for me at a formative time of my life, and still significantly informs my work as a performance practitioner, researcher, and educator.

IF THE "FIELD" IS EVERYWHERE, WHERE IS "ABROAD?"

To a certain extent, the phrase "conducting research abroad" implies that a necessary geographical distance must separate the researcher's home from "the field," whatever and wherever the location. In "Undoing Fieldwork: Personal, Political, Theoretical and Methodological Implications," Deborah D'Amico-Samuels objects that "the field is everywhere, . . . the world [is] a shared field, in which our methods and conclusions have meanings which impact on our own lives and those of the people who allow us to share theirs."[3] She therefore calls for a reflexive, and ethical approach to ethnography in which researchers, once they have returned to the security and comfort of their "natural" academic environment, retain an awareness of their privileged positionality. She states "We need to observe the life we participate in when we are 'back from the field' critically, and question the roles we play with respect to those from all over the world who are affected by our actions as anthropologists and as participants in institutions, communities and families in our corner of this very unequal world."[4]

The blurring of boundaries between "field" and "home" may also derive from the researcher's particular positionality. For example, I am a French citizen with an American PhD, am currently teaching performance practice and theory at an English-speaking Canadian university, and have a long-standing research interest in Polish director Jerzy Grotowski's cross-cultural investigation of performance. Consequently, I am always 'conducting research abroad,' whether I am in the United States, Canada, Poland, or even France, since "abroad" has paradoxically become what I now call "home." The feeling of relief usually associated with 're-turning home from the field' is not something to which I can look forward, since, for me, the field is indeed everywhere and I am almost always simultaneously an insider and an outsider. Prior to further introducing my current research project, which is situated at the intersection of the fields of performance studies and cultural anthropology, I will first contextualize my approach by examining its interdisciplinary affiliations.

CRISES AND REVOLUTIONS IN THE SOCIAL SCIENCES

My doctoral and postdoctoral research in the anthropology of performance and experimental ethnography led me to investigate how the type of critical reflexivity advocated by Mohanty has informed the discipline of anthropology in the last two decades, a period marked by what has been described by social scientists as an epistemological and methodological revolution. Denzin and Lincoln discuss this revolution's key paradigm shifts in *Turning Points in Qualitative Research: Tying Knots in a Handkerchief*, stating that in the 1980's, qualitative research was reintroduced into the fields of sociology and education, introduced into nursing and clinical research, and adopted in other areas of social and human sciences, thereby undermining the dominance of quantitative research. Denzin and Lincoln identify "the triple crises of authority, representation, and praxis" as having brought about a deep questioning of the nature and function of the social sciences, lead-ing to a systematic reevaluation of research methodologies, and producing new understandings of the various ways in which researchers create reality through their representational, textual, and interpretive practices. They conclude that "the two crises of authority and representation shaped the third, asking how praxis or action was defined under a new interpretive regime."[5]

This radical critique of quantitative research grounded in the contested notion of scientific objectivity has so profoundly affected the ways in which research as praxis is conducted in the social sciences that, according to Denzin and Lincoln, it is no longer possible for researchers to claim that they are able to "directly capture and hence represent lived experience."[6] Since they can only "know the other" through their own "practices of representation," the knowledge they produce is "always partial, incomplete, and situated."[7] Moreover, knowledge production is always informed "implicitly or explicitly by the social, cultural, class, and gendered location"[8] of the producer. Finally, this revolution of representation, authority, and legitimization integrates the perspectives of those whose voices were previously silenced, including women and non-Western and Indigenous researchers (such as Linda Tuhiwai Smith), who have developed alternative methodologies and representational devices grounded in their critique of dominant approaches. As we will see, performance has become an important component of these new methodologies.

A POSTCOLONIAL CRITIQUE OF "OBJECTIVITY"

As demonstrated by postcolonial critics such as Edward Said, Homi Bhabha, and Gayatri Spivak, colonization has had a critical impact on identity formation among both colonized and colonizing cultures. Cultural theorist Stuart Hall, who deconstructs the notion of the "Other" contends that positionality, agency, performance, and identity are interrelated. He states: "Identities are the names we give to the different ways we are positioned by, and position ourselves within, the narratives of the past."[9] Hall infers that colonial subjects are not only "constructed as different and other within the categories of knowledge of the West"[10] by colonial regimes, but that the latter have the power to make the colonized see and experience themselves as "Other"[11] He therefore contends that cultural identity is not an essence but a positioning.[12] Cross-cultural research therefore necessarily implicates researchers in a complex network of positionalities involving different cultural groups whose histories may vary from engaging in colonial exploitation to resisting the colonial power apparatus. This means that researchers must carefully probe the culturally and historically specific assumptions underpinning the frameworks through which methodological approaches are developed.

If early colonial discourse clearly relied on a Eurocentric worldview to justify inhumane practices such as slavery, the first professional Western anthropologists were empowered by this kind of discourse and earned their reputation thanks to their alleged ability to represent other cultures objectively by simply "being there," as Clifford Geertz puts it, and observing the Other. The postcolonial critique of Western anthropological discourse has helped to foreground the material realities of fieldwork, especially in terms of the power differential between ethnographers and informants. From a postcolonial perspective, the intrusive presence of the Western observer is acknowledged as one fraught with the history of Western imperialism, implying a positionality that needs to be constantly redefined and questioned. This critique undertakes to systematically expose the foundation of anthropological discourse in the hope of converting the ethnographer's much vaunted objectivity into a sense of intellectual honesty grounded in reflexive and dialogical methodologies. James Clifford, whose historical and literary critique of anthropological discourse and practice has been particularly influential, indicts ethnographic writing which "speaks with automatic authority for others defined as unable to speak for themselves."[13] The new model he proposes is one in which "the writer's "voice" pervades and situates the analysis, and objective, distancing rhetoric is renounced [while] the evocative, performative elements of ethnography are legitimated."[14]

Building upon this welcomed legitimization of the performative, D. Soyini Madison remarks that the "dynamics of transformation" characterizing performance can become particularly productive for researchers who are committed to "intervention and change."[15] Indeed, the intersubjectivity and self-reflexivity inherent to the experience of performance can undermine claims to objectivity based on the privileging of sight, acknowledged to be culturally specific rather than universal. Having disrupted a long ethnographic tradition premised on the belief that it is through detached observation of human behavior that one may come to a scientific understanding of human subjects, the performative perspective provides an alternative research model, since, as noted by anthropologist Victor Turner, "in performance [man] reveals himself to himself."[16]

AT THE CROSSROADS OF PERFORMANCE AND ANTHROPOLOGY

Victor Turner, who died in 1983, is considered to have pioneered performance studies with theatre director and theorist Richard Schechner. Their collaboration in the late seventies led to the development of a new field of interdisciplinary and cross-cultural research. In 1980, the New York University Graduate Drama Department, chaired by Schechner, became the first Department of Performance Studies, followed by the creation of a similar department at Northwestern University under the leadership of Conquergood. The points of convergence between Turner's, Schechner's, and Conquergood's respective conceptions of performance have largely contributed to defining the field of performance studies, which combines academic research on performance with anthropological fieldwork as well as social activism and advocacy. Using the concept of performance as a lens through which to examine a wide range of performance-based practices previously excluded by the narrower scope of theatre studies, including ritual performance practices and performance in everyday life, this interdisciplinary field of research challenges culturally and historically specific conceptions of theatre by posing the deceptively simple question: "What is performance?" The breadth of inquiry of performance studies and its openness to cross-fertilization has therefore offered researchers new perspectives in an era of epistemological and methodological turmoil.

Because of its alliance with the discipline of anthropology, the field of performance studies is largely indebted to traditional ethnographic approaches relying on the "participant observation" methodology—a methodology so widely used by anthropologists that it is considered to be the cornerstone of ethnographic fieldwork. However, "participant observation" relies of the now highly contested claim that the ethnographer is an objective observer. In *Writing Culture*, Clifford foregrounds the assumptions underlying this approach when he remarks: "The predominant metaphors in anthropological research have been participant-observation, data collection, and cultural description, all of which presuppose a standpoint outside—looking at, objectifying, or, somewhat closer, "reading," a given reality" [17] and doing so "without being seen."[18]

Interestingly, Turner began to question the notion of "participant observation" precisely because of his growing interest in performance. In "Dramatic Ritual/Ritual Drama: Performative and Reflexive Anthropology," for example, Turner contends that anthropology entails studying what it means to be human. Having pointed out that, as with the members of the cultures they study, ethnographers, too, are human, he suggests that it is pointless for them to systematically disavow their own experience and feelings.[19] It is Turner's collaboration with Schechner which convinced him that performance was an experiential process that afforded a particular form of reflexivity where one could be "at once one's own subject and direct object"[20] - that is to say, observe and participate simultaneously as an embodied agent.

Building on Turner's insight, as well as on his own collaboration with director Peter Brook on the theatre production *The Ik*, which was based on ethnographic research, Colin Turnbull deplores the fact that while anthropologists are trained to observe, they often overlook participation. He declares that "we do not even bother to train ourselves for "participation," which we too often reduce to childish role-playing, ignoring the rigorous preparation and training readily available through the disciplines of theatre."[21] Turnbull contends that this inability and/or unwillingness to become involved physically and emotionally results in a "failure to be fully human, . . . treating [others] as though they were indeed not full human beings themselves but as things that could be satisfactorily examined and explained through the artifice of reason alone."[22] Consequently, what is usually left out of these re-constructions of cultural processes is embodiment, whether it be the embodied experience of the culture-bearers themselves or the embodied relationship between ethnographers and their informants that develops over time.

In their efforts to account for embodied experience, researchers have been experimenting with alternative approaches that include personal narratives, auto-observation, literary tales, critical autobiography, reflexive ethnography, co-constructed narrative, Indigenous anthropology, anthropological poetics, and performance ethnography. Conquergood hence redefines culture "as a set of performance practices."[23] Echoing Conquergood, Madison considers performance to be key to our critical understanding of what it means to be human. Borrowing

Turner's notion of "*homo performans*," she envisions human beings as a "performing species" and posits performance as "necessary to our survival."[24]

Given the embodied nature of performance processes, the concept of embodiment has, in turn, become pivotal to the work of researchers belonging to what one may call the post-Victor Turner generation. Kirsten Hastrup, an anthropologist who became a close collaborator of experimental theatre director Eugenio Barba, notes in *A Passage to Anthropology* that "most cultural knowledge is stored in action rather than words," and specifies that such embodied knowledge is transmitted through psychophysical involvement in cultural processes.[25] Hastrup derives from her encounter with theatre that the concept of embodied experience becomes pivotal whenever researchers attempt to account for what Barba defines as the "body-in-life." She situates flesh and blood human agents within a corporeal field "with which every individual is inextricably linked by way of the physical, sensing and moving body."[26] She infers from this embodied condition that "the point from which we experience the world is in constant motion . . . there is no seeing the world from above."[27]

The potentially imperialist connotations of the phrase "conducting research abroad" thus derive from the belief that researchers can have a bird-eye view of the world by keeping a distance with their object of study, as if their mind could somehow safely hover above "the field" while their body remained anchored in the gritty materiality of fieldwork. If self-reflexivity can help to account for the impact that one's presence as an outsider may have on the cultural processes being researched, it can also lead to self-indulgence if it is not underpinned by a commitment to experiential participation in these processes and by the recognition that one's approach should be significantly informed (and possibly transformed) by the epistemologies and methodologies of cultural insiders.

INTEGRATING INDIGENOUS PERSPECTIVES

For Denzin, whose approach is largely influenced by Conquergood's interdisciplinary research, the most challenging questions emerge from ethnography's failure to satisfactorily account for lived experience, which tends to be absent from most ethnographic texts. While acknowledging that "experiences are constantly out of reach of language and discourse and on the borderline of consciousness and awareness," so that it is impossible to "represent a life as it is actually lived or experienced," Denzin suggests that meaningful representations are transmitted through proverbs, stories, folktales, and other forms of cultural performances, which he identifies as "the realm of lived experience that is recoverable."[28] These "re-tellings" do not claim to capture the original meaning of an experience but to evoke lived experience through new expressions of this experience.[29]

Denzin envisions such cultural performances as powerful tools for the investigation of "the world of human experience from the point of view of the historically and culturally situated individual."[30] One of the main proponents of performance ethnography in the post-Victor Turner era, Denzin states that "the world is a performance, not a text," and that "every performance, every identity [is] a new representation of meaning and experience," as well as a site of struggle, negotiation, and hope, "a site where the performance of possibilities occurs."[31] Denzin draws from Conquergood's approach to define the term performance as "a way of revealing agency, . . . a way of bringing culture and the person into play, . . . as a path to understanding, a tool for engaging collaboratively the meanings of experience."[32]

Moreover, Denzin integrates the critique of Euro-American anthropology produced by Indigenous researchers such as Maori scholars Linda Tuhiwai Smith and Russell Bishop, a critique which calls for the legitimization, in the academy, of embodied knowledge as a counter-hegemonic mode of inquiry. In the *Handbook of Critical & Indigenous Methodologies*, the editors, Denzin, Lincoln and Smith, advocate a performance-based approach to critical qualitative research informed by Indigenous methodologies and designed to "create a space for critical, collaborative, dialogical work."[33] They state: "there is much to learn from Indigenous scholars about how radical democratic practices can be made to work."[34] For example, the Maori

> value dialogue as a method for assessing knowledge claims. The Maori moral position also privileges storytelling, listening, voice, and personal performance narratives. . . . This is a performative, pedagogical ethic, grounded in the ritual, sacred spaces of family, community, and everyday moral life. It is not imposed by some external, bureaucratic agency. This view of knowing parallels the commitment within certain forms of Red pedagogy to the performative as a way of being, as a way of knowing, as a way of expressing moral and spiritual ties to the community."[35]

The editors consider performance to be central to Indigenous worldviews because "meaning and resistance are embodied in the act of performance itself. The performative is where the soul of the culture resides. In their sacred and secular performances, the members of a culture honor one another and the culture itself."[36] Since performance processes are vital to the embodied transmission of traditional knowledge, such processes significantly inform the decolonizing research methodologies developed collaboratively by the Indigenous and non-Indigenous scholars who are committed to the radical democratic practice defined by Denzin, Lincoln and Smith. This integration of the performative opens up new possibilities for research grounded in Indigenous practices that legitimize other ways of knowing.

Denzin, Lincoln and Smith support the view by Indigenous scholars that "Indigenous knowledge systems are too frequently made into objects of study, treated as if they were instances of quaint folk theory held by members of a primitive culture. The decolonizing project reverses this equation, making Western systems of knowledge the object of critique and inquiry."[37] The Indigenous critique of the use of theory in the Western academy challenges "critical theory's criteria for self-determination and empowerment" because, from an Indigenous perspective, such criteria "perpetuate neocolonial sentiments while turning the indigenous person into an essentialized "other" who is spoken for."[38] Indigenous critics such as Bishop and Smith point out that critical theory has "failed to address how Indigenous cultures and their epistemologies were sites of resistance and empowerment."[39]

Moreover, Indigenous critics argue that there is "a pressing need to decolonize and reconstruct those structures within the academy that privilege Western knowledge systems and their epistemologies."[40] For critical theorists, the most challenging aspect of this Indigenous critique may very well lie in its definition of research itself. Indeed, for Indigenous scholars, "the purpose of research is not the production of new knowledge per se. Rather, the purposes are pedagogical, political, moral, and ethical, involving . . . a commitment to praxis, justice, an ethic of resistance, and a performative pedagogy that resists oppression."[41] Moreover, from an Indigenous perspective, "the central tensions in the world today go beyond the crises in capitalism and neoliberalism's version of democracy."[42] For, according to Native Canadian, Hawaiian, Maori, and American Indian pedagogy, "the central crisis is spiritual, 'rooted in the increasingly virulent relationship between human beings and the rest of nature."[43] In response to this crisis, Indigenous activists propose a respectful performance pedagogy [that] works to construct a vision of the person, ecology, and environment that is compatible with Indigenous worldviews.[44]

In *Decolonizing Methodologies*, Smith stresses that "Indigenous communities have something to offer to the non-Indigenous world [such as] Indigenous peoples' ideas and beliefs about the origins of the world, their explanations of the environment, often embedded in complicated metaphors and mythic tales [which] are now sought as the basis for thinking more laterally about current theories about the environment, the earth and the universe."[45] She specifies that Indigenous perspectives on research are informed by "arguments of different Indigenous peoples based on spiritual relationships to the universe, to the landscape and to stones, rocks, insects and other things, seen and unseen," which, she remarks, "have been difficult arguments for Western systems of knowledge to deal with or accept."[46] She concludes that such arguments "give a partial indication of the different world views and alternative ways of coming to know, and of being, which still endure within the Indigenous world [and which are] critical sites of resistance for indigenous peoples."[47]

Accordingly, if Indigenous and non-Indigenous scholars are to collaboratively produce decolonizing research methodologies that promote the radical democratic practice advocated by Denzin, Lincoln and Smith, "a new set of moral and ethical research protocols is needed," and the editors of the *Handbook of Indigenous and Critical Methodologies* suggest that such protocols must be informed by communitarian principles of sharing, reciprocity, and relationality.[48] This is especially crucial to the integration of Indigenous ethical and moral perspectives which call for "a collaborative social science research model that makes the researcher responsible not to a discipline (or institution) but rather to those studied."[49] Having researched and taught the anthropology of performance and experimental ethnography as a postdoctoral fellow in the UC Santa Cruz Anthropology Department, I am committed to investigating how the Indigenous critique of Western research models might inform interdisciplinary and cross-cultural research approaches and shape the emerging field of performance as research.

PERFORMANCE AS RESEARCH, AND RESEARCH AS CEREMONY

Integrating Indigenous research principles has helped me to address the practice/theory divide which characterizes performance research in the academy and which severely undermines practice-based research endeavors requiring the building of relationships based on trust, respect, and reciprocity. *Meetings with Remarkable Women - Tu es la fille de quelqu'un/You Are Someone's Daughter*, the SSHRC-funded research project.[50] I am currently conducting research on women who contributed to the cross-cultural, practice-based research of influential experimental theatre director Jerzy Grotowski. Indeed, their experience of being "researched" by theatre scholars and turned into informants, case studies and objects of inquiry has understandably led performance practitioners belonging to the Grotowski diaspora to mistrust most research endeavors, especially those supported by a large amount of university funding, a sure sign that there must be a hidden agenda. And in fact, there always is, since the academy sets the criteria for successful research, such as dissemination by means of peer-reviewed academic publications addressed primarily to an academic audience. This practice thereby excludes most practitioners from the debate even when claiming to support process-oriented and practice-based projects grounded in the notion of "performance as research" or "practice as research in performance."

On January 26, 1998, at the end of his last Collège de France lecture[51] as Professor of Theatre Anthropology, Grotowski declared, as if in conclusion, that asking questions only with the mind merely amounted to playing a game of ideas that was neither interesting nor true. This critical stance towards the production of abstract intellectual constructs that replace performance practice as such, was constantly balanced, in Grotowski's analysis of his own work, with the exacting demand for rigor and consistency that characterized his life-long practice-based research. This explains why practitioners in the Grotowski diaspora would be so acutely aware that academic approaches to performance often colonizes practice to fit pre-established theoretical frameworks. Such a process reduces it to lifeless formulas bound to fail to convey the kind of embodied knowledge that is gained through "doing." They are also weary of researchers who fall into the other extreme by mystifying artistic practice to liberate it from theory's grasp. In both cases, academic research misrepresents, disrespects and dishonors the work of artists who have dedicated their life to very sophisticated ways of conducting research through practice.

In the field of performance studies, the gap that separates performance scholars from performance practitioners has been described by Conquergood as an "apartheid of knowledges" and defined by Shannon Jackson as an insidious "division of labor" privileging those who think over those who do. Interestingly, Cree scholar Shawn Wilson points to a similar disjunction between Western and Indigenous scholars in his work *Research Is Ceremony: Indigenous Research Methods*, published in 2008: "As part of their white privilege, there is no requirement for [dominant system academics] to be able to see other ways of being and doing, or even to recognize that they exist. Oftentimes, then, ideas coming from a different worldview are outside their entire mindset and way of thinking. The ability to bridge this gap becomes important in order to ease the tension that it creates."[52] Because of the complex negotiations in which I am engaged due to my positionality as a performance practitioner and scholar, I have witnessed and experienced tensions not unlike those described by Wilson as I straddle two worlds that often seem irreconcilable. While such research approaches are designed by and for Indigenous scholars and activists working within their own communities, they raise questions that are more pertinent to my experience as a researcher, practitioner and educator than the questions raised by those whom Wilson identifies as "dominant system academics."

Indeed, Grotowski's practice-based performance research tends to be dismissed by many theatre scholars and critics for being suspiciously "esoteric" or even dangerously "mystical." This stems from Grotowski's controversial decision in 1970, after having garnered international acclaim over the past decade as the Polish Laboratory Theatre's artistic director, to abandon theatre production all together in order to focus on practical research. Such research entailed long-term collaboration with holders of traditional embodied knowledge pertaining to world performance traditions often linked to ancient ritual practices.

Indigenous research principles are particularly productive for the development of my project for several reasons, which include: the marginality of Grotowski's research in mainstream theatre studies in spite of the fact that theatre historians consider the Polish director to be as influential as Stanislavski and Brecht, two other major twentieth century theatre innovators; the peripheral position of women in the official histories of Grotowski's work and the ensuing lack of knowledge about their contribution to that work; the interconnection of science, art and spirituality as well as the importance of the senses and intuition in this type of approach and the sense of relationality that characterizes the Grotowskian performer's kinesthetic connection to human and non-human partners, including nature, whose organicity the training often emulates.

In *Research Is Ceremony*, Wilson refers to researchers from a number of Indigenous cultures who point out that science, art, and religion are integrated rather than distinct in traditional Indigenous knowledge. Wilson foregrounds the importance of approaching knowledge through the senses and the intuition as well as through the intellect, and stresses that, from an Indigenous perspective, knowledge is relational and shared. One is answerable to all of one's relations—including one's environment, one's ancestors, and the world at large—when one is conducting research.[53] Grounding Indigenous Research in the three R's: "Respect, Reciprocity and Relationality," Wilson specifies that "respect is more than just saying please and thank you, and reciprocity is more than giving a gift." He provides the example of Cree Elders, who conceive of respect as a basic law of life that "regulates how we treat Mother Earth, the plants, the animals, and our brothers and sisters of all races. . . . Respect means that you listen intently to others' ideas, that you do not insist that your idea prevails."[54] Indigenous research criteria are thus meant to ensure that the research conducted by Indigenous scholars "will be honored and respected by their own people. So much the better if dominant universities and researchers adopt them as well."[55]

These criteria are so fundamental to Indigenous communities that they "will not allow entry by researchers, Indigenous and non-Indigenous, until they have met the community's conditions." According to some of the key principles outlined by Wilson, Aboriginal people themselves must approve the research and research methods; researchers must be willing and able to engage in a "deep listening and hearing with more than the ears" in order to develop a "reflective, non-judgmental consideration of what is being seen and heard" along with "an awareness and connection between logic of mind and the feelings of the heart"; finally, researchers bear the "responsibility to act with fidelity in relationship to what has been heard, observed, and learnt."[56]

Relationality as defined by Wilson includes a spiritual relationship with the land, animals and plants, ancestors and future generations, and the cosmos. The cosmic scope of relationality can also be understood in terms of ecological balance. In *Relational Being: Beyond Self and Community*, Kenneth J. Gergen argues that a sustainable relationship between human beings and the natural world environment is critical to the survival of all forms of life on earth: "To understand the world in which we live as constituted by independent species, forms, types, or entities is to threaten the well-being of the planet. . . . Whatever value we place upon ourselves and others, and whatever hope we may have for the future, depends on the welfare of relationship."[57] Furthermore, for Wilson, research itself hinges upon relationality. Indeed, he stresses "the importance of spirituality in research itself" and suggests that research is ceremony because it is about making connections and strengthening them: "there is a lot of work, dedication and time spent in building up the relationships with the cosmos that allow the visible ceremony to happen."[58] Wilson's use of the term ceremony is, of course, culturally specific, yet his choice to equate research and ceremony points to new possibilities for both Indigenous and non-Indigenous researchers. Participating in a ceremony entails carrying out a series of actions which, if performed competently and in accordance with traditional knowledge, can activate, sustain and revitalize relationships to others, to the entire community, and to the world at large. There are striking parallels between this conception of ceremony and the practical research carried out by Grotowski. Furthermore, the transmission processes connecting one generation to the next in the Grotowski diaspora hinge upon the kind of competence that guarantees efficacy within traditional ritual practices. Given such parallels, envisioning this project as an investigation of research as ceremony can perhaps become a way of foregrounding the question of relationality within the research process itself.

EXPERIENCING THE INTERRELATION OF EMBODIMENT, TRANSMISSION, AND CREATIVITY

As with Grotowski, his collaborators envision artistic research as primarily practice-based, and consider that one must "do" to understand and not the other way around. Consequently, these artists share their research through the workshops they teach and the performances they create. In order to know them, it is therefore necessary to establish a relationship with them based on embodied participation in their work. My research approach thus hinges upon creating possibilities for this kind of relationship to develop through repeated encounters with women's creative research in the Grotowski diaspora.

The main practice-based component of my research thus involved organizing a month-long Laboratory of Creative Research that took place in Poland from July 7 to August 5, 2009 hosted by the Grotowski Institute for the "2009, Year of Grotowski" (UNESCO). This Laboratory included five work sessions led by Rena Mirecka (Poland), Katharina Seyferth (Germany), Ang Gey Pin (Singapore), Dora Arreola (Mexico), and Iben Nagel Rasmussen (Denmark), a three-day theatre festival featuring the current creative work of these artists, as well as two days of meetings with other women whose work was influenced by Grotowski.

There were seventeen international participants from eleven different countries who took part in all five work sessions, including myself and four University of British Columbia, Okanagan students. Being involved in these five work sessions entailed what American anthropologist Stoller calls "lending one's body to the world" so that conducting research may become a form of apprenticeship through which one learns from others instead of studying them. Experiencing intensive daily physical training with five different work leaders who have themselves invested many years of their lives in this process of self-cultivation, to borrow fifteenth-century Japanese Noh master Zeami's terminology, is an experiential approach to research hinging upon direct transmission of embodied knowledge.

The transmission processes underpinning the teachings of the five work leaders are diverse yet linked by common principles and recurring key elements within the training itself. For example, Rena Mirecka, after twenty-five years of collaboration with Grotowski as a founding member of his Laboratory Theatre, went on to develop her own paratheatrical research; Katharina Seyferth, who belongs to what might be called the second generation, was a member of the core group conducting practice-based research in the forest of Brzezinka, near Wroclaw, Poland, at a time of transition between the paratheatrical period and the period known as Theatre of Sources, which focused on world performance traditions grounded in ancient ritual practices. In spite of the differences in their respective approaches, relationship to the natural world is central to both Mirecka's and Seyferth's creative research, and it is significant that both of them chose to lead their work session in Brzezinka.

The paratheatrical research of Rena Mirecka is informed by Hinduism and Native American spirituality, and situates human beings in relation to "Mother Earth," "Father Sky" and the four cardinal directions, North, South, East and West, which are themselves linked to the four elements, air, water, fire, and earth, and to the four colors, white, red, yellow and black. Her teaching relies on seemingly very simple principles that are put into practice in her work: it is in giving that we receive; focusing only on the mind creates an imbalance; every single detail must be attended to yet there must be joy and sorrow because that's part of life, and doing things mechanically or technically is not alive. She explains that experiencing the connection between movement and sound is like stepping lightly into a canoe—only after developing a friendship with the water can we navigate the river; this journey requires great commitment, the ability to let go of fear, shame, and will, to accept oneself and others as we are.

As for Seyferth, she draws from her direct connection to Grotowski's post-theatrical research as a core member of the group which was based in the forest of Brzezinka. In addition to teaching physical training belonging to the theatrical, paratheatrical and Theatre of Sources periods, she leads participants into the heart of the forest by night for unusual expeditions. This summer, we thus marched in a line following in her brisk footstep, at times running in her stride through the darkness, barely avoiding ditches, puddles, and stinging nettles, at times lying down onto the soft, cool earth to contemplate the starry sky towards which rose the trees of the forest of Brzezinka. We were also invited to explore the forest on our own by daylight, to discover a particular area, place, or spot with which to build a relation by developing a site-specific action that would eventually be shared with others.

Both Mirecka and Seyferth use elements of Yoga when teaching physical training. Mirecka also integrates work on shakras and mantras, and her Indian work session assistant, Anant Sharma, introduced participants to ragas. Mirecka and Seyferth both speak about the training as a preparation for a journey into "the unknown": precise and rigorous physical work provides a structure taking the doer farther and deeper each time, beyond perceived limitations. During this training, it is crucial to take time to delve into the organicity and flow of the body in movement, for Mirecka and Seyferth stress that personal associations only emerge from a total commitment of the body to deep work. This is the necessary condition for something unexpected to take place—which becomes a point of entry into the unknown. Finally, Mirecka and Seyferth both make clear that although the training is physically demanding, the point is not to be exhausted but to find an organic way of working that energizes the body, which can only happen when going beyond tiredness and discovering another quality of energy. This is how one finds "the life" that turns mere exercises into creative exploration.

Seyferth specified during her work session that simplicity should ensue from the work, so that the training is a preparation enabling something to emerge by itself: unknown, surprising, alive, unpredictable. She also stated that judging or being judged during the work must be avoided, as well as talking about the work afterwards, because the workspace must remain a space in which one feels free to explore. Similar principles linked the respective approaches of the other work leaders involved in this research project, with the most central element being what Grotowski himself termed "organicity."

During his Collège de France lectures, Grotowski defined "organicity" by stating that it referred to the existence of the genuine living process which characterized an "expression not elaborated in advance." Grotowski provided the example of the movement of trees swaying in the wind, or the ebb and flow of the ocean on the shore. He remarked that the expressiveness that could be perceived in nature by the viewer appeared without the purpose of illustrating, representing or expressing anything. Without the presence of the viewer, these natural phenomena kept occurring and recurring, unnoticed. A key principle of

Grotowski's work is that "the form should be preceded by what must precede it, that is, preceded by a process which leads to the form."[59] In his Collège de France lectures, Grotowski remarked that a truly creative organic process was always connected personal associations, which could be linked to something that had happened to us in the past, or something that could have happened, or that we think should have happened: "something rooted in the personal life, for example a longing never nurtured."

When Grotowski spoke about "la lignée organique au théâtre et dans le rituel," the title of his Collège de France lectures, he established a link between aesthetic and ritual performance practices, suggesting that theatre and ritual were related because of the live process they had in common and that may be described as a transformation of energy generating a different quality of perception—Grotowski employed the English term "awareness." Floyd Favel, a Cree artist who worked with Rena Mirecka and with Grotowski at the beginning of the Art as Vehicle period, defines this type of process as linking theatre, tradition, and ritual: "Theatre and ritual traditions share the same characteristics: narrative, action, and the use of a specialized or sacred space. But theatre comes from across the Big Water and our traditions originate here. Both of these mediums have different objectives and goals. Where these two mediums connect is at the spiritual level. In the moment of performance, higher self is activated, and it is at this higher plane that theatre and tradition are connected and related."[60] The connection that Favel establishes between performance and ritual arts is informed by his participation Art as vehicle, the ultimate phase of Grotowski's research focused on ancient traditional vibratory songs through which he believed it was possible to become reconnected with one's ancestors.

TU ES LA FILLE DE QUELQU'UN

Although I later had the opportunity to work directly with several of Grotowski's collaborators, I initially trained in Paris in the 1990s with French actors Caroline Boué-Erhardt and Bertrand Quoniam, who had themselves trained with Ludwig Flaszen and Zygmunt Molik, two founding members of Grotowski's Laboratory Theatre. I therefore identify with what I would call the Grotowski diaspora's lost generation—a generation upon whom Grotowski's influence is, at best, invisible, as he noted during his Collège de France lectures. While there is a certain sense of freedom and independence that comes with not being a legitimate inheritor, with not having to "defend" or "preserve" Grotowski's legacy, I am also aware that reconnecting with one's sources and ancestry was key to Grotowski's research, especially in his investigation of traditional songs.

Indeed, Grotowski stated: "As one says in a French expression, 'Tu es le fils de quelqu'un' [You are someone's son]. You are not a vagabond, you come from somewhere, from some country, from some place, from some landscape. . . . Because he who began to sing the first words was someone's son, from somewhere, from some place, so, if you refind this, you are someone's son. If you do not refind it, you are not someone's son; you are cut off, sterile, barren."[61] While this statement seems to be focusing solely on sons, and can, at first sight, appear patriarchal, I have chosen to believe that it should not be taken literally, for surely women also experience the need to know where they come from, that is to say, the need to be someone's daughter.

According to Grotowski, what enables traditional songs to reach us across hundreds of years is the particular vibratory quality linked to the precision of the song's structure, so that it is necessary to search for the vocal and physical score inscribed within each particular song. When a competent performer actively and attentively embodies a traditional song, it can become a vehicle that reconnects her/him to those who first sang this song. One might even say that the ancestral embodied knowledge encoded in traditional songs is part of our DNA—or, if willing to take the risk of sounding much less scientific, one might suggest that it constitutes a trace of our humanity. If so, it is only when we remember how to sing that we can truly call ourselves someone's son or daughter. Interestingly, traditional songs have a central place in the teaching of Grotowski's women collaborators, and working with some of these artists has led me to reconnect with traditional songs in the ancient Occitan language, which my maternal grandmother spoke with her sisters, brothers, parents and grandparents. It has also compelled me to find out more about the creative research of women in the Grotowski diaspora, and to understand what motivated them to dedicate much of their life to this research.

I chose to pursue Grotowski-based training because I sensed that it could provide women with creative agency beyond the limitations placed upon them by the conventions of psychological realism. The assumptions underlying such conventions have been scrutinized by feminist theorists, who contend that realist theatre naturalizes the normative gender roles it reproduces on stage. Hence, performers working in realist theatre are often type-cast in accordance with the gender roles society expects them to play in real life. By taking on these roles, performers become complicit with the naturalization process at work in realist theatre, while at the same time being deeply shaped by these representations.

This critique of psychological realism is substantiated by American experimental theatre director Joseph Chaikin when he declares in *The Presence of the Actor*: "My early training for the theatre taught me to represent other people by their stereotype—or taught me, in fact, to become the stereotype." Chaikin indicts "the actor as salesman," whose job it is to make a "recommendation to the types within the audience as to how they should classify themselves."[62] In an attempt to break with realism, Chaikin and the collective of the Open Theatre developed physically-based training that was influenced by their encounter with Grotowski. Chaikin's aim was to alter "the limitations of life as it is lived," for he was convinced that "when the theatre is limited to the socially possible, it is confined by the same forces that limit society."[63]

Can Grotowski-based training provide performers with the creative agency summoned by Chaikin? Having renounced theatre at the height of his company's international acclaim, Grotowski asked: "This life that you are living, is it enough?" and declared: "No, such life is not sufficient. So one does something, one proposes something, one accomplishes something which is the response to this deficiency. . . . Art is deeply rebellious. [It] pushes back the limits imposed by society or, in tyrannical systems, imposed by power."[64] This conception of artistic practice may be attributed to the oppressive political and social circumstances of Grotowski's Poland and to his witnessing of the destruction and suffering perpetrated by Nazism and Stalinism. In any case, the urgency that animated Grotowski's commitment to artistic practice also deeply informed his research on aesthetic and ritual performance processes. My research project, which focuses on daughters rather than sons, investigates how their belonging to different cultures and traditions has informed their perspective on performance, creativity, and agency.

LOOKING FOR TRACES: TOWARDS AN ARCHEOLOGY OF EXPERIENCE

Why is Grotowski's approach still relevant today? Since the second half of the twentieth century, performance has been increasingly placed in the service of the commercial cultural industry. In the 1960s, Chaikin indicted the figure of the "actor-as-salesman," which in the twenty-first century has become the "actor-as-brand-name," that is to say, a corporately owned human being whose labor of embodiment is instrumental to the commodification of social role-models sanctioned by economically dominant cultures and naturalized by global media networks. Angela McRobbie hence examines the extent to which the globalization of the beauty-fashion industry complex affects the lives of women across social and cultural divides in the so-called postfeminist era.

In contrast, Grotowski's process-oriented investigation of the human creative potential, informed by performance traditions hinging upon the transmission of embodied knowledge, may be perceived as providing performers with the creative means to resist the hegemony of corporate consumerist culture ruled by ruthless competition and shaped by the tides of market forces. Grotowski, who notoriously coined the phrase "poor theatre," speaks about the existential quest he considers to be central to artistic research in the following terms:

> No one who denies the quest will be happy. Many people do reject it; they feel obliged to smile, as if they were advertising toothpaste. But why are they so sad? . . . One has not [to] learn but [to] unlearn, not to know how to do, but how not to do, and always facing doing; to risk total defeat; not a defeat in the eyes of others, which is less important, but a defeat of a missed gift, an unsuccessful meeting with someone, that is to say an unsuccessful meeting with oneself.[65]

Might the conception of performance developed by Grotowski and his collaborators provide women with an alternative form of embodied agency otherwise unavailable to them in more conventional forms of theatre practice? Can physically-based training focused on impulses, associations and organicity lead women performers to undertake their own journeys into the unknown? If this process-oriented approach can enable women to explore 'what could have happened, what should have happened, and what is rooted in their personal lives and linked to a longing never nurtured,' how might women claim the power of performance and transmit it to others in order to change lives?

Among the women from different cultures and generations who have been in direct contact with Grotowski's work, the ones involved in this project clearly assert their independence and artistic autonomy, while acknowledging the significant influence of Grotowski's approach on their own work, yet in a markedly different way from the male collaborators and official inheritors. They thus seem freer to investigate the interrelation between theatre, tradition and ritual, and their respective approaches, while extremely diverse, are often situated at the intersection of Art as Presentation and Art as Vehicle, two categories that defined the theatrical and post-theatrical periods of Grotowski's work and that remained distinct in his terminology—hence the importance of the perspectives contributed by artists such as Rena Mirecka, Katharina Seyferth, Iben Nagel Rasmussen, Ang Gey Pin, Dora Arreola and the other women encountered during this summer's meetings in Poland.

What does the experiential dimension of embodied research leaves us with? Traces—the traces of an organic lineage linking theatre, paratheatre and ritual, beyond the conceptual categories separating them. Indeed, because this type of performance training requires engaging one's whole being—body, mind and heart—it becomes impossible to distinguish between being, doing, sensing, feeling, imagining, remembering, thinking and understanding. Different layers of consciousness seem to be activated simultaneously without canceling each other out. The perception of self and other merges with the experience of time and space, which expand beyond everyday life notions of duration and location. Everything in the world seems interconnected, and everyone seems to exist in relation to everything. It becomes impossible to distinguish between inner and outer, impulse and action, movement and repose. Boundaries dissolve to let life flow through with a rush of fresh associations in its wake. Images and sensations linger in the body memory as sole recording technology—a sedimentation process occurs and an archeology of experience becomes possible. Millions of years elapse in the blink of an eye, leaving traces of tectonic shifts and volcanic eruptions in the geological layers of the skin, deep into nerve tissue, bone, marrow and blood. "If research doesn't change you as a person, then you haven't done it right," cautions Wilson.[66]

NOTES

1   J.N. Mohanty, "The Other Culture," *Phenomenology of the Cultural Disciplines*, ed. Mano Daniel and Lester Embree (Dordrecht: Kluwer, 1994), 145.

2   Mohanty, "The Other Culture," 135–146.

3   Deborah D'Amico-Samuels, "Undoing Fieldwork: Personal, Political, Theoretical and Methodological Implications," *Decolonizing Anthropology, Moving Further Toward an Anthropology for Liberation*, ed. Faye V. Harrison (Wash-

ington: Association of Black Anthropologists/American Anthropological Association, 1991), 82–83.

4   D'Amico-Samuels, "Undoing Fieldwork," 82.

5   Lincoln and Denzin, *Turning Points*, 3.

6   Lincoln and Denzin, *Turning Points*, 17.

7   Lincoln and Denzin, *Turning Points*, 17.

8   Lincoln and Denzin, *Turning Points*, 17.

9   Stuart Hall, "Cultural Identity and Diaspora," *Colonial Discourse and Post-Colonial Theory*, ed. Patrick Williams and Laura Chrisman (1990. New York: Columbia University Press, 1993), 394.

10   Hall, "Cultural Identity," 394.

11   Hall, "Cultural Identity," 395.

12   Hall, "Cultural Identity," 395.

13   James Clifford and George E. Marcus, eds, *Writing Culture: The Poetics and Politics of Ethnography* (Berkeley: University of California Press, 1986), 9.

14   Clifford and Marcus, *Writing Culture*, 12.

15   D. Soyini Madison, *Critical Ethnography: Methods, Ethics, and Performance* (Thousand Oaks: Sage, 2005), 170.

16   Madison, *Critical Ethnography*, 150.

17   Clifford and Marcus, *Writing Culture*, 9.

18   Clifford and Marcus, *Writing Culture*, 12.

19   Victor Turner, "Dramatic Ritual/Ritual Drama: Performative and Reflexive Anthropology," *Interculturalism and Performance: Writings from PAJ*, ed. Bonnie Marranca and Gautam Dasgupta (New York: PAJ), 101.

20   Turner, "Dramatic Ritual/Ritual Drama," 111.

21   Colin Turnbull, "Liminality: a Synthesis of Subjective and Objective Experience," *By Means of Performance: Intercultural Studies of Theatre and Ritual*, ed. Richard Schechner and Willa Appel (Cambridge University Press, 1990), 50.

22   Turnbull, "Liminality, " 51.

23   Dwight Conquergood, "Performance Studies: Interventions and Radical Research," *TDR* T174 (Summer 2002): 140.

24   Madison, *Critical Ethnography*, 150.

25   Kirsten Hastrup, "The Motivated Body: on the Locus of Agency," *A Passage to Anthropology: Between Experience and Theory* (London and New York: Routledge, 1995), 82.

26   Hastrup, "The Motivated Body," 95.

27   Hastrup, "The Motivated Body," 95.

28   Norman K. Denzin, *Interpretive Ethnography, Ethnographic Practices for the Twenty-First Century* (Thousand Oaks: Sage, 1997), 61.

29   Denzin, *Interpretive Ethnography*, 61.

30   Denzin, *Interpretive Ethnography*, 87.

31   Norman K. Denzin, *Performance Ethnography: Critical Pedagogy and the Politics of Culture* (Thousand Oaks: Sage, 2003), 328.

32   Denzin, *Performance Ethnography*, 9–10; 19.

33   Norman K. Denzin, Yvonna S. Lincoln and Linda Tuhiwai Smith, ed. *Handbook of Critical & Indigenous Methodologies* (Thousand Oaks: Sage, 2008), 5.

34   Denzin, Lincoln and Smith, *Critical & Indigenous Methodologies*, 14.

35   Denzin, Lincoln and Smith, *Critical & Indigenous Methodologies*, 14: citing Collins (1991), Bishop (1998), Grande (2000), and Graveline (2000).

36   Denzin, Lincoln and Smith, *Critical & Indigenous Methodologies*, 14.

37   Denzin, Lincoln and Smith, *Critical & Indigenous Methodologies*, 6.

38   Denzin, Lincoln and Smith, *Critical & Indigenous Methodologies*, 5: citing Bishop (2005).

39   Denzin, Lincoln and Smith, *Critical & Indigenous Methodologies*, 9.

40   Denzin, Lincoln and Smith, *Critical & Indigenous Methodologies*, 6: citing Mutuaand Swadener (2004), Semali and Kincheloe (1999).

41   Denzin, Lincoln and Smith, *Critical & Indigenous Methodologies*, 14: citing Christians (2002).

42   Denzin, Lincoln and Smith, *Critical & Indigenous Methodologies*, 13.

43   Denzin, Lincoln and Smith, *Critical & Indigenous Methodologies*, 13: citing Grande (2000).

44   Denzin, Lincoln and Smith, *Critical & Indigenous Methodologies*, 13.

45   Linda Tuhiwai Smith, *Decolonizing Methodologies: Research and Indigenous Peoples* (London: Zed Books, 1999), 159.

46   Smith, *Decolonizing Methodologies*, 74.

47   Smith, *Decolonizing Methodologies*, 74.

48   Denzin, Lincoln, and Smith, *Critical & Indigenous Methodologies*, 14.

49   Denzin, Lincoln, and Smith, *Critical & Indigenous Methodologies*, 15.

50   *Meetings with Remarkable Women/Tu es la fille de quelqu'un* is funded by a SSHRC Standard Research Grant and a SSHRC Research/Creation in Fine Arts Grant (Social Sciences and Humanities Research Council of Canada).

51   Grotowski gave a series of public lectures titled "La Lignée Organique au Théâtre et dans le Rituel" between March 97 and January 98 in Paris (1997: March 24, June 2, June 16, June 23, October 6, October 13, October 20. 1998: Jan 12 and 26). The inaugural lecture took place on March 24, 1997, at Peter Brook's Théâtre des Bouffes du Nord. Grotowski spoke in French. I attended these talks and documented them in the Polish theatre journal *Didaskalia*.

52   Shawn Wilson, *Research Is Ceremony: Indigenous Research Methods* (Halifax and Winnipeg: Fernwood Publishing, 2008), 44.

53   Wilson, *Research Is Ceremony*, 56.

54   Wilson, *Research Is Ceremony*, 58.

55   Wilson, *Research Is Ceremony*, 59.

56   Wilson, *Research Is Ceremony*, 59.

57   Kenneth J. Gergen, *Relational Being: Beyond Self and Community* (Oxford: Oxford University Press, 2009), 396.

58   Wilson, *Research Is Ceremony*, 89–90.

59   Jerzy Grotowski, "C'était une sorte de volcan," Interview: 8, 9, 10 February, 1991, Paris. (*Gurdjieff*. Dossiers H. Lausanne: L' Age d'Homme, 1993), 102.

60 Floyd Favel, "Poetry, Remnants and Ruins: Aboriginal Theatre in Canada," *Canadian Theatre Review* 139 (Summer 2009): 33.

61 Jerzy Grotowski, "Tu es le fils de quelqu'un [You Are Someone's Son]" (1989), trans. James Slowiak and the author, *The Grotowski Sourcebook*, ed. Richard Schechner and Lisa Wolford (Routledge: London and New York, 1997), 304.

62 Joseph Chaikin, *The Presence of the Actor* (New York: Theatre Communications Group, 1972), 12.

63 Chaikin, *The Presence of the Actor*, 22 – 3.

64 Grotowski, "Tu es le fils de quelqu'un," 295.

65 Jerzy Grotowski, "Holiday [Swieto]" (1972), trans. Boleslaw Taborski, *The Grotowski Sourcebook*, ed. Richard Schechner and Lisa Wolford (Routledge: London and New York, 1997), 117–18 .

66 Wilson, *Research Is Ceremony*, 135.

CHAPTER ELEVEN

Counter-Movement: Researchers from Abroad and the Reconfiguration of the Research Location

By Sami Hanna and Mustafa Sever

INTRODUCTION

Since it first opened up the doors of its institutions of higher education to foreign enrollment in the 1920s, the United States has become a popular destination for international students from more than two hundred countries around the world. According to the statistics of the U.S. Immigration and Customs Enforcement Bureau[1], a total of 583, 959 international students are currently enrolled at American universities and colleges, 75 percent of whom attend the top ten majors of study, with the most popular subjects being business, management, marketing, and related support services. Education, which ranks last among the top ten, attracts around twenty thousand international students.

The Bureau's statistics also indicate that 107,513 foreign students are currently pursuing doctoral degrees in the United States. These students, like their domestic counterparts, engage in various research practices throughout the duration of their study. As two fellow international students ourselves, our interest in international students' research choices and practices has developed from our observations that there seems to be a tendency for orienting one's research towards one's own—either within the communities found in one's own home country, or towards one's respective diasporic, ethnocultural group inside the United States. This inclination to research one's own adds another layer to the methodological discussion of the Self and Other in relation to questions of representation in qualitative inquiries. One of the main challenges of conducting ethnographic research has been the politics of relationship with one's participants: the degree of objectivity we must maintain towards our participants in relation to the barrier that sets us apart from them, the barrier as seen in the hyphen between researcher-participant. In other words, do we, as researchers, maintain our distance from our participants, or do we draw closer to them in order to better articulate their own understandings of the sociocultural phenomena that we have chosen to study?

Richard Rorty explains this as an opposition between "desire for objectivity" and "desire for solidarity."[2] Until the 1970s, the dominance of positivistic approaches in social sciences—investigating social phenomena through methods of natural sciences—meant weaker ties between ethnography and social reality by distancing the ethnographer from his/her subjects for the sake of enhancing objectivity. This dominance, however, has been undermined with the interventions of critical, postmodernist and post-structuralist approaches, which appropriated "truth" and "social reality" as the continuous production of interaction rather than fixed and pre-existing to human conditions. Prior to postmodernist and poststructuralist interventions that sought to question or deconstruct, a common approach for the ethnographic researcher had been to keep a certain distance from his/her participants. More recently, however, such an assumption of objectivity has been considerably critiqued by approaches that advocate closer association with participants in order to better reflect their voices and their understandings of the phenomena the researcher chooses to investigate. Such dynamic of keeping vis-à-vis overcoming the distance between researcher (Self) and participants (Others) has been represented as a "hyphen," the barrier that sets one apart from the other.[3] In what follows, we examine how the specifics of doing research on one's own ethnocultural folk outside the boundaries of the homeland may unfold in ways not limited to the above discussion of keeping or overcoming the hyphen.

FROM BEING HERE TO BEING THERE

The major concern of this chapter underlies the movement of researchers from their research "stations" to the locations of possible field instances to be examined. To a considerable extent, this movement has been referred to as *Being Here* to *Being There*, to use the famous binary description from Geertz.[4] During the days of anthropological investigations of other cultures, specifically those different from our normative native culture, the spatial relationship between these two poles was physical, not only in the obvious terms of leaving one's (Western) home country to travel to a target (non-Western) "field," but also due to the geopolitical and historical opposition that exists between the contexts of Here and There. In other words, Here and There unequivocally meant two different places in the world: two countries, a country and an island, a country and a tribal community, etc. Conceptualizations of being Here and There reflect the manifestations of the differential power positions two places may hold. The power balance between East and West, in which the latter has held the advantageous pole for centuries, makes it a classical example of how ethnographic stories, obliviously or not, have produced and perpetuated this imbalance through exoticizing, stereotyping, and misrepresenting. However, the practice and implications of the powerful investigating the weak/suppressed/disadvantaged should not be limited to broader contexts such as

East and West alone. This holds true for every context where spatial segregation, for example, is the norm: within the same country, in a single neighborhood or locale, etc.

Attention in ethnographic research, thus, shifted towards subjects of research whose appeal was no longer an exotic foreignness; yet it was gradually the sameness of one's own group that became visible. In this sense, the anthropological enterprise took a sociological turn that was, above all, spatial—pertaining to space, a condition that came to introduce changes to the practice in methodological and conceptual ways. Ethnographers began to conceive the relationship between the location of research and the subjects of research as an inseparable element of ethnographic imagination that needed to be incorporated into the methodological and conceptual framework as something susceptible to change (e.g., within the same city, people who live in the downtown part experience social realities differently from those who live in the suburbs). The assumption of similarity, however, did not abolish the Geertzian binary of "Being Here" and "Being There," but simply infused it with a reconfiguration of spatiality: Here started to mean "the academy" and There "the field," according to Segall.[5] For example, ethnographic researchers no longer have to travel long miles to reach their sites, but can simply drive down the street to a school, a mall, or a prison to conduct their data collection, and can then return to their offices or apartments to analyze and interpret such data. The reconfigured spatiality, Segall argues, has not only made it more difficult to discern clear boundaries between Here and There as physical entities, but has also problematized the "hyphen"[6] that used to set boundaries between the Self (researchers) and Other (subjects of research). The geopolitical physicality of the concept of space—which marks the actuality that the space is not neutral but governed by various political discourses—has thus started to gradually clear the stage for relations that can still be described as physical (as in the simple act of leaving one's university campus to observe a classroom). They can also display non-geopolitical differentiations as is the case of research *within* a locality, a neighborhood, a city, etc. In other words, if location was the main marker of other-ness in ethnography, the differentiation from Self is now established through the workings of ethnographic writing, or the text of ethnography.

Thus, instead of inscribing physical location as the primary marking of difference, difference is now located discursively/textually in that the occupiers are represented according to the epistemological schemas that the researcher holds in his/her mind prior to research. This has specific implications on the research process altogether, the There of research having now become part of the interior of the ethnographic text. This means that the researcher needs to address the question of his/her relationship with his/her participants differently. One approach is to become conscious and reflective of the tensions and dynamics that such a relationship may entail, which in technical terms is usually referred to as "reflexivity." Another option the researcher may have is to think of this relationship in terms of where he/she stands vis-à-vis the participants, and how his/her identities as a human being and researcher may impact his/her experiences throughout and after fieldwork. This is referred to as standpoint or positionality. One reason for using *positionality* instead of the easier *position* may come from the function of the suffix—*ity*, which suggests a "state" or "quality," whose constitution need not be organic—taken for granted, inherited and/or biologically pre-dispositioned, but that can very well be acquired. This usage goes hand in hand with the new understanding of the researcher as not simply a detached fieldworker with one identity, but as someone who negotiates multiple identities within and without the field. A researcher can have different positionalities (identities) that bring him/her closer to or farther from the subjects of research. For example, one is not only a woman, but also a mother, a feminist, a Marxist, a lesbian, and so on. By contrast, Here is the understanding of identity as more or less organic: it has gained political, socioeconomic, ideological, gendered, and cultural signifiers and meanings. A researcher may not be able to change his/her organic identities (for example, race and ethnicity), but he/she can acquire affiliations that are not determined by genes, such as those referenced by religion, politics, theory, and socioeconomics. One's position as Euroamerican, which for the sake of argument can be said to be generally a position of privilege, may be mitigated by a positionality of, say, activist feminism that seeks to address conditions of racism against women of color.

With reference to the argument that we make in this chapter, we believe that the spatial binary of Here/There is significant primarily because of the contrastive character of what we propose—researchers not going abroad, but instead conducting research "Here." This binary is also relevant because of the specific underpinnings of studying one's own folk when the one who studies and those whom he/she examines bear relations that are not entirely nativist to the space inhabited. This simply means that certain groups/individuals inhabit a location to which they have migrated, rather than the one into which they were born. One should be aware, however, of the necessary qualifications that need to accompany any articulation of the "native" in a country as politically and historically specific to the condition of settler coloniality as the United States is. In other words, the designation "native" is not mechanical or straightforward, but results from different appropriations of power and political realities. In the context of our study, we examine international students, who, by definition, came to the United States on temporary "non-immigrant" visas to complete a program of study, with the expectation that once their degrees have been conferred, they will return to our home countries of origin. Burnapp[7] argues that the journey these students undergo can be identified with the movement "from a known *place* into something at first unknown—a *space*—which with time itself becomes known as a *place*."[8]

They are, then, transient sojourners in another culture, but above all they are transient researchers with a There that is different from the two There's mentioned above: academy/field and home/foreign country. An international graduate student's There is consequential to his/her being physically away from his/her home country. At the same time, however, this physical There is now the Here of the academy as an entity that contributes considerably to the experiences of the transience of study and stay. On the other hand, we have groups who are ethnoculturally and/or nationally similar to those international students, a basis that seems to foreground some of the research choices of these students In other words, international students tend (and are encouraged) to study people who are similar to them, i.e., groups that are culturally, religiously, linguistically similar. These groups can be identified as diasporic, i.e., people who migrated to other countries from the ones into which they were born, without neglecting that a person can be keen to different self-identifications that are determined by generational and socioeconomic considerations. (Experiences of first- and second-generation immigrants in the United States, for example, significantly differ from each other in regards to adaptation, linguistic abilities, perceptions of the host society, etc.) Besides, it is not entirely clear what similarities and differences may exist between transient and diasporic entities. One reason for this uncertainty may be that the examination of international students and their respective diasporic groups has focused on specific aspects of each group in separation from the other, rather than the interaction between the two groups.

Our attention, however, is focused on the reasons why one's own ethnocultural "folk" may become an obvious choice for international students specifically when conducting graduate and post-graduate research, not abroad, but inside the United States. Of course, any such choice is filtered through many academic, personal, and financial considerations. But in the case of international students, deciding on the subjects of research may come before thinking through the research problem/questions. This may relate to the fact that it is not uncommon to seek known faces in an unknown land, i.e., to choose to work with someone with whom one is most comfortable or with whom one might have similarities. At the same time, there is the fundamental question of who can represent whom, and how this element of representation interplays with the politics of insider-ness/outsider-ness. For example, it is not very common for a Kenyan student to decide to conduct research on certain aspects of the mainstream U.S. society, whereas American researchers regularly travel to many African countries to carry out their fieldwork. Of course this example does not only refer to how national, racial or ethnic differences play a role on conducting research abroad. Instead it points to the ways in which power is embedded into ethnographic practices and curiosities. Choosing to study one's own culture and people in diaspora should not overshadow another practice that is also common these days. For example, a PhD student from China studying in the United States goes back to Guangzhou to collect data on the transformation of the public educational system in that province, and then comes back to the United States in order to present her findings. It is the location of this research interaction on which we focus, realizing how common the movement from Here (United States) to There (country of origin) might be. Such movement falls in line with these native researchers' attempt to problematize claims of authentic knowledge of their folk within the homeland which is not unlike what has been observed through and because of the interpretative turn in ethnographic research at various sociology departments in the West.

In our chapter, we wish to articulate a counter-movement; instead of *going* abroad, we, as international graduate students, *come* from abroad in order to engage in research and fieldwork Here. Even more interesting is how international graduate students come to terms with the particulars of conducting fieldwork

Here versus There, and the different choices and decisions they must make with regards to these issues. As we mentioned above, many choose to return to their native environments in order to conduct fieldwork, but many others decide to remain in the United States and instead research contexts that bear some similarity, mostly ethnocultural, to their own background. Consequently, the question becomes, why don't the latter choose to research outside of that which relates to their own "folk?" From our own experiences as doctoral students in education, studying one's folk is not a codified requirement, so to speak, but is rather a strong suggestion that is communicated in many ways. When we were considering potential research sites for classroom projects or dissertations, the piece of advice that we received from advisors, professors, and classmates was to work on and with people who spoke our languages and shared our ethnocultural backgrounds. The implication behind this advice was that as an "insider," it would be much easier to gather authentic knowledge from subjects with whom we share ethno-cultural similarities. As a result, one of us ended up conducting a research study on the experiences of his fellow Turks in an urban, Northeastern site in the United States. The suggestion that one's folk may be the obvious object of study was further highlighted by what we have observed as a trend at the conferences we have attended, and at which we presented, as well as in the dissertations that we discuss here: a Turkish Language Education student studying the experiences of her fellow nationals, who may be struggling with academic English; a Kenyan Education student studying the schooling experiences of Kenyan immigrants in two major U.S. cities; and a Curriculum and Instruction student from the People's Republic of China researching the perceptions of daughters to Chinese immigrants of schooling, family, and identity at a local Chinese church and a Chinese cultural center.

It is important to point out that ours is not a study of the specifics of conducting research by international students in the United States as demonstrated in their own dissertations. Rather, our focus is primarily on the question of choice, i.e., why one would observe one's own folk for ethnographic investigation but not others. Therefore, we did not follow a formalized approach to analyzing the dissertations that we decided to include as examples of what we seek to articulate. Instead, we sought to problematize the choice international researchers in the United States make in studying their respective diasporic groups. This approach is conscious of the implications that the research location (physical in its expression of certain geopolitical and historical realities) has on the relationship between the researchers and their participants, as well as the reconfiguration of the dialectic Here-There.

THE REFLEXIVE GAZE AND THE RECONFIGURATION OF LOCATION

While we do not claim to wholly address how one chooses to investigate one's folk while studying in the United States, we argue that it is possible to attempt an explanation by examining one central part of ethnography today, i.e., reflexivity. The focus on reflexivity is inseparable from the shift that the configuration of location has undergone—location as less physically determined than expressed through the discourse of ethnography. As a result, the geopolitical particulars of a given space become secondary, which is different from the initial theorization of Geertz's Here and There as physical and ethnological oppositions.[9] Segall's iteration that discourse has now become practice, and practice discourse, is indicative of the postmodernist attempt to expose the inner workings of ethnography through its own text.[10] Put differently, discourse and ethnographic practice are interrelated and impact the outcomes of research considerably. Being reflexive about research practices may provide the opportunity to distinguish different voices and discourses embedded into ethnographic texts. Instead of the Geertzian fleshing out of text with thick descriptions from the field, researchers now seek to bring out the components of the research process that form the ethnographic text. Making the interior of an ethnographic text known can nowadays be achieved by confessional moods and modes, an inclination to talk about research practices in order to counter the possible influences of personal, cultural or methodological biases; such as stereotypes about cultural norms, perceptions of women, negligence of extraneous variables; which might impact research outcomes, where the "I," "They," "How," and "Why," and, to a lesser degree, the "where," of the research are expected to be laid bare for the reader.

The only constituent from the list above that is not capitalized is the "where" of research. Recent discursive trends in the field of ethnographic research have somehow de-essentialized location as an exclusive physical (geopolitical) entity. Space is no longer a physical entity that is constructed only by its native population but a political one invented and susceptible to change by different attributions. To compensate for this displacement of fixed physicality, Segall argues for the duality of discourse-as-practice and practice-as-discourse, where location has been reconfigured as no longer entirely geopolitical, but one that rather primarily becomes discursive/textual.[11] In this manner, it may not be absolutely necessary for researchers to travel to where space is still natively populated, i.e., Kenyans in Kenya, Syrians in Syria, etc. Instead, researchers can now investigate Kenyan and Syrian phenomena in transnational spaces outside of Kenya and Syria, relying mainly on "native" networks to locate potential research participants who not only live, but who also interpret these phenomena in their diasporic experiences. Seeking out "native" networks in diaspora appears essential in the methodological approaches of the international students' dissertations that we examined. If this seems like a reasonable means for the researcher to identify a field in a non-native environment, then, at a more structural level, the language of "networking" and "networks" suggests a different mode of delimitation that may transcend space as a physical attribution. A network allows the researcher's boundedness to the field and to his/her subjects of research to become more relational than locational. The nodes and ties of networks are no longer topographic or physical, but are instead relational and affective. Consequently, one may look at the field as less a matter of geopolitical opposition, i.e., either a Here or a There, than an entity that has been mitigated and even undermined by the novel diasporic interaction between the Here's and There's of ethnography, pre-, through-, and post-fieldwork. When looking for participants, international students often primarily seek the help of institutions of national and religious solidarity (community centers, churches and mosques), designated public spaces (language schools, national food restaurants or refugee camps), and meeting places for special events (parties, weddings, and national or religious celebrations). The following quotes provide examples of the utilization of these types of networks:

> As for the research on Japanese students, I have visited the JSA [Japanese Student Association] meetings at UCLA and the meetings of Japanese Cultural Club in Little Tokyo where many Japanese students who are studying at American universities visit to learn English or to teach the Japanese language to American people who also visit there (Mitsuhashi).[12]

> I recruited my three research informants through an acquaintance of mine at the local Christian church for ethnic Chinese. I was looking for three young women who had been born in China and had possibly had some schooling there, and who were attending a mainstream American secondary school in Littletown (Sun).[13]

The role that native researchers play during and after researching their folk in migratory sites instead of sites of permanent residence still materializes within a physical space. For example, when a Turkish student studying in the United States researches the schooling experiences of Turkish-Americans in Little Istanbul in Jersey City, the research does not take place or shape in vacuum, but within the specifics of a physical location, such as the Northeastern United States, the State of New Jersey, the city itself, etc. In other words, the physical dimension of location need not be a determining feature only in relation to the Geertzian binary of absolute Here and There. The location of fieldwork, in our opinion, will still influence the process of *graphing* the ethno, i.e., collecting data and interacting with the research participants, as well as writing. At the same time, location not only plays an important role in how researchers reflexively understand their identities in the field (as insiders in their diasporic communities, for instance), but also in how these researchers are seen in the eyes of their participants. If a researcher sees herself as an insider within the context of her diasporic research, her participants may not share this perception of her as such. They might identify her as the "one from the university," or "the educated woman who wants to tell our stories," views that are similar to those encountered by a returning native researcher in her home country, where she is perceived as "the one who's been in America." It may be the case that participants of our research do not necessarily share our understanding of location as a material boundedness that has been displaced in the village into which globalization has transformed the world. A site of migration and diasporic settlement is far from immune to the influences of the location such as physical conditions, dominant economic activities, and linguistic preferences: a Chinatown in California is a San Francisco Chinatown, a Turkish community is a Turkish community in New York City, and so forth. Thus, when an international graduate student from Honduras chooses to study familial influences on the education of second-generation Latinos and Latinas in the U.S. city where he/she is pursuing his/her studies, she is still doing so within a physical location that is bounded by the geopolitical and historical underpinnings of this diasporic space.

One of us, Mustafa, conducted his first qualitative research study in the United States on the schooling experiences of first-generation Turkish-Americans. His decision to study his own folk was not dissimilar from the choices made by his classmates, international as well as domestic from minority groups, when seeking out their research participants: African-Americans chose to study African-Americans; Latinos, Latinos; and Chinese, Chinese. When he started his fieldwork, however, the initial association of linguistic and cultural insider-ness soon gave way to a different vision after the first interviews. Almost all of the participants were either native or native-like speakers of English, adding another dimension of complexity to the project. Survival for these participants in a foreign country was not only a reaction to specific social, cultural, and political stimuli of the host society. It was also an engagement with one's cultural roots and cultural maintenance in diaspora, and with investing culturally and emotionally in the home country/culture while establishing connections with one's own people living in diaspora. In addition, it marked a need to come to terms with how these elements came to unfold at the level of the individual imagining of what Turkishness meant. This complex picture stood at odds with the researcher's initial goal to simply present the "schooling experiences of Turkish people living in the United States." The presumption that being Turkish would help the writer capture such experiences better than researchers with different ethnocultural backgrounds led him to focus on the romantic episodes of his participants' personal histories during the first few years of settlement. These encounters were not dissimilar from what he himself went through at the time, such as difficulties associated with adapting to a new culture, problems with peer groups, language proficiency, etc. But the participants' relationships to U.S. society and its institutions were more evolved than an adaptation framework could accommodate. Even when the writer thought that his Turkishness might at least enable him to track the residuals of the participants' early years of migration, it turned out that the migratory space had impacted these very residuals, so that to now claim shared Turkishness appeared to be somewhat essentialist. One remarkable example was the participants' perceptions of the "Turkish father" as a traditional authority figure. The Turkish authoritarian father figure that emerged in the informants' narratives was quite different from how it has been perceived in the home culture, where he is still seen as a traditional power holder and gatekeeper. The diasporic father figure was instead one who was culturally expected to protect the family from possible cultural contaminations that would come from contact with the host culture. Another departure was the complaint of one of the research participants that his father had never "gone fishing with him." This "fun" side to the father-son relationship was absent when the same writer investigated fatherhood experiences in his Master's thesis while he was still in Turkey. The diasporic father figure in this sense was neither Turkish nor American for many of the research participants. Because of a positionality of similarity that the writer assumed, he expected that a diasporic perception of the Turkish father figure would be but an extension of the traditional Turkish view. What unfolded instead was more or less a "hybrid" figure, with elements derived from both the native and diasporic contexts. This positionality of the oneness of culture and language, which maintained a presumption of insider-ness to the writer throughout his fieldwork, prevented him from articulating his participants' experiences as Turkish-Americans outside the framework of Turkishness.

Investing only in similarities may hinder an acknowledgement of the impact of the differential geopolitical and historical realities of the diasporic space, and how these interact with and transform the experiences of the inhabitants of this space in various ways. According to Homi Bhabha, the specific character of the diasporic space makes it a "third space," neither a "first" space where nativity is organic, nor a "second" space where foreignness is unchallenged.[14] Levitt and Khagram argue that such third or transnational spaces introduce a critique of conventional research methodologies that tend to take nation-states for granted, therefore neglecting the effects of transnational phenomena particularly upon immigrant groups living outside of their countries of origin, whatever the context (East or West) or the country may be.[15] Physical distance, Levitt and Khagram add, does not discourage immigrant communities from investing in their home countries. "Home" seems to always influence these transnational communities through cultural and social ties that are maintained across nation-states borders. Against this argument that the border and the nation-state as rational units of sociological analysis are actually eroding, or need to be eroded, Waldinger suggests that transnationalism as an ultimate analysis unit for Latino diasporic conditions in the United States needs further validation.[16] He suggests that "[m]igrant cross-state social action comes in a variety of types, with the direction of conditioning factors differing from one type to another," and, despite acts of border-crossing, "neither transnational*ism* as a condition of being, nor *transmigrants*, as a distinctive class of people is commonly found."[17]

In such third spaces, claims to Turkishness or any other native authenticities that roam above any physicality of location is suspect precisely because migratory experiences are influenced by the materiality of the host country/culture. These experiences are not totally unbounded, following Khagram and Levitt's call to look at any bordering as archaic[18]; on the contrary, their boundedness is above all an impact of the diasporic space. We believe that a transnational theorization of demographic, social, and cultural border-crossings should not diminish the fact that states, and their borders, are still determined through legal codes that give shape, undermine, or enhance transnational mobilizations and flows. A free flow of transnational labor of any kind, for instance, is, by far, more hindered than the flow of transnational investment capital precisely because of the active statist legislative role in sanctioning one but not the other. In the same vein, the militarization of borders, the U.S.-Mexican border as a primary example, is par excellence a statist action, even when supplemented by fragmented para-statist and non-statist interventions: the Minutemen in Arizona, U.S.-Mexican border "civil" vigilantes. Another example may further clarify our argument that boundedness to a space/location is by no means an archaic unit of analysis. Even though fortune cookies are associated with *the* Chinese culture, they were actually invented in California, and many of those living within China are not familiar with them. In this sense, the diasporic commodity of the fortune cookie is bounded to the field of its Western circulation, if not to an assumed cultural geopolitical boundedness to which we refer today as China. If one accepts the transnational call for disposing of the statist boundary as a unit undermining a true understanding of the world today, this should not mean that the very concept of boundedness should also become archaic. Boundedness can still be configured in different forms that are material and influenced by history and geopolitics.

Therefore, rather than eliminating the hyphen between "self" and "other," insiders and outsiders, it becomes problematized along new lines. What may contribute to a researcher's sense of insider-ness while abroad is not only the common background he/she shares with his/her research participants, nor the language they share, but the realization that he/she shares with her informants the experience of being abroad. Such realization brings new meanings and manifestations to the dynamic of insider-ness/outsider-ness into the picture. One of these novel dimensions may be associated with what Relph identifies as "emphatic insider-ness."[19] This takes place in the emotional connectedness a researcher establishes with a group or a place, not necessarily on only the basis of "real" commonalities, but also out of the workings of the researcher's field-related sense of identity and positioning. This explains why neither language nor culture may be sufficient means to assume an insider's positioning when conducting research in a native environment. In parallel, when conducting research abroad, the way in which the researcher claims linguistic and cultural oneness with his/her research participants may be contradicted by those very participants' different understanding of solidarity and insider-ness. Although the level of nativity of the researcher in relation to his/her native informants determines his oneness with them, his/her insider-ness is also dependent on the context of the research and its specifics. Thus, assuming insider-ness on the basis of shared language and culture as main indices of familiarity may not hold true in all instances. The privilege of the researcher—a person temporarily engaged with his/her participants' experiences and lives, who then returns to his/her academic world—is a mark of differentiation that language and culture may not be able to gloss over.

Assuming oneness with participants based on specific indices of nativity, mainly language and culture, may sometimes marginalize other important factors of differentiation in diaspora, such as power and privilege, such as the relationship of international researchers, on the one hand, and migratory research subjects, on the other, to this diasporic location of research. What may contribute to underestimating the differential role of location are the very mechanisms that guide present day ethnographic practices—as we mention above, reflexivity is one such mechanism. In identifying and defining reflexivity, Pillow's model presents four kinds of reflexivity: a) reflexivity as recognition of self; b) as recognition of others; c) as truth; and, d) as transcendence.[20] We limit our discussion to the first three types. This is because, reflexivity as transcendence is more a philosophical discussion concerning "freeing the self" from all the biases carried into the field. What connects the first two is the question of positionality. Positionality here means that the researcher tries to make clear the processes of writing and negotiating his/her different identities/biases within and without the field. It is also indicative of the researcher's attempt to overcome the hyphen, to come closer to his/her research subjects, and establish some solidarity with them. The latter quality usually emerges from a type of commitment on the part of the researcher, be it political, cultural, linguistic, gendered, etc., to articulate and communicate a sense of oneness with participants—or, solidarity as effect of similarity, in Pillow's words.[21]

Let us, then, try to identify the kind of similarity that may define the relationship of graduate international students with the respective diasporic communities in the United States whom they choose to research. Above all, there is the presumed (organic) similarity of belonging to the same ethnocultural or national group. It is the desire to "affirm oneness"[22] that may orient native investigations of diaspora within that diaspora. A South Korean researcher does not need to remind his/her South Korean informants living in the United States of her ethnocultural identity, for it is implied for both her and her participants. Thus the researchers need to invoke the positionality of the "I," the need to confess one's self, becomes less demanding, specifically because the organic is still one of the contributing factors, rather than the overdetermining factor, or the thing that has been entirely disavowed. By contrast, a White, middle-class female researcher investigating women factory workers in her own U.S. community may use reflexivity to confess her socioeconomic privilege (outsider-ness), but she may also resort to her gendered solidarity with those women (insider-ness) to suggest sameness. Oneness here has to be confessed and is not straightforwardly assumed due to one degree or another of ethnocultural similarity. The following testimony demonstrates how invoking, i.e., confessing, oneness is not necessary when this oneness is implied and presumed:

> I am a Kenyan who had, at the time of this field work, lived and studied in the Midwest for almost nine years. Once my respondents knew who I was, they felt a connection and trusted me. They felt that I was one of them and this gave me credibility and enabled me to gain access into their world and space. This insider position provided some advantages: first and most important, my respondents understood that we had some shared experiences and therefore they trusted me and felt comfortable with my intentions (Njeru).[23]

Here, "trust" and "connection" seem to flow naturally from the presumed oneness that the label "Kenyan" brings into the picture. As an implied organic commonality, Kenyan identity appears to be sufficient for this particular researcher to self-identify as an insider. But what about the location of this presumed oneness? It is not within a Kenyan context that this researcher reflects on what made his informants trust him. It is, instead, a diasporic location for the participants, and, as one of those international students who are expected to return home after completing their studies in the United States, the transient location for the researcher. These two contexts mark the major difference between two temporalities of space: whereas for the researcher the location may still be defined as There, it is a more ambivalent identification for the participants. Location, in this sense, is not another index of similarity as some researchers may assume. Postmodernist influences on academic ethnographic training may have contributed to this de-focusing of the materiality of location,[24] when the physical boundedness of location as present outside the text becomes easier to displace for the sake of introducing a discursive reconfiguration of site.

The third type from Pillow's model is reflexivity as truth, a dimension that concerns the notion of voice. For a reflexive practice to be able to reflect the reality of the examined community, it has to develop an attempt at true voicing, meaning that the voice of the author should not be the only one that populates the ethnographic text. Instead, the multiple voices of the participants should be incorporated as well. At the same time, in order for such incorporation to be truly reflective of participants' voices, it has to allow the participants' own words and interpretations to emerge in the text, with as little authorial intervention (editing, interpretation) as possible. This simply means that the researcher, when writing ethnography, tries to communicate his/her participants' own interpretations and understandings of the researched phenomena, rather than using his/her narrative to interpret their interpretations. In other words, the researcher will not impose the epistemological maps in his/her mind unto the phenomena under scrutiny. If we understand authorial editing as a form of translation, we have to remember that it can be one of two kinds as far as ethnography is concerned: translation as bimodal, where one meaning is transposed from one language into another; and translation as unimodal within one and the same language. If conducting research abroad involves some degree of the former, native researchers commonly use the same linguistic medium as their native informants of diaspora, i.e., where the first language within diasporic communities continues to be spoken and written. Here, speaking the same language may be taken as a marker of similarity, and this may have some impact on how researchers identify their ability to interpret what their informants tell them with as little unimodal translation as possible, the presumption of oneness thus becoming an act of disavowal of editing and translation. As Tatar expresses it, "[s]haring the same cultural background with my participants, I could easily relate to their ideas and interpretations."[25]

CONCLUSION

Instead of examining what "going abroad" may mean when one chooses to conduct ethnographic research, we have focused on those graduate students who engage in what can be seen as a counter-movement: international students at U.S. universities who remain in the United States in order to research their own diasporic folks at sites that may, as orthonyms of an original, still signify one native condition or another. Little Tokyo, Little Russia, Chinatown, and Koreatown may bear some marks of oneness in the eye of the researcher, but the locational realities of their being entities *grounded/bounded* in Los Angeles, San Antonio, San Francisco, or Toronto should not become invisible due to the collapsing of the boundary between practice and discourse. Such collapsing is often supplemented by reflexive practices that prioritize specific attributes of oneness, while de-focusing marks of differentiation, primarily location as configured differently for the international researcher, on the one hand, and his/her research participants, on the other. If reflexivity reconfigures the notion of location as less physical/material than discursive/textual, the assumption of unbounded similarity displaces location for the sake of projecting space that is not interrupted by the questions of geopolitics and history. Thus, such a counter-movement presents transient researchers with new complexities that go beyond the straightforward assumptions of similarity and insider-ness, challenging some of their conceptions about locational (bounded) materiality as having become but an archaic formulation in an age of global transformations/mobilizations.

NOTES

1   U.S. Immigration and Customs Enforcement (ICE), "International Students SEVIS by the Numbers," *ICE Web* 2006, http://www.ice.gov/sevis/numbers/student/ (accessed March 5, 2007).
2   Richard Rorty, "Solidarity or Objectivity?" in *Post-Analytic Philosophy*, ed. John Rajchman and Cornel West (New York: Columbia University Press, 1985), 3–19.
3   Michelle Fine, "Working the Hyphens: Reinventing Self and Other in Qualitative Research," in *Handbook of Qualitative Research*, ed. Norman K. Denzin and Yvonna S. Lincoln (Thousand Oaks, Calif.: Sage Publications, 1994), 70–82.
4   Clifford Geertz, *Works and Lives: The Anthropologist as Author* (Stanford, CA: Stanford University Press,1988), 150–151.
5   Avner Segall, "Critical Ethnography and the Invocation of Voice: From the Field/in the Field—Single Exposure, Double Standard?" *Qualitative Studies in Education* 14, no. 4 (July 2001): 579–592.
6   Fine, "Working the Hyphens," 70–82.
7   Dave Burnapp, "Trajectories of Adjustment of International Students: U-curve, Learning Curve, or Third Space?" *Intercultural Education* 17, no. 1 (March 2006): 81–93.
8   Burnapp, "Trajectories of Adjustment," 83.
9   Geertz, *Works and Lives,* 143–144.
10 Segall, "Critical Ethnography and the Invocation of Voice," 583–584.
11 Segall, "Critical Ethnography and the Invocation of Voice," 583.
12 Kyoko Mitsuhashi, "Gender Consciousness among Japanese Students who are Studying at American Universities" (PhD diss., University of California, Los Angeles, 2004), 66.
13 Yu-Chi Sun, "Three Chinese Immigrant Daughters: Their Perceptions of Schooling, Family, and Identity" (PhD diss., Pennsylvania State University, 2004), 19.

14   Homi Bhabha, *The Location of Culture* (New York: Routledge, 1994), 315–353.

15   Sanjeev Khagram and Peggy Levitt. "Towards a Field of Transnational Studies and a Sociological Transnationalism Research Program." *Harvard University, The Hauser Center for Nonprofit Organizations Working Paper No. 24* 2004, http://papers.ssrn.com/sol3/papers.cfm?abstract_id=556993 (accessed October 10, 2007).

16   Roger D. Waldinger, "Between 'here' and 'there:' Immigrant Cross-Border Activities and Loyalties," *International Migration Review* 42, no.1 (March 2008): 3–29.

17   Waldinger, "Between 'here' and 'there,'" 4.

18   Khagram and Levitt. "Towards a Field of Transnational Studies."

19   Burnapp, "Trajectories of Adjustment," 84.

20   Wanda Pillow, "Confession, Catharsis, or Cure? Rethinking the Uses of Reflexivity as Methodological Power in Qualitative Research," *Qualitative Studies in Education* 16, no. 2 (March 2003): 175–196.

21   Pillow, "Confession, Catharsis, or Cure?" 182.

22   Daphne Patai, "U.S. Academics and Third World Women: Is Ethical Research Possible?" in *Women's Words: The Feminist Practice of Oral History*, ed. Sherna Berger Gluck and Daphne Patai (New York: Routledge, 1991), 144.

23   Grace Muthoni Njeru, "The Experiences of Kenyan students in two Midwest U.S. States: Benefits, Challenges & Coping Strategies" (PhD diss., University of Missouri, Columbia, 2006), 51.

24   Segall, "Critical Ethnography and the Invocation of Voice," 579.

25   Sibel Tatar, "Turkish Graduate Students' Perceptions of Participating in U.S. Classrooms" (PhD diss., Indiana University, 2003), 62.

CHAPTER TWELVE

Back from the Field: Positionality, Methodology, and Practice

By Lise-Hélène Smith and Anjana Narayan

The lived experience of gathering and sharing knowledge in cultures unlike our own simply remains too multi-faceted and unpredictable to fit any fabricated category. In this light, this book only claims to provide insights into what conducting research away from one's home may be like, and to raise some of the concerns that have transpired in recent years during the process of data collection. While various profiles of researchers emerge from the chapters included in this collection, contributing authors have in common their foresight, determination, and courage, all of which are welcome, if not necessary, allies to the pursuit of research beyond borders. It is our hope that their stories both instructed and inspired you to approach global research with even more care, more consideration, and more dedication. We must never forget that research is contextual by nature and that it is our responsibility to be conscious of its processes and methods. In this chapter, we offer a synthesis of the practical and methodological challenges that many chapters have discussed. By building upon some of them, we hope to help future researchers navigate the complex yet exhilarating world of research beyond borders.

BEYOND THE INSIDER-OUTSIDER MODEL

While there has been much debate about the insider/outsider dilemma in the domestic context, globalization has extended the research process to the non-Western world which hosts some of the poorest and most exploited groups. When collecting data, the researcher's relationship to the researched is inevitably unequal and unbalanced.[1] Because researchers occupy privileged positions while research participants find themselves often occupying much more vulnerable ones, researchers have to be very aware of not only socio-economic disparities, but also of differing standards of living, lifestyles, and cultural perspectives.[2]

This asymmetrical power relationship raises essential methodological questions. The research process, for example, cannot be separated from questions of identity or identification that revolve around ethnicity, religion, class, or gender to name a few factors that affect data collection and its results. Difference between

195

the researcher and his or her research participants can lead to either appreciation or opposition, which can both alter the accuracy of the data collected. When conducting qualitative research, one way to prevent such inaccuracies in the data collection is to minimize the disparity between the researcher and the researched. This is often referred to as "ethnic" or "cultural matching," which relies on the assumption that common ground between the researcher and the researched might help establish a good rapport, facilitate interaction, and lead to fruitful conversations.[3] It can also minimize marginalization, create a rapport free of tensions and contribute to the legitimacy of the research project in the eyes of the participants.

Historically, scholars conducting cross-cultural research have been and are still encouraged to practice ethnic or cultural matching. On the one hand, if researchers are readily accepted, they may be able to understand cultural nuances and capture subtleties more easily, thus building trust and encouraging participation. As Dwyder and Buckle emphasize, "The benefit to being a member of the group one is studying is acceptance. One's membership automatically provides a level of trust and openness in your participants that would likely not have been present otherwise."[4] Hence, ethnic matching might be conducive to more equal relations, allow for the collection of more sensitive information, or result in the collaboration of a larger number of participants because of easier access. On the other hand, it can also enhance other differences that might have been otherwise disregarded by the research participants.[5] For example, participants may hone in on the researchers' differing age, upbringing or status if they claim ethnic matching and reject them on those grounds more easily than if they were assumed to be outsiders from the start. Although claiming to see through the same lens as one's research participants can reduce distance and lead to increased acceptance, it can also mask significant differences.[6] Assuming a shared heritage or background can result in damaging misunderstandings or in the participants' omission of critical information.[7]

With insider membership, a commitment to the participant community combined with careful bracketing, disciplined self-reflexivity, and detailed analysis to uncover one's biases as well as those of the participants can, however, help reduce the risk of inaccuracy.[8] To have an impact on methodologies and results, however, reflection on self, process, representation and power differentials needs to occur throughout the research process rather than simply as a final introspective step.[9] This type of self-critical monitoring is only possible if one adopts the same attitude as the researcher who does not benefit from an insider status. Whether conducting qualitative or quantitative research, oftentimes the outsider researcher must remain particularly "open, honest, deeply interested in the experience of one's research participants, and committed to accurately and adequately representing their experience."[10] Hence prudence, honesty, respect and good will remain necessary to the successful undertaking of cross-cultural research, whatever the status of the researcher.

If the researcher and participants do not share the same background or culture, building trust becomes essential to the successful collection of data, if only to secure access to archives, for example. This is even more difficult if the researcher can be associated with a group that has historically oppressed or colonized the participants. In unequal power relations, historically or otherwise, there is always the risk of imposing dominant ideology or truths onto participating communities, especially during qualitative research; this risk cannot be ignored.[11] Awareness of one's positionality as well as awareness of the multiplicity of experiences, meanings, and interpretations is crucial for the outside researcher to start understanding the lives of research participants.[12] Working across difference thus requires that one neither marginalizes nor appropriates the experiences of research participants by paying attention to variations in their individual experiences.[13] Working through difference may also entail not only the acknowledgement but also the accommodation of difference so as to find a comfortable common ground.[14]

For outsider researchers conducting qualitative research, data collection often depends on the establishment of a good rapport with the local community to gain legitimacy. This can be achieved, for example, by taking part in the community's daily activities, by carefully abiding by the local customs, or by creating an advisory committee consisting of community members.[15] Showing genuine interest in the community and adopting a non-authoritarian stance can help bridge differences and encourage active collaboration.[16] To prevent exploitative practices, outsider researchers should be careful to explain their research intentions and objectives, to establish and justify their interest in the study questions, and to commit to providing feedback to the community.[17] As truthfulness and transparency demonstrate respect that, in turn, commonly yields trust, respecting the participant community is essential to gaining the trust of its members so that one may become perceived as an "acceptable outsider doing "useful" research."[18] Oftentimes, obtaining access requires that the researcher be cognizant of interviewees' needs.[19] Formulating interview questions to empower one's study participants can also help shift unequal power relations "from a position of vulnerability to one of knowledge or strength."[20] Likewise, creating a safe space conducive to sharing and joining over commonalities constitutes an important aspect of cross-cultural qualitative research.[21] Yet the argument also has been made that a more distant outsider perspective that relies less on building trust may lead to more objective results.[22] As a researcher with outsider status puts it, being "as much an outsider as you can get" may also mean that one holds "no preconceptions, no vested interests."[23] As such, the objectivity, reflexibility, and/or authenticity of a research project is less likely to be questioned when the researcher is an outsider rather than an insider to the study participants.[24]

Although the focus has shifted from obtaining objective or authentic data to more subjective and sensitive interpretations of data, accuracy of results still remains very much a concern for both insider and outsider researchers.[25] Yet to claim insider or outsider status can actually mask the shifting nature of one's positionality, thus distorting the data gathered. As researchers, we may never be completely inside or outside our research communities, with which we constantly renegotiate our relationships.[26] As such, the researcher's status is never fixed, but fluctuates with time, moving to and from insider and outsider status with the evolution of the research project. What is more, these positionalities may not be mutually exclusive but rather inform each other. As a researcher may be both an insider and an outsider to a given community, to claim insider or outsider status may be to homogenize the complexity of identity formation, of identification, and/or of socio-cultural perception. Just as culture is ever shifting, so is cultural identity. As Stuart Hall puts it, cultural identities are "a matter of 'becoming' as well as of 'being' . . . Far from being eternally fixed in some essentialised past, they are subject to the continuous 'play' of history, culture and power."[27] The insider/outsider model may simply be too monolithic or dichotomous to acknowledge the complexity of cultural exchanges that can take place in spite of, or perhaps because of, disparities that exist between the researcher and the researched.

As a result, it may be fair to say that most researchers occupy "the space between" or "third space" to use Dwyder and Buckle's terminology, a space that affords deep knowledge of the experience one studies even if one does not share such experience (although one may or may not share the participants' heritage).[28] For postcolonial theorist Homi Bhabha, the "in-between" or "third space of enunciation" is the precondition for the articulation of cultural difference, which relies on cultural translation and negotiation "of elements that are *neither the One . . . nor the other . . . but something else besides* which contests the terms and territories of both."[29] The notion of "neither" "nor" "but something else" that constantly demands the cautious renegotiation of positionalities can perhaps best describe the researcher's status and assist future researchers in preparing for fieldwork overseas.

LINGUISTIC COMPETENCY AND CULTURAL FILTERS

This emphasis on truthful communication raises the obvious question of language proficiency, especially the researcher's linguistic training and competency. Interestingly, cross-cultural qualitative research is increasingly conducted by researchers who do not speak the language of their research participants. Yet knowledge of the participants' language does not suffice during the data collection process to create a basis for shared knowledge or understanding across cultures.[30] Too often, researchers are forced to hire local, bilingual individuals to act as interpreters, unless they can demonstrate appropriate language proficiency combined with an intimate knowledge of the local culture, or what Gabriela Pohl calls "communicative competence."[31] Both are necessary to reach conceptual equivalence in the target language. As Reiche and Harzing stress, such equivalency is crucial during the translation process to ensure the accuracy of the study results and avoid cultural misunderstandings.[32] Several types of equivalence must be achieved to produce meaningful translation, including semantic, idiomatic and experiential in addition to conceptual equivalence.[33]

In spite of the artificiality created by the intervention of an interpreter, it is difficult not to rely on language assistants even when one is conducting qualitative cross-cultural survey research that only requires the use of questionnaires to obtain data. Even if the researcher can establish whether a concept exists in another culture and if its connotations are similar in both cultures, it is difficult to assess the quality of a translated questionnaire. Available strategies all seem to come with noticeable shortcomings. Such strategies may include using back-translation, which entails translating questions back into the original language to check for accuracy of meaning; utilizing a bilingual method, which entails having a number of bilingual individuals fill out the same questionnaire and comparing results for inconsistencies; or finally relying on a committee procedure, which entails gathering a group of bilingual individuals to translate a questionnaire jointly, thus minimizing the risk of errors.[34] However, the accuracy of these strategies is often so contested that a researcher may be equally criticized for employing them or for not employing them.[35] What is more, these strategies are only useful if the respondents are monolingual and may actually fail if questionnaires are filled out by bilingual individuals who will likely approach each question with their own cultural assumptions, thus altering the study results.[36]

More often than not, however, the intervention of language assistants, whether as transcribers, translators or interpreters, is simply a necessity to the pursuit of qualitative overseas research. Paradoxically, as Steen Mangen notes, issues of language competencies are commonly downgraded in much cross-national research[37] even though language assistants are often inseparable from the research process itself. Language assistants' demeanor or attitude towards the study, the reliability of their translation and the accuracy with which they report the participants' words back to the researcher can all have tremendous impact on the results of the study.[38] Language assistants play a crucial role in the acquisition of data, especially as researchers rely on them to extract meaning, deduce or draw conclusion from conversations with their research participants. In short, these assistants often become critics in their own right who can easily (even if not intentionally) either hinder or facilitate data collection.[39] Yet the importance of these intermediaries both as linguistic and cultural bridges is often understated—that is, when their presence is even acknowledged in the final, printed results of a study. Of course, relying on interpreters increases the distance between the researcher and the respondents, which can be problematic when trying to capture linguistic or cultural nuances. On the other hand, a reliable interpreter can become a researcher's best ally by navigating with mastery a cultural matrix that is at best only familiar to the researcher.[40] Since language assistants can be vital to the process of knowledge formation, to cross-cultural interpretation and to overseas qualitative research generally, they should be acknowledged as such.

As Monique Hennink notes,[41] despite their significant contribution, language assistants are greatly undervalued members of the research team. Their efforts are not reflected (and often not acknowledged) in documented research reports, while their skills in interaction and communication are lost or ignored in the translated English version. Hennink argues that "cross-cultural research is therefore conducted with an unquestioning acceptance of the use of language assistants. A language assistant is seen as a neutral mouthpiece," which is a gross misinterpretation of the pivotal role they play in the research process.[42] Hennink suggests that language assistants need to be given greater visibility and due acknowledgement. This would considerably improve research in several areas: greater transparency, clarity, and accuracy at all phases of the data collection process, better control over the research project, and high-quality research outcomes.[43] Translators and interpreters must be provided with adequate training to complement their skills in communication, interaction, and interpretation with awareness about their role in the data filtering process, with due attention to the fine nuances of key terminology and cultural contexts, which are essential to avoid misinterpretation or misconception.[44] Such a strategy, Hennink argues, would mutually benefit language assistants and researchers: the former would have a better understanding of their role, responsibilities, and function in the community under study, while the researchers would have wider scope in selecting language assistants with adequate training and aptitude for particular research settings.

ACQUIRING RESEARCH SKILLS AND BUILDING NETWORKS

If, indeed, we as scholars are interested in understanding, supporting and, working for social change around the world, we need to avoid the convenient approach of fitting experiences into existing theoretical conceptualizations and instead focus on trying to explain experiences of diverse populations and further challenge theories. This effort extends to training the next generation of scholars as the learning process remains very much discipline-based on American campuses and comes with its own conventions and biases, in spite of increasing globalization and the blurring of national boundaries. It is a common belief that culturally-ingrained research biases can best be corrected through immersion in another cultural setting.[45] Engaging in research abroad requires students to exercise their critical skills while allowing them to acquaint themselves with academic inquiry.[46] Independent research abroad hence benefits students in more than one way: it provides students with the opportunity to apply and expand upon acquired knowledge; it complements and enriches theoretical knowledge with hands-on experience that broadens students' perspectives; and it empowers students by allowing them to both test and hone acquired skills. Simply put, as Mel Bolen expresses it, "undergraduate research abroad can demonstrate that the cultural context of learning enhances the disciplinary knowledge gained."[47] As such, overseas research encourages students to become more cognizant of assumptions that inform their academic work generally. Overall, engaging in independent research abroad allows students to take away new depths of insight to their majors and to gain a new sense of accomplishment or self-confidence in the process.[48]

Successful research abroad, however, requires a set of skills that students may not possess or may not have had to acquire on their home campus. Conducting research overseas requires navigating another cultural context and interacting outside of the familiar classroom setting with people who are neither one's peers nor one's instructors.[49] To set up their research project effectively, students will undoubtedly have to contact local individuals and organizations, become familiar with local customs, and develop a plan on how to secure access to the necessary information. As Larry Hubbell points out, establishing personal contacts from overseas can be quite challenging, in spite of the availability of the Internet, as individuals seldom respond to emails or phone calls from strangers unless one can claim to have been referred by a person they know.[50] Securing the name and support of at least one contact prior to one's departure can thus be instrumental to a research project and so can securing the names of other recommended contacts. Hence, a well-thought out research plan with achievable goals and appropriate, often lengthy, preparations are key to the success of fieldwork abroad.

Preparing to work in an international context means that students must learn to ask the right questions, seek assistance both academically and financially, and anticipate the skills they will need to conduct cross cultural research. Defining a research project often means asking faculty members for assistance, whether it is in shaping the project goals and their feasibility, in securing grants, or in establishing contacts in the host culture. Although seeking faculty support and involvement is essential to the success of a student's research project, there is no single model of supervision. Ideally, each student would be supported by a faculty member at their home institution while also benefiting from local contacts at their research site. Faculty can assist students not only with clarifying expectations and determining the level of oversight that the project will entail, but also with recruiting participants at the site or with establishing how authorship should be credited.[51] In addition, faculty members can guide students through the research preparations by asking appropriate questions to encourage students to examine the cultural context of their research and help them frame their project effectively. For example, asking students why and how they chose their research site, what they hope to learn from conducting research in the host culture they have chosen, how they will ensure that the project is culturally appropriate or that their research goals are plausible, how their project is relevant to the local people and how they plan on sharing results in a useful and efficient way, can help ensure the success of the students' undertaking.[52] Similarly, as Martin and Bolen suggest, faculty members can also help students realize which skills they have acquired through the experience by encouraging self-assessment and reflexibility throughout the process: "What did you do to get this information? Did you have someone specific in the culture that gave you good advice? How did you find this person? What steps did you take when you succeeded in doing a piece of your research? When you did not succeed how did you figure out what went wrong? What did you do to try again?"[53] In raising these questions or bringing these considerations to the forefront, faculty members can help students contextualize their project and ensure not only its cultural relevance but also its ethical basis. Faculty members can encourage students to draft a formal research proposal, thus compelling interested students to generate a plausible research question, to choose a method of data collection, to create research instruments if necessary, and to formulate a plan to analyze the collected data.[54] Ultimately, if framed appropriately, conducting research abroad can teach students to "transcend cultural differences in constructive ways and to adapt to differing cultural modes" which higher education strives to encourage.[55]

Enrolling in a Study Abroad Program can sometimes provide some local support to complement any faculty supervision on the home campus. Study Abroad Programs often facilitate or enable a student's research project by providing the student with an established infrastructure that provides room and board, with direct contacts and with easy access to the local culture. What is more, Streitwieser and Sobania argue that by "engaging local people, culture, and taking classes in local institutions in the host country, students gain the insight to begin extracting the essence of the host culture."[56] It can be easier or less intimidating to graft an independent research project to a Study Abroad Program than to find housing and make all living arrangements on one's own. In addition, some programs such as those proposed by the School of International Training (SIT) have a built-in research component through their Field Study Seminar which requires students to spend four to six weeks collecting data to complete an Independent Study Project.[57] Even when conducting research independently from a Study Abroad Program, students should not underestimate the invaluable resource that such programs represent, particularly to establish contacts in the host culture prior to traveling. For example, local professors who are teaching some of the study abroad courses in the host country can become powerful allies during the research process. Arranging to speak with students who have recently returned from studying in the host culture can also be extremely informative in preparing for a trip. Because former participants often agree to disclose their contact information to new or potential applicants, the usefulness of a Study Abroad program in the host culture selected should not be neglected, even when designing an independent research project.

THE POLITICS OF DATA COLLECTION AND KNOWLEDGE PRODUCTION OR DISSEMINATION

Several other challenges arise at the data collection stage and during both knowledge production and knowledge dissemination. During the process of data collection, the first challenge may well consist of aligning social science research projects with funding requirements and publishing guidelines. Funding sources are more likely to provide grants for research that demonstrates "scientific merit," and can be translated into "quantitative data." Consequently, social science researchers have developed a strong attraction to quantitative data, even when it may not be the most plausible methodology for the study.

As Bandana Purkayastha, et al. note,[58] quantitative research is often not feasible for social sciences research in developing countries. For instance, accurate and updated data on demographics, statistics, or census data may be impossible to obtain in regions with a weak public administrative infrastructure. Moreover, despite "scientific merit" criterion, there are certain areas of social science research where quantitative research is not conducive to unbiased, accurate, and complete findings, leaving qualitative research as the only viable choice. For example, as Purkayastha et al. demonstrate, quantitative research on gender in a country like India would result in heavily biased or incomplete results, because the data analysis would fail to capture women's voices, or even accurately convey their day-to-day lives in a gendered setting. What is more, a region like the Indian subcontinent presents a number of challenges—linguistic and geographical diversity, bewildering differences between urban and rural settings, vast differences in communication facilities and general infrastructure, numerous daily challenges in procuring labor resources—all of which require money, time, labor, and resources, and are not conducive to quantitative analysis.

Several types of social science inquiry require archival research, which alone can present numerous challenges. While most public information is now present online and easily accessible in the West, developing countries do not have either the technological infrastructure or resources to computerize their library systems. Researchers who are used to digital catalogs must painstakingly navigate through handwritten ones, which are often indecipherable due to technical jargon or lack of a clear system. When visiting brick-and-mortar libraries, researchers have to contend with bureaucratic red tape that often seems incomprehensible. Library administrators often require documents to prove scholastic qualifications or to allow access to certain archives. The researcher may face access restrictions that were never mentioned before, or bewildering demands such as providing a high school diploma instead of evidence of one's Masters or even Doctoral degree. Conducting fieldwork in non-Western countries can be physically, mentally and emotionally draining as well as time-consuming, often involving long hours of travel, poor transportation and communications infrastructure, and frustrating efforts to reach out to local entities without success, apart from language problems. When collecting data, researchers must have the cultural capabilities to work successfully under these circumstances.

Given the numerous—and often unexpected—hurdles, researchers should take the necessary precautions to minimize these contingencies. The most effective way is to prepare before leaving home, by using academic email lists to contact fellow researchers or academicians in the country of the study. Having such contacts also helps with developing a basic vocabulary for official rules, such as the local terms for "certificate" or "letter of introduction." Compiling a list of individual contacts from one's home institution and the country of research has proved to be a valuable strategy, as it gives the researcher some standing in the scholastic community. Making contact information easily visible on key documents also helps, as it increases credibility or legitimacy. Garnering the support of community stalwarts or collaborating with reputable organizations may not only prove worthwhile, but also strengthen the research project. Such persons or organizations have specialist knowledge about local culture, are trusted by the community, and can help the researcher design surveys and compile questionnaires that have greater relevance to the study. Data collection that coincides with community goals may also earn community support for the project. Friendly courtesy, good manners, and respect for people will always open doors that would otherwise have been firmly shut. Whatever the research methodology, when collecting data in developing countries, researchers should also pay close attention to possible differences in key research terminology. For instance, as Purkayastha et al. highlight, Americans tend to equate the terms "fieldwork" and "ethnography" while in some Asian countries different levels of participant observation, such as structured or semi-structured interviews, are associated with these terms, which may also include quantitative analysis through surveys.[59]

At the knowledge production and dissemination stage, one core issue is that there is no market demand for non-English scholarship in the West. As Bandana Purkayastha and Mangala Subramaniam[60] note, the knowledge produced by non-English scholarship is most often treated as addressing specific cases that describe groups in situated contexts, rather than as sources of theory or sources of policy-making. Knowledge produced and disseminated in languages other than English is undervalued and deemed less relevant. For example, Bandana Purkayastha and Mangala Subramaniam highlight that the large and valuable body of research in local languages on women's experiences in India and Africa is never used in knowledge production in the West, nor is non-English scholarship produced by outsiders within Europe and America. This division represents a serious short-coming of meritorious scholarship and creates insurmountable barriers to publishing in peer-reviewed journals.

Another major challenge at the knowledge production and dissemination stage is the lingering distrust of Western researchers in many non-Western countries whose inhabitants often associate research with exploitation. As Richa Nagar (2002)[61] points out, this distrust stems from the fact that individuals in non-Western cultures believe previous research conducted in local settings to have not only failed to contribute anything of value to their community, but also misrepresented their culture. According to Nagar, there are several effective ways to address this challenge. First, she calls for a more widespread dissemination of knowledge. In other words, instead of confining knowledge production and dissemination to academic groups (i.e., academic publications), one should make it accessible to a wider audience that includes the participants, the community, and the region where the research was conducted (i.e., non-academic documentation, including reports, newspaper articles in local languages, and other popular communication media). Wider knowledge dissemination can be used by target audiences in multiple locations and at multiple levels, replacing existing knowledge hierarchies with shared knowledge. Second, she argues that this strategy needs institutional support to be effective enough to yield positive benefits. Academic institutions have to recognize and actively support "non-academic" analyses as research products as well as acknowledge the researcher's skill and commitment in terms of both time and effort, instead of dismissing them as supplementary activities. Finally, Nagar emphasizes that academics need to ensure institutional recognition of the fact that knowledge is never the product of any one person, and therefore cannot be owned by a single entity. Such recognition would replace the concept of sole ownership with a policy that acknowledges and promotes collaborative effort with multiple participants—social activists, biographers, research assistants.

INSTITUTIONAL REVIEW BOARDS

Whenever a research project relies on the contribution of individuals, federal regulation requires that the project be approved by an Institutional Review Board. An institutional review board (IRB) is a committee that is officially appointed to supervise all biomedical and behavioral research that includes human subjects. Its primary objective is to protect the human rights and welfare of all research subjects involved. The IRB committee reviews every protocol to ensure that the research project and methodology are valid and that the risks to the participants are minimal or reasonable. A significant component of the protocol submitted to the IRB includes a document known as the "informed consent" form, which is intended to provide participants with sufficient information to make an educated decision about whether to participate in the study. Informed consent is one of the primary ethical requirements of all research requiring interaction with human subjects.

In the last decade, gaining informed consent from individuals whose lives and customs are being researched has become a topic of significant controversy when it comes to ethical research practices, especially in the context of cross-cultural and international research. In his award-winning essay on informed consent,[62] Ben Campbell identifies three necessary components to obtain valid informed consent from either the participant or his or her surrogate: first, participants (or surrogates) must be fully informed about the research goal and methods, as well as the possible risks/rewards and alternatives; second, they must demonstrate an understanding of such disclosure particularly in terms of how it affects their particular situation; and third, they must decide to participate freely, without any undue persuasion, pressure, or coercion. Based on a comprehensive literature review conducted by Wiles et al.,[63] obtaining informed consent meaningfully can present quite a challenge. According to these authors, the issues that arise during the process of securing informal consent in cross-cultural settings go significantly beyond merely providing due disclosure to help participants make informed decisions. Instead, they include complex and conflicting factors, including complying with relevant laws and regulations; achieving a subtle balance between competing interests (the research objectives versus the participants' best interests and those of the gatekeepers); and carefully framing the definition and connotation of key terms such as "voluntary," "consent," and "competence" to avoid possible misinterpretations.

Several scholars have highlighted researchers' own conflicting interests when negotiating this delicate balance and providing participants with information on their research plans and goals. On the one hand, researchers clearly need to provide sufficient information to enable participants to make informed decisions about participation. On the other hand, they also want to avoid providing information that might be misinterpreted and deter individuals from participating, since the study can only take place if enough individuals are successfully recruited. This delicate, but common balancing act can take on insurmountable proportions when linguistic, cultural, and ethical differences, to name just a few, must also be taken into consideration.

While some literature addresses the challenges of information provision to "hard to reach" or socially excluded groups such as children, the elderly, or individuals with mental health problems, little has been written about the specific set of challenges that researchers encounter in an international context. Informed consent as is currently implemented places considerable importance on the written document and consent documents can be too overwhelming and intimidating to potential participants.[64] According to Liamputtong,[65] several research subjects view any form of formal documentation as threatening in light their vulnerable status (such is commonly the case for certain ethnic groups and refugees), or as violating their anonymity as research participants. Many resent it as unnecessary red tape. Additionally, issues of illiteracy have to be considered since several ethnic participants are illiterate in their native language and may fail to grasp the implications of informed consent. Because of these difficulties, modifying the forms even slightly may help researchers handle disclosure of information more successfully in cross-cultural contexts. Some of these modifications could include limiting the informed consent form to one page (which many IRBS allow), writing the form in clear, simple, and concise language using short sentences, or omitting altogether the injury and liability clauses that can be baffling or insulting to potential participants. Other strategies to consider, for example when confronted with illiterate participants, could include reading the form out loud to secure verbal rather than written consent with the help of a recording device. Ultimately, ensuring that potential participants understand the information presented is the critical component of the informed consent process.

Because of the importance of communication, linguistic competency presents an additional challenge in the case of the IRB-mandated translation forms for non-native English speakers, as mentioned earlier. As Nancy Kass[66] points out, translation is an inexact science, and key terminology—such as "research," "confidential" or "validity"—may not have a close enough counterpart in a local language, rendering these terms virtually meaningless to participants. Researchers have to consider how these terms can best be explained, how linguistic limitations may impact participants' understanding of these concepts (and to what extent), and the overall effect of linguistic inaccuracies on the validity of the research study. Scholars such as Ben Campbell even raise doubts about whether informed consent can be considered valid when the research participants have limited access to education and little or no understanding of the key terminology. Yet, according to Campbell, while differences in language and culture can severely impede a proper understanding of the research constituents, there is no evidence that understanding differs between participants in Western and non-Western regions. Campbell suggests that the researcher should recognize the potential risk of an improper understanding of key concepts in either setting, rather than focus on select participants' inability to understand discipline-specific terminology. Toward this end, he recommends adapting proven models to local cultures and settings, which, admissibly, can present a difficult challenge. As an example, Campbell refers to a two-year study in Tibet by Adams et al.[67] on informed consent in a cross-cultural setting. Its findings demonstrate that universally accepted paradigms of understanding need to be resized and adapted to local cultural settings, with an emphasis on intent instead of specific content, so as to be equally understood in both contexts across multiple disciplines. In cross-cultural settings, customizing the standard methods to obtain informed consent is an effective strategy to improve cultural understanding and develop more effective research techniques.[68] Thus, considering from whose perspective terms such as "understanding" or "comprehension" are defined merits our attention and need to be addressed more effectively in international contexts.

The issue of informed consent is intricately related to competence in making the voluntary decision or choice to participate, especially in the context of participants regarded as "vulnerable." Such participants are sometimes not considered competent enough to give informed consent at the initiation of the research project or to give continued informed consent over its duration.[69] [70] This demographic typically includes children and the young, the mentally incapacitated, and those with learning disabilities, but it should be extended in scope to include individuals who have experienced traumatic situations and those who live in developing regions (particularly countries that have suffered the ravages of territorial, racial or political upheaval, resulting in mass migration), as well as indigent populations (a large proportion of which is afflicted with AIDS/HIV), and displaced individuals. Although the latter groups merit rigorous ethical oversight, the poorly accessible, unstable, or volatile regions they inhabit make this a daunting task.

Research focusing on these particular groups have given rise to the contentious debate on whether a research should adopt the "individual model" or the "community model" when seeking informed consent.[71] To ensure that the individual rights of vulnerable groups are protected, ethics committees require that researchers follow certain protocols, such as approaching such participants with sensitivity, obtaining valid and voluntary informed consent, providing justifiable reasons for the group's inclusion, and describing the process that was followed to obtain consent. When following the individual model, proxy consent from a parent or relative may be used in the case of individuals with impaired capacity or limited competence. This model addresses the socio-cultural limitations of the participants by customizing the consent form to a culture-specific setting, often by involving reputable and trusted community stalwarts. Some scholars, however, challenge the very labels of "vulnerable" and "incompetent" (as well as proxy rights), viewing them as violations of individual rights in two primary aspects: they worry that over-zealous gatekeepers may deprive individuals from participating in research while less competent gatekeepers may fail to allow individuals to choose to participate in research with full awareness of the alternatives.[72] [73] In addition, the question of "competency" itself has generated considerable debate. A number of scholars argue that it is an essentially modern Western concept that does not apply to societies grounded in "groupness" or communities that have a different cultural and social hierarchy (such as participants requiring consent from the titular head of the household or a community leader). In such cases, group and community rights have to be safeguarded above individual rights, according to a community model. Such a model indeed de-stigmatizes incompetency and upholds the culture-specific hierarchical integrity of communal and family structures.

Overall, scholars have often questioned the applicability of the IRB procedures and guidelines in a cross-cultural setting where Western cultural values are virtually alien or inappropriate. The thrust of the argument is that IRB principles are a reflection and product of Western thought that has little to no applicability in a broader context. Yet, it is clear to all that research participants should be protected, whether physically, emotionally, or legally. While several countries have different sets of standards for human research subject, others have simply no procedural standards in place.[74] Consequently, researchers are increasingly stressing the need for more dialogue and debate on constraints across institutional and geographical lines as well as the need to move beyond codified and regulated model of ethics to alternative approaches to ethical and just research.[75]

This book was intended to serve as a resourceful body of knowledge that would successfully promote theoretical, empirical, and methodological cross-fertilization between different academic disciplines and practices while inspiring young scholars in their novel, but just research efforts overseas. In the process of becoming bona fide global citizens, scholars conducting research abroad have been successful at blurring the geopolitical boundaries that have, more often than not, caused divisions and tensions in the past. This collection stresses the importance of expecting the unexpected and the need to challenge both ideologies and methodologies while remaining mindful of individuals and their communities. We hope that the wisdoms of contributing authors will help young scholars generate new discourses as well as new ways of gathering and sharing knowledge in all its cultural implications.

NOTES

1 Theodoros Iosifides, "Qualitative Migration Research: Some New Reflections Six Years Later," *The Qualitative Report* 8, no. 3 (September 2003): 442.
2 S.R. Benatar, "Reflections and Recommendations on Research Ethics in Developing Countries," *Social Science and Medicine* 54 (2001): 1131–1141.
3 Chih Soong Sin, "Ethnic Matching in Qualitative Research: Reversing the Gaze on 'White Others' and 'White' as 'Other,'" *Qualitative Research* 7, no. 4 (2007): 477–499.
4 Sonya Corbin Dwyder and Jennifer L. Buckle, "The Space Between: On Being an Insider-Outsider in Qualitative Research," *International Journal of Qualitative Methods* 8, no1 (2009): 58.
5 Yasemin Gunaratnma, *Researching "Race" and Ethnicity: Methods, Knowledge and Power* (London: Sage Publications, 2003).
6 Tanya Bakhru, "Negotiating and Navigating the Rough Terrain of Transnational Feminist Research," *Journal of International Women's Studies* 10, no. 2 (November 2008): 207.
7 Dwyder and Buckle, "The Space Between," 58.
8 Dwyder and Buckle, "The Space Between," 58.
9 Farhana Sultana, "Reflexivity, Positionality and Participatory Ethics: Negotiating Fieldwork Dilemmas in International Research," *ACME* 6, no. 3 (2007): 376.
10 Dwyder and Buckle, "The Space Between," 59.

11 Iosifides, "Qualitative Migration Research," 442.

12 Iosifides, "Qualitative Migration Research," 442.

13 Tanya Bakhru, "Negotiating and Navigating," 208.

14 Irene Donohoue Clyne, "Finding Common Ground: Cross-Cultural Research in the Muslim Community," University of Melbourne at http://www.aare.edu. au/01pap/don01569.htm.

15 Pranee Liamputtong, "Doing Research in a Cross-Cultural Context: Methodological and Ethical Challenges" Doing Cross-Cultural Research, ed. Pranee Liamputtong, 34 (Springer Netherlands, 2008): 3–20.

16 Roberta G. Sands, Joretha N. Bourjolly, and Dorit Roer-Strier, "Crossing Cultural Barriers in Research Interviewing," Qualitative Social Work 6, no. 3 (September 2007): 367.

17 Clyne, "Finding Common Ground" at http://www.aare.edu.au/01pap/ don01569.htm

18 Sultana, "Reflexivity," 379.

19 Larry D. Hubell, "False Starts, Suspicious Interviewees, and Nearly Impossible Tasks: Some Reflections on the Difficulties of Conducting Research Abroad," The Qualitative Report 8, no. 2 (June 2003): 200.

20 Sands, "Crossing Cultural Barriers," 367.

21 Sands, "Crossing Cultural Barriers," 367–368.

22 Jan Ritchie, Anthony B. Zwi, Ilse Blignault, Anne Bunde-Birouste, Derrick Silove, "Insider-Outsider Positions in Health-Development Research: Reflections For Practice," Development in Practice 19, no. 1 (February 2009): 110.

23 Jan Ritchie, "Insider-Outsider Positions," 108.

24 Dwyder and Buckle, "The Space Between," 57.

25 Dwyder and Buckle, "The Space Between," 58.

26 Bakhru, "Negotiating," 209.

27 Stuart Hall, "Cultural Identity and Diaspora," Colonial Discourse and Post-Colonial Theory: A Reader, eds. Patrick William and Laura Chrisman (New York: Columbia University Press, 1994), 394.

28 Dwyder and Buckle, "The Space Between," 61.

29 Homi Bhabha, Location of Culture (London: Routledge, 1994), 13.

30 Monir Tayeb, "Conducting Research Across Cultures: Overcoming Drawback and Obstacles," International Journal of Cross-Cultural Management 1, no. 1 (2001): 10.

31 Gabriela Pohl, "Cross-Cultural Pragmatic Failure and Implications for Language Teaching," SLLT 4 (2004) at http://www.usq.edu.au/users/sonjb/sllt/4/ Pohl04.html

32 B. Sebastian Reiche and Anne-Wil Harzing, "Key Issues in International Survey Research" (June 26, 2007) at http://www.harzing.com/intresearch_keyissues.htm

33 Leonardo Oliveira Reis, "Translating Questionnaires for Use in Cross-Cultural Research: Are We doing the Right Thing?" Actas Urológicas Espanolas 33, no. 1 (2009): 5–7.

34 Reiche and Harzing, "Key Issues" at http://www.harzing.com/intresearch_keyissues.htm

35 Janet Harkness, "In the Pursuit of Quality: Issues for Cross-National Survey Research," *Cross-National Research Methodology and Practice*, eds. Hantrais and Mangen (London and New York: Routledge, 2007), 44–45.

36 Reis, "Translating Questionnaires."

37 Steen Mangen, "Qualitative Research Methods in Cross-national settings," *Cross-National Research Methodology and Practice*, eds. Hantrais and Mangen. (London and New York: Routledge, 2007), 21.

38 Monique M. Hennink, "Language and Communication in Cross-Cultural Qualitative Research," *Doing Cross-Cultural Research: Ethical and Methodological Perspectives*, ed. Pranee Liamputtong, Social Indicators Research Series 34 (Netherlands: Springer, 2008), 21–33.

39 Hennink, "Language," 25.

40 Molly Andrews, "Against Good Advice: Reflections on conducting research in a country where you don't speak the language," *Oral History Review* 22, no. 2 (1995): 75–86.

41 Monique M. Hennink, "Language and Communication in Cross-Cultural Qualitative Research," in *Doing Cross-Cultural Research: Ethical and Methodological Perspectives*, ed. Pranee Liamputtong, Social Indicators Research Series 34 (Netherlands: Springer, 2008), 21–33.

42 Hennink, "Language," 26.

43 Hennink, "Language," 30.

44 Hennink, "Language," 29.

45 Mel Bolen and Pat Martin, "Undergraduate Research Abroad: Challenges and Rewards - Why Encourage Research Abroad?" *Frontiers: The Interdisciplinary Journal of Study Abroad* XII (November 2005): xi.

46 Berhnard Streitwieser and Neal Sobania, "Overseeing Study Abroad Research: Challenges, Responsibilities and the Institutional Review Board," *Frontiers: The Interdisciplinary Journal of Study Abroad* XVI (Spring 2008): 6.

47 Bolen and Martin, "Undergraduate Research Abroad," xii.

48 Ray Segebrecht, "Undergraduate Research Aboard" (September 2009) at http://www.kansan.com/news/2009/sep/11/undergraduates_research_abroad/

49 Bolen and Martin, "Undergraduate Research Abroad," xi.

50 Hubell, "False Starts," 200.

51 E. Plante, "International Research Collaborations: Promoting International Student Research," *The ASHA Leader* 12 (November 2007): 15–17.

52 Bolen and Martin, "Undergraduate Research Abroad," xii.

53 Bolen and Martin, "Undergraduate Research Abroad," xii.

54 Streitwieser and Sobania, "Overseeing Study Abroad Research," 9.

55 Bolen and Martin, "Undergraduate Research Abroad," xii.

56 Streitwieser and Sobania, "Overseeing Study Abroad Research," 5–6.

57 Streitwieser and Sobania, "Overseeing Study Abroad Research," 6.

58 Bandana Purkayastha, et al., "The Study of Gender in India: A Partial Review," *Gender & Society* 4 (2003): 17.

59 Purkayastha, et al. "Gender in India," 508

60 Bandana Purkayastha and Mangala Subramaniam, *The Power of Women's Informal Networks: Lessons in Social Change from South Asia and West Africa* (Lamham, Maryland, Lexington, 2004), 1–9.

61 Richa Nagar, "Footloose Researchers, "Traveling" Theories, and the Politics of Transnational Feminist Praxis," *Gender, Place, and Culture,* 9 no. 2 (2002): 179–186.

62 Campbell, Ben. "Informed Consent in Developing Countries: Myth or Reality?" (2009) at http://www.dartmouth.edu/~ethics/docs/Campbell_informed-consent.pdf, 2.

63 Rose Wiles, Sue Heath, Graham Crow, and Vikki Charles, "Informed Consent in Social Research: A Literature Review," *Sociological Research Online* 12, no. 2 (March 30, 2007) at http://www.socresonline.org.uk/12/2/wiles.html

64 Susan Y. Wood, Barbara A. Friedland, C. Elizabeth McGrory, "Informed Consent: From Good Intentions to Sound Practices: A report of a Seminar 24–25 May 2001" (Population Council New York, NY, 2002) at http://www.popcouncil.org/pdfs/ebert/informedconsent.pdf

65 Pranee Liamputtong, "Doing Research in a Cross-Cultural Context: Methodological and Ethical Challenges," in *Doing Cross-Cultural Research* ed. Pranee Liamputtong, 34 (Netherlands: Springer, 2008), 3–20

66 Nancy E. Kass, "Human Rights, Politics, and Reviews of Research Ethics," Johns Hopkins Bloomberg School of Public Health, at www.myoops.org/twocw/jhsph/courses/ . . . /PDFs/InformedConsent.pdf.

67 Vincanne Adams, et al, "Informed Consent in Cross-Cultural Perspective: Clinical Research in the Tibetan Autonomous Region," *PRC, Cult Med Psychiatry* 31 (2007): 445–472.

68 Mary C. Beach, Somnath Sana, and Lisa A. Cooper, "The Role and Relationship of Cultural Competence and Patient-Centeredness in Health Care Quality," The Commonwealth Fund (2006).

69 Chris Robinson in *Doing Research with Children and Young People,* eds. Lewis, Ding, Kellet, and Robinson (London: Sage, 2003).

70 J. Rodgers, "Trying to Get it Right: Undertaking Research Involving People With Learning Difficulties," *Disability and Society* 14, no. 4 (1999): 1–33.

71 Dawson Lisa and Nancy Kass, "View of U.S. Researchers about Informed Consent in International Collaborative Research," *Social Science and Medicine* 61 (2005): 1211–1222.

72 Sue Heath, Vikki Charles, Graham Crow, and Rose Wiles, "Informed Consent, Gatekeepers and Go-betweens," Paper presented at the International Association Sixth International Conference on Social Science Methodology, Amsterdam. (August 2004). Available at http://www.sociologyandsocialpolicy.soton.ac.uk/Proj/Informed_Consent/Resources.htm

73   T. Miller and L. Bell, "Consenting To What? Issues of Access, Gate-keeping and 'Informed' Consent," in *Ethics in Qualitative Research* eds. M. Mauthner, M. Birch, J. Jessop, and T. Miller (London: Sage, 2002).

74   Yasmin A. Ranney, "Ethical Dilemmas in Comparative/Cross-Cultural Qualitative Research." Paper Presented at the 1st International Congress of Qualitative Inquiry, University of Illinois, Urbana, Champaign, May 5–7, 2005.

75   Deborah G. Martin, "Bureacratizing Ethics: Institutional Review Boards an Participatory Research" (ACME Editorial Collective, 2007): 319–328.

Bibliography

Adams, Vincanne, et al. "Informed Consent in Cross-Cultural Perspective: Clinical Research in the Tibetan Autonomous Region." PRC, *Cult Med Psychiatry* 31 (2007): 445–472.

Alderson, Priscilla. *Listening to Children: Children, Ethics and Social Research.* Illford, Essex: Barnardo's, 1995.

Amelina, Anna. "Searching for an Appropriate Research Strategy on Transnational Migration: The Logic of Multi-Sited Research and the Advantage of the Cultural Interferences Approach." *FSQ* 10, no. 1 (2010): 9.

Ames Marquez, Alcides, and Bernard Francou. "Cordillera Blanca glaciares en la historia." *Bulletin de L'Institut Français d'Études Andines* 24, no. 1 (1995): 37–64.

Arcese, Peter, and Anthony R. E. Sinclair. "The Role of Protected Areas as Ecological Baselines." *Journal of Wildlife Management* 61, no. 3 (July 1997): 587–602.

Bakhru, Tany. "Negotiating and Navigating the Rough Terrain of Transnational Feminist Research." *Journal of International Women's Studies* 10, no. 2 (November 2008): 207.

Beach, B.C., S. Sana and L.A. Cooper, "The Role and Relationship of Cultural Competence and Patient-Centeredness in Health Care Quality." *The Commonwealth Fund* (2006).

Beaucarnot, Claudie. *Diary, 1943.* March 1990.

Bebbington, Anthony. "Liberation ecologies: environment, development, social movements." In *Movements, Modernizations, and Markets: Indigenous Organizations and Agrarian Strategies in Ecuador,* edited by R. Peet and M. Watts, 86–109. London: Routledge, 1996.

Beck, Ulrich and Natan Sznaider. "Unpacking Cosmopolitanism for the Social Sciences: A Research Agenda." *The British Journal of Sociology* 57, no. 1 (2006): 1–23.

Becker, Heike. "This New Thing That Came with Independence: Gender Aspects of Traditional Authorities and Customary Courts in Northern Namibia." Paper presented at the Africa Seminar, Centre for African Studies, University of Cape Town, October 2, 1996.

Benatar, S.R. "Reflections and Recommendations on Research Ethics in Developing Countries." *Social Science and Medicine* 54 (2001): 1131–1141.

Bernard, H. R. *Research Methods in Anthropology: Qualitative and Quantitative Approaches*. 2nd ed. Walnut Creek, California: Altamira Press, 1995.

Bernard, H. Russell. email communication, April 9, 2007.

Bhabha, Homi. *The Location of Culture*. London and New York: Routledge, 1994.

Blee, Kathleen M. "Becoming a Racist: Women in Contemporary Ku Klux Klan and Neo-Nazi Groups." *Gender and Society* 10, no. 6 (1996): 680–702.

Bolen, Eric G., and William L. Robinson. *Wildlife Ecology and Management*. 5th ed. Benjamin Cummings Publishing Company, 2002.

Bolen, Mel and Pat Martin. "Undergraduate Research Abroad: Challenges and Rewards-Why Encourage Research Abroad?" *Frontiers: The Interdisciplinary Journal of Study Abroad*, xi.

Boyden, Jo, and Judith Ennew, eds. *Children in Focus—a Manual for Participatory Research with Children*. Stockholm: Grafisk Press, 1997.

Boydston, Erin E., Karen M. Kapheim, Heather E. Watts, Micaela Szykman, and Kay E. Holekamp, "Altered Behavior in Spotted Hyenas Associated With Increased Human Activity." *Animal Conservation* 6, no. 3 (August 2003): 207–219.

Bronfenbrenner, Urie. *The Ecology of Human Development: Experiments by Nature and Design*. Cambridge, MA: Harvard University Press, 1979.

———. "Environments in Developmental Perspective: Theoretical and Operational Models." In *Measuring Environment across the Life Span: Emerging Methods and Concepts*, edited by Sarah L. Friedman and Theodore D. Wachs, 3–28. Washington, D.C.: American Psychological Association, 1999.

Buchan, Nancy R., Rachel T. Croson, and Robyn M. Dawes. "Swift Neighbors and Persistent Strangers: A Cross-Cultural Investigation of Trust and Reciprocity in Social Exchange." *American Journal of Sociology* 108, no. 1 (2002): 168–206.

Burawoy, Michael, Alice Burton, Ann Arnett Ferguson, and Kathryn J. Fox. *Ethnography Unbound: Power and Resistance in the Modern Metropolis*. Berkeley: University of California Press, 1991.

Burke, Timothy J. "Easily Distracted: Culture, Politics, Academia, and other Shiny Objects." http://weblogs.swarthmore.edu/burke (accessed in June 2008).

Burnapp, Dave. "Trajectories of Adjustment of International Students: U-curve, Learning Curve, or Third Space?" *Intercultural Education* 17, no. 1 (March 2006): 81–93.

Caballero Guerrero, J. "Comparacion De Cuatro Tratamientos De Manejo Para La Proteccion De La Peta De Agua (Podocnemis Unifilis), Troschel 1840, Y Estimación De La Supervivencia De Las Crias En Las Playas Del Río Itenéz." Universidad Autonoma Gabriel Rene Moreno, 1996.

Campbell, Ben. "Informed Consent in Developing Countries: Myth or Reality?" (2009). http://www.dartmouth.edu/~ethics/docs/Campbell_informed-consent.pdf (accessed September 23, 2009).

Cappelli, Adriano. *Lexicon abbreviaturarum: Dizionario di abbreviature latine ed italiane*. 6th ed. Milan: Ulrico Hoepli, 1979.

Carey, Mark. *Separate but Integrated: A History of Isolation and Market Participation Among Nicaragua's Mayangna Indians*. MA thesis, University of Montana, 1998.

——. "Beyond the Archive: A Practical Guide for Research in Latin America." *Brújula* 5, no. 1 (Dec. 2006): 173–176.

——. "La influencia Mayangna en la historia de la Costa Atlántica nicaragüense." *Revista de Historia* 14 (2002): 73–88.

——. "Living and Dying With Glaciers: People's Historical Vulnerability to Avalanches and Outburst Floods in Peru." *Global and Planetary Change* 47 (2005): 122–134.

——. "The Politics of Place: Inhabiting and Defending Glacier Hazard Zones in Peru's Cordillera Blanca." In *Darkening Peaks: Glacial Retreat, Science, and Society*, edited by Ben Orlove, Ellen Wiegandt, and Brian Luckman, 229–240. Berkeley: University of California Press, 2008.

——. *In the Shadow of Melting Glaciers: Climate Change and Andean Society*. New York: Oxford University Press, in press.

Castro de León, Z. "Geografía Histórica De La Tortuga Del Orinoco." Universidad Central de Venezuela, Facultad de Humanidades y Educación, Escuela de Historia, 1986.

CBS. *2001 Population and Housing Census. Basic Analysis with Highlights*. National Report. Windhoek, Namibia: Central Bureau of Statistics, National Planning Commission, 2003.

——. *Namibia Household Income & Expenditure Survey 2003/2004*. Preliminary Report. Windhoek, Namibia: Central Bureau of Statistics, National Planning Commission, 2006.

Chaikin, Joseph. *The Presence of the Actor*. New York: Theatre Communications Group, 1972.

Chataway, Cynthia J. "Negotiating the Observer-Observed Relationship." In *From Subjects to Subjectivities: A Handbook of Interpretive and Participatory Methods*, edited by Deborah L. Tolman and Mary Brydon-Miller, 239–55. New York, NY: New York University Press, 2001.

Clifford, James, and George E. Marcus, eds. *Writing Culture: The Poetics and Politics of Ethnography*. Berkeley: University of California Press, 1986.

Clyne, Irene Donohoue. "Finding Common Ground: Cross-Cultural Research in the Muslim Community." University of Melbourne. http://www.aare.edu.au/01pap/don01569.htm. (accessed on September 21, 2009)

Cochran, Moncrieff, and J Brassard. "Child Development and Personal Social Networks." *Child Development* 50 (1979): 609–16.

Commission française du guide des sources de l'histoire des nations. Sources de L'Histoire de L'Asie et de L'Océanie dans les archives et bibliothèques françaises. 2 vols. New York/Detroit: K. G. Saur; Distributed by Gale Research Co., 1981.

Compas, Bruce E., Jennifer K. Connor-Smith, Heidi Saltzman, Alexandra Harding Thomsen, and Martha E. Wadsworth. "Coping with Stress During Childhood and Adolescence: Problems, Progress, and Potential in Theory and Research." *Psychological Bulletin* 127, no. 1 (2001): 87–127.

Conquergood, Dwight. "Performance Studies: Interventions and Radical Research." *TDR* T-174 (Summer 2002): 145–156.

Cook, Karen S. "Networks, Norms, and Trust: The Social Psychology of Social Capital." 2004 Cooley Mead Award Address." *Social Psychology Quarterly* 68, no. 1 (2005): 4–14.

Cook, Karen S., Russell Harding, and Margaret Levi. *Cooperation without Trust?* Vol. IX, Russell Sage Foundation Series on Trust. New York: Russell Sage Foundation, 2005.

Cook, Karen S., Toshio Yamagishi, Coye Cheshire, Robin Cooper, Masafumi Matsuda, and Rie Mashima. "Trust Building Via Risk Taking: A Cross-Societal Experiment." *Social Psychology Quarterly* 68, no. 2 (2005): 121–42.

Corin, Ellen. "Uncertainty in Clinical Practice." *Working with culture*. Montreal, Canada: McGill University Summer Program in Social and Cultural Psychiatry, 2007.

Corsaro, William A. *The Sociology of Childhood*. Edited by York Bradshaw, Joya Misra and Vincent Roscigno. 2nd ed. Sociology for a New Century Series. Thousand Oaks, Calif.: Pine Forge Press, 2005.

Cronon, William. "The Trouble with Wilderness; or, Getting Back to the Wrong Nature." In *Uncommon Ground: Rethinking the Human Place in Nature*, edited by William Cronon, 69–90. New York: W.W. Norton and Company, 1996.

Crow, Ben. "Understanding Famine and Hunger." In *Poverty and Development in the 1990s*, edited by Tim Allen and Alan Thomas. Oxford: Oxford University Press, 1992.

Cupples, Julia and Sarah Kindon. "Far from Being 'Home Alone': The dynamics of accompanied fieldwork." *Singapore Journal of Tropical Geography*, 24, no. 2 (2003): 211–228.

D'Amico-Samuels, Deborah. "Undoing Fieldwork: Personal, Political, Theoretical and Methodological Implications." In *Decolonizing Anthropology, Moving Further Toward an Anthropology for Liberation*, edited by Faye V. Harrison, 68–87. Washington: Association of Black Anthropologists/American Anthropological Association, 1991.

De Tona, Carla. "But What is Interesting is the Story of Why and How Migration Happened," *Forum Qualitative Sozialforschung/Forum: Qualitative Social Research* [Online Journal] 7, no. 3: Article 13, paragraph 27. Available at: http://www.qualitative-research.net/fqs-texte/3-06/06-3-13-e.htm (accessed on January 13, 2007).

Decoux, Jean. *A la barre de L'Indochine: Histoire de mon gouvernement général (1940–1945)*. Paris: Plon, 1949.

Del Testa, David W. "'Paint the Trains Red:' Labor, Nationalism, and the Railroads in French Colonial Indochina, 1898–1945." PhD diss., Department of History, University of California, 2001.

Denzin, Norman K. *Performance Ethnography: Critical Pedagogy and the Politics of Culture.* Thousand Oaks: Sage, 2003.

———. *Interpretive Ethnography, Ethnographic Practices for the Twenty-First Century.* Thousand Oaks: Sage, 1997.

Denzin, Norman K., Yvonna S. Lincoln, and Linda Tuhiwai Smith, eds. *Handbook of Critical & Indigenous Methodologies.* Thousand Oaks: Sage, 2008.

Descours-Gatin, Chantal et al., Guide de Recherches sur Le Vietnam: Bibliographies, archives et bibliothèques de France. Paris: Éditions L'Harmattan, 1983.

Diener, Ingolf. "Ethnicity and Nation-Building: Towards Unity Respectful of Heterogeneity?" In *Contemporary Namibia: The First Landmarks of a Post-Apartheid Society,* edited by Ingolf Diener and Olivier Graefe, 231–57. Windhoek, Namibia: Gamsberg Macmillan, 2001.

Dimond, S., and J. Lazarus. "The Problem of Vigilance in Animal Life." *Brain, Behavior and Evolution* 9, no. 1 (1974): 60–79.

Dirks, K. T., and D. L. Ferrin. "Trust in Leadership: Meta-Analytic Findings and Implications for Research and Practice." *Journal of Applied Psychology* 87, no. 4 (2002): 611–28.

Duffy, Gavan. "Events and Versions: Reconstructing Event Data Analysis." *International Interactions* 20, nos. 1-2 (1994): 147–167.

Dwyder, Sonya Corbin and Jennifer L. Buckle. "The Space Between: On Being an Insider-Outsider in Qualitative Research." *International Journal of Qualitative Methods* 8, no. 1 (2009): 58.

Emerson, Richard. "Power-Dependence Relations." *American Sociological Review* 27, no. 1 (1962): 31–41.

Ergueta, P., and C. de Morales. *Libro Rojo De Los Vertebrados De Bolivia.* Gland, Switzerland: International Union for the Conservation of Nature, 1996.

Evans, Sterling. *The Green Republic: A Conservation History of Costa Rica.* Austin: University of Texas Press, 1999.

Falla, Jonathan. *True Love and Bartholomew: Rebels on the Burmese Border.* Cambridge: Cambridge University Press, 1991.

Favel, Floyd. "Poetry, Remnants and Ruins: Aboriginal Theatre in Canada," *Canadian Theatre Review* 139 (Summer 2009): 31–35.

Fine, Michelle. "Working the Hyphens: Reinventing Self and Other in Qualitative Research." In *Handbook of Qualitative Research,* edited by Norman K. Denzin and Yvonna S. Lincoln, 70–82. Thousand Oaks, Calif.: Sage, 1994.

Fine, Michelle. "Working the Hyphens: Reinventing Self and Other in Qualitative Research." In *Handbook of Qualitative Research,* edited by Norman K. Denzin and Yvonna S. Lincoln, 70–82. Thousand Oaks, Calif.: Sage Publications, 1994.

Fischer, Julia, Dawn M. Kitchen, Robert M. Seyfarth, and Dorothy L. Cheney. "Baboon Loud Calls Advertise Male Quality: Acoustic Features and their Relation to Rank, Age, and Exhaustion." *Behavioral Ecology and Sociobiology* 56, no. 2 (June 2004): 140–148.

Frank, Lawrence G., Kay E. Holekamp, and Laura Smale. "Dominance, Demography, and Reproductive Success of Female Spotted Hyenas." In *Serengeti II: Dy-*

namics, Management, and Conservation of an Ecosystem, edited by Anthony Ronald Entrican Sinclair and Peter Arcese, 364–384. Chicago: University of Chicago Press, 1995.

Frohlick, Susan E. "'You Brought Your Baby to Base Camp?' Families and Field Sites." *Great Lakes Geographer* 9, no. 1 (2002): 49–58.

Fukuyama, Francis. *Trust: Social Virtues and the Creation of Prosperity.* New York: Free Press, 1995.

Gambetta, Diego. "Can We Trust Trust?" In *Trust: Making and Breaking Cooperative Relations,* edited by Diego Gambetta, 213–37. New York: Basil Blackwell, 1988.

Gatenby, Bev, and Maria Humphries. "Feminist Participatory Action Research: Methodological and Ethical Issues." *Women's Studies International Forum* 23, no. 1 (2000): 89–105.

Gaventa, John, and Andrea Cornwall. "Power and Knowledge." In *Handbook of Action Research: Participative Inquiry and Practice,* edited by Peter Reason and Hilary Bradbury, 70–80. Thousand Oaks, Calif.: Sage, 2001.

Gazquez, Denis and Agathe Larcher-Goscha. *Publications officielles de L'Indochine coloniale: Inventaire analytique (1859–1954).* Paris: Bibliothèque nationale de France, 2004.

Geertz, Clifford. *Works and Lives: The Anthropologist as Author.* Stanford, CA: Stanford University Press, 1988.

Gergen, Kenneth J. *Relational Being: Beyond Self and Community.* Oxford: Oxford University Press, 2009.

Gill, Hannah E. "Finding a Middle Ground between Extremes: Notes on Researching Transnational Crime and Violence." *Anthropology Matters Journal* 6, no. 2 (2004): 1–9.

Godoy, Ricardo. "The Effects of Rural Education on the Use of the Tropical Rain Forest by the Sumu Indians of Nicaragua: Possible Pathways, Qualitative Finds and Policy Options." *Human Organization* 53, no. 3 (1994): 233–44.

———. *Indians, Markets, and Rainforests: Theory, Methods, Analysis.* New York: Columbia University Press, 2001.

Godoy, Ricardo, Nicholas Brokaw, David Wilkie, D. Colón, A. Palermo, S. Lye, and S. Wei. "Of Trade and Cognition: Markets and the Loss of Folk Knowledge among the Tawahka Indians of the Honduran Rain Forest." *Journal of Anthropological Research* 54, no. 26 (1998): 219–33.

Godoy, Ricardo, Nicholas Brokaw, and David Wilkie. "The Effect of Income on the Extraction of Non-Timber Tropical Forest Products: Model, Hypotheses, and Preliminary Findings from the Sumu Indians of Nicaragua." *Human Ecology* 23, no. 1 (1995): 29–52.

Gottlieb, Benjamin H. *Coping with Chronic Stress.* Edited by Donald Meichenbaum. The Plenum Press Series on Stress and Coping. New York: Plenum Press, 1997.

Gould, Stephen J. *The Hedgehog, the Fox, and the Magister's Pox: Mending the Gap Between Science and the Humanities.* New York: Harmony Books, 2003.

Grandjean, Philippe. *L'Indochine face au Japon, 1940–1945: Decoux-De Gaulle, un malentendu fatal*. Paris: Éditions L'Harmattan, 2004.

Grotowski, Jerzy. "C'était une sorte de volcan." Interview. February 8, 9, 10, 1991. Paris. *Gurdjieff. Dossiers H*. Lausanne: L'Age d'Homme, 1993: 98–115.

———. "Holiday." Translated by Boleslaw Taborski. *TDR* T-58 (June 1973): 113–135.

———. "Tu es le fils de quelqu'un [You Are Someone's Son]." Translated by Jacques Chwat. *TDR* T-115 (Fall 1987): 30–40.

———. *Towards a Poor Theatre*. New York: Simon and Schuster, 1968.

Guba, Egon G, and Yvonna S. Lincoln. "Competing Paradigms in Qualitative Research." In *Handbook of Qualitative Research*, edited by Norman K. Denzin and Yvonna S. Lincoln, 105–17. Thousand Oaks, Calif.: Sage, 1994.

———. *Fourth Generation Evaluation*. Newbury Park, Calif.: Sage, 1989.

Guha, Ramachandra. "Radical American Environmentalism and Wilderness Preservation: A Third World Critique." *Environmental Ethics* 11 (Spring 1989): 71–83.

Gunaratnma, Yasemin. *Researching "Race" and Ethnicity: Methods, Knowledge and Power*. London: Sage Publications, 2003.

Habermas, Jürgen. *Legitimation Crisis*. Cambridge: Polity Press, 1988.

Hall, Stuart. "Cultural Identity and Diaspora." In *Colonial Discourse and Post-Colonial Theory*, edited by Patrick Williams and Laura Chrisman, 392–403. 1990. New York: Columbia U P, 1993.

Harding, Russell. "Conceptions and Explanations of Trust." In *Trust in Society*, edited by Karen S. Cook, 3–39. New York: Russell Sage Foundation, 2001.

Hardy, Andrew. *Red Hills: Migrants and the State in the Highlands of Vietnam*. Honolulu: University of Hawaii Press, 2003.

Harkness, Janet. "In the Pursuit of Quality: Issues for Cross-National Survey Research." In *Cross-National Research Methodology and Practice*, edited by Hantrais and Mangen. London and New York: Routledge, 2007.

Harrison, Jane, Lesley MacGibbon, and Missy Morton. "Regimes of Trustworthiness in Qualitative Research: The Rigors of Reciprocity." *Qualitative Inquiry* 7, no. 3 (2001): 323–45.

Hastrup, Kirsten. "The Motivated Body: on the Locus of Agency." In *A Passage to Anthropology: Between Experience and Theory*, 77–98. London and New York: Routledge, 1995.

Hays-Mitchell, Maureen. "Danger, Fulfillment, and Responsibility in A Violence-Plagued Society." *The Geographical Review* 91, nos. 1–2 (2001): 311–321.

Hazan, Cindy, and Phillip R. Shaver. "Attachment as an Organizational Framework for Research on Close Relationships." In *Close Relationships: Key Readings*, edited by Harry T. Reis and Caryl E. Rusbult, 153–74. New York: Psychology Press, 2004.

Healy, Lynne M. *International Social Work: Professional Action in an Interdependent World*. New York: Oxford University Press, 2001.

Heath, S., V. Charles, G. Crow, and R. Wiles. "Informed Consent, Gatekeepers and Gobetweens." Paper presented at the International Association Sixth International Conference on Social Science Methodology, Amsterdam. (August,

2004).   http://www.sociologyandsocialpolicy.soton.ac.uk/Proj/Informed_
Consent/Resources.htm. (accessed on November 17, 2009).

Heaney, Christopher. "Bonesmen: Did Yale Plunder Peru?" *The New Republic*
(Oct. 23, 2006): 14–19.

———. "Finders Keepers? After Almost a Century, Peru Revives the Drama of Hiram Bingham, 5,000 artifacts, and Machu Picchu." *Legal Affairs* (March-April
2006). http://www.legalaffairs.org/issues/March-April-2006/scene_Heaney_
marapr06.msp (accessed on November 21, 2007).

Heimer, Carol A. "Solving the Problem of Trust." In *Trust in Society*, edited by
Karen S. Cook, 40–88. New York: Russell Sage Foundation, 2001.

Hennink, Monique M. "Language and Communication in Cross-Cultural Qualitative
Research." In *Doing Cross-Cultural Research: Ethical and Methodological Perspec-
tives*, edited by Pranee Liamputtong. 21–33. Social Indicators Research Series 34
(Springer, Netherlands: Springer Publishers, 2008).

Herlihy, Peter H. "Indigenous Peoples and Biosphere Reserve Conservation in the
Mosquitia Rain Forest Corridor, Honduras." In *Conservation Through Cultural Survival: Indigenous Peoples and Protected Areas*, edited by Stan Stevens,
99–129. Washington, D.C.: Island Press, 1997.

Hirabayashi, Lane Ryo. *The Politics of Fieldwork: Research in an American Concentration Camp*. Tucson: The University of Arizona Press, 1999.

Hofer, Heribert, and Marion L. East "Population Dynamics, Population Size, and
the Commuting System of Serengeti Spotted Hyenas." In *Serengeti II: Dynamics, Management, and Conservation of an Ecosystem*, edited by Anthony
Ronald Entrican Sinclair and Peter Arcese, 332–63. Chicago: University of
Chicago Press, 1995.

Holekamp, Kay E., Laura Smale, R. Berg, and Susan M. Cooper. "Hunting Rates
and Hunting Success in the Spotted Hyena (Crocuta crocuta)." *Journal of Zoology* 242, no.1 (May 1997): 1–15.

Holekamp, Kay E., Micaela Szykman, Erin E. Boydston, and Laura Smale. "Association of Seasonal Reproductive Patterns With Changing Food Availability
in an Equatorial Carnivore, the Spotted Hyaena (Crocuta crocuta)." *Journal of
Reproductive Fertility* 116, no. 1 (May 1999): 87–93.

Howard, Sarah M. "Land Conflict and Mayangna Territorial Rights in Nicaragua's
Bosawás Reserve." *Bulletin of Latin American Research* 17, no. 1 (1998): 17–34.

Hubell, Larry D. "False Starts, Suspicious Interviewees, and Nearly Impossible
Tasks: Some Reflections on the Difficulties of Conducting Research Abroad."
The Qualitative Report 8, no. 2 (June 2003): 200.

"Indochine," Wargnier, Regis. VHS, Los Angeles, Sony Picture Classics, 1992.

Iosifides, Theodoros. "Qualitative Migration Research: Some New Reflections Six
Years Later." *The Qualitative Report* 8, no. 3 (September 2003): 442.

Jackson, Shannon. *Professing Performance: Theatre in the Academy from Philology
to Performativity*. Cambridge: Cambridge University Press, 2004.

Jennings, Eric. *Vichy in the Tropics: Petain's National Revolution in Madagascar,
Guadeloupe, and Indochina, 1940–1944*. Stanford: Stanford University Press,
2004.

Johns, A. D. "Continuing Problems for Amazon River Turtles." *Oryx* 21, no. 1 (1987): 25–28.

Jones, James H. *Bad Blood: The Tuskegee Syphilis Experiment*, Revised Edition. New York: Free Press, 1993.

Kamminga, Evelien. "Herero and Owambo Collective Decision-Making Mechanisms and the Implications for Children's Rights Realizations in Namibia." Windhoek, Namibia: UNICEF, 2000.

Kaplan, Alice. *French Lessons: A Memoir*. Chicago: University of Chicago Press, 1993.

Kaser, Georg, and Henry Osmaston. *Tropical Glaciers*. New York: Cambridge University Press, 2002.

Khagram, Sanjeev and Peggy Levitt. "Towards a Field of Transnational Studies and a Sociological Transnationalism Research Program." *Harvard University, The Hauser Center for Nonprofit Organizations Working Paper No. 24*. 2004. http://papers.ssrn.com/sol3/papers.cfm?abstract_id=556993 (accessed on October 10, 2007).

Kirsch, Gesa and Liz Rohan, *Beyond the Archives: Stories About Research as a Lived Process*. Carbondale: University of Southern Illinois Press, 2008.

Kitchen, Dawn M., Robert M. Seyfarth, Julia Fischer, and Dorothy L. Cheney. "Loud Calls as Indicators of Dominance in Male Baboons (Papio cynocephalus ursinus)." *Behavioral Ecology and Sociobiology* 53, no. 6 (May 2003): 374–384.

Koehn, Daryl. *Rethinking Feminist Ethics: Care, Trust, and Empathy*. New York: Routledge, 1998.

Kramer, Roderick M. "Divergent Realities and Convergent Disappointments in the Hierarchic Relation: Trust and Intuitive Auditor at Work." In *Trust in Organizations: Frontiers of Theory and Research*, edited by Roderick M. Kramer and Tom R. Tyler. Thousand Oaks, Calif.: Sage, 1996.

Krech III, Shepard. *The Ecological Indian: Myth and History*. New York: W.W. Norton & Company, 1999.

Kruuk, Hans. *The Spotted Hyena: A Study of Predation and Social Behavior*. Chicago: University of Chicago Press, 1972.

"L' Amant [The Lover]," Annaud, Jean-Jacques. VHS, Los Angeles, Metro-Goldwyn-Mayer, 1992.

Langfred, C. W. "Too Much of a Good Thing? Negative Effects of High Trust and Individual Autonomy in Self-Managing Teams." *Academy of Management Journal* 47 (2004): 385–99.

Lather, Patti. *Getting Smart: Feminist Research and Pedagogy with/in the Postmodern*. New York: Routledge, 1991.

Lawrence, Mark Atwood. *Assuming the Burden: Europe and the American Commitment to the War in Vietnam*. Edited by Fredrik and Christopher E. Goscha, Series "From Indochina to Vietnam: Revolution and War in a Global Perspective." Berkeley: University of California Press, 2005.

Lazarus, Richard S., and Susan Folkman. *Stress, Appraisal, and Coping*. New York: Springer, 1984.

Levi, Margaret, and Laura Stoker. "Political Trust and Trustworthiness." *Annual Review of Political Science 3* (2000): 475–507.

Levin, Daniel Z., Ellen M. Whitener, and Rob Cross. "Perceived Trustworthiness of Knowledge Sources: The Moderating Impact of Relationship Length." *Journal of Applied Psychology* 91, no. 5 (2006): 1163–71.

Levitt, Peggy and Sanjay Khagram. "Towards a Field of Transnational Studies and a Sociological Transnationalism Research Program." Hauser Center for Non-profit Organizations, Social Science Research Network, Working Paper, no. 24 (2005): 16.

Lewicki, Roy J., D. McAllister, and R. Bies. "Trust and Distrust: New Relationships and Realities." *Academy of Management Review* 23 (1998): 439–58.

Lewicki, Roy J., Edward C. Tomlinson, and Nicole Gillespie. "Models of Interpersonal Trust Development: Theoretical Approaches, Empirical Evidence, and Future Directions." *Journal of Management* 32, no. 6 (2006): 991–1002.

Lewis, C. S. *The Discarded Image.* Cambridge: Cambridge University Press, 1964.

Liamputtong, Pranee. "Doing Research in a Cross-Cultural Context: Methodological and Ethical Challenges." In *Doing Cross-Cultural Research*, edited by Pranee Liamputtong. Social Indicators Research Series 34. Springer, Netherlands: Springer Publishers, 2008.

Lincoln, Yvonna S., and Norman K. Denzin, eds. *Turning Points in Qualitative Research: Tying Knots in a Handkerchief.* Walnut Creek: Altamira, 2003.

Lipinge, Scholastika, Kathe Hofnie, and Steve Friedman. *The Relationship between Gender Roles and HIV Infection in Namibia* 8. Windhoek, Namibia: University of Namibia Press, 2004.

Lisa, Dawson and Nancy Kass. "View of U.S. Researchers about Informed Consent in International Collaborative Research." *Social Science and Medicine* 61 (2005): 1211–1222.

Lubell, Mark. "Familiarity Breeds Trust: Collective Action in a Policy Domain." *The Journal of Politics* 69, no. 1 (2007): 237–50.

MacMillan, Margaret. *Dangerous Games: The Uses and Abuses of History.* New York: Modern Library, 2009.

Madison, D. Soyini. *Critical Ethnography: Methods, Ethics, and Performance.* Thousand Oaks: Sage, 2005.

Maguire, Patricia. "Uneven Ground: Feminisms and Action Research." In *Handbook of Action Research*, edited by Peter Reason and Hilary Bradbury, 59–69. London: Sage, 2000.

Maitam, Jean-Jacques. *A House Divided (Viet Nam).* Greensboro, NC: Tudor Books, 2002.

Mangen, Steen. "Qualitative Research Methods in Cross-national settings." In *Cross-National Research Methodology and Practice*, edited by Hantrais and Mangen. London and New York: Routledge, 2007.

Marcoy, P. *Travels in South America: From the Pacific Ocean to the Atlantic Ocean.* New York: Scribner, Armstrong and Co., 1875.

Mayer, R. C., J. H. Davis, and F. D. Schoorman. "An Integrative Model of Organizational Trust." *Academy of Management Review* 20 (1995): 709–34.

McClennen, Sophia A. "Area Studies Beyond Ontology: Notes on Latin American Studies, American Studies, and Inter-American Studies." *A Contracorriente* 5, no. 1 (Fall 2007): 173–184.

McRobbie, Angela. *The Aftermath of Feminism: Gender, Culture and Social Change.* London: Sage, 2008.

Mendelsohn, John, Alice Jarvis, Carole Roberts, and Tony Robertson. *Atlas of Namibia: A Portrait of the Land and Its People.* 1st ed. Cape Town: David Philip, 2002.

Messick, David M., and Roderick M. Kramer. "Trust as a Form of Shallow Morality." In *Trust in Society*, edited by Karen S. Cook, 89–117. New York: Russell Sage Foundation, 2001.

Mikulincer, Mario. "Attachment Working Models and the Sense of Trust: An Exploration of Interaction Goals and Affect Regulation." In *Close Relationships: Key Readings*, edited by Harry T Reis and Caryl E Rusbult, 175–91. New York: Psychology Press, 2004.

Miller, T. and L. Bell. "Consenting To What? Issues of Access, Gate-keeping and 'Informed' Consent." In *Ethics in Qualitative Research*, edited by M. Mauthner, M. Birch, J. Jessop, and T. Miller. London: Sage, 2002.

Mills, M. Gus L. *Kalahari Hyenas: Comparative Behavioural Ecology of Two Species.* London: Unwin Hyman, 1990.

Mills, M. Gus L., and Heribert Hofer. *Hyaenas: Status Survey and Conservation Action Plan.* IUCN/SSC Hyaena Specialist Group. IUCN, Gland, Switzerland and Cambridge, 1998.

Ministerio de Desarollo Sostenible y Medio Ambiente. *Plan De Manejo Parque Nacional Noel Kempff Mercado.* Santa Cruz, Bolivia: Fundación Amigos de la Naturaleza and The Nature Conservancy, 1996.

Mitsuhashi, Kyoko. "Gender Consciousness among Japanese Students who are Studying at American Universities." PhD diss., University of California, Los Angeles, 2004.

Mohanty, J. N. "The Other Culture." In *Phenomenology of the Cultural Disciplines*, edited by Mano Daniel and Lester Embree, 135–146. Dordrecht. Dordrecht: Kluwer, 1994.

MOHSS, and Macro International. *Namibia Demographic and Health Survey 2006–2007.* Windhoek, Namibia and Calverton, MD, USA: Ministry of Health and Social Services (Namibia) and Macro International, 2008.

MOHSS. *Report of the 2008 National HIV Sentinel Survey.* Windhoek, Namibia: Ministry of Health and Social Services, 2008.

Mufune, Pempelani. "Youth Problems in Namibia." In *Challenges for Anthropology in the "African Renaissance." A Southern African Contribution*, edited by Debie LeBeau and Robert J Gordon, 177–90. Windhoek, Namibia: University of Namibia Press, 2002.

Nagar, Richa. "Footloose Researchers, 'Traveling' Theories, and the Politics of Transnational Feminist Praxis." *Gender, Place, and Culture* 9, no. 2 (2002): 179–186.

Neumann, Roderick P. *Imposing Wilderness: Struggles Over Livelihood and Nature Preservation in Africa.* Berkeley: University of California Press, 1998.

Njeru, Grace Muthoni. "The Experiences of Kenyan Students in Two Midwest U.S. States: Benefits, Challenges & Coping Strategies." PhD diss., University of Missouri, Columbia, 2006.

Ojasti, J. *Wildlife Utilization in Latin America: Current Situation and Prospects for Sustainable Management*: FAO, 1996.

Olesen, Virginia. "Early Millennial Feminist Qualitative Research: Challenges and Contours." In *The Sage Handbook of Qualitative Research*, edited by Norman K. Denzin and Yvonna S. Lincoln, 235–63. Thousand Oaks, Calif.: Sage, 2005.

Orwell, George. *Burmese Days*. New York: Harvest, 1934.

Oyewùmi, Oyèronké. *The Invention of Women*. Minneapolis: University of Minnesota Press, 1997.

Packer, Craig. *Into Africa*. Chicago: the University of Chicago Press, 1994.

Pangle, Wiline M. "Threat-sensitive Behavior and its Ontogenic Development in Top Mammalian Carnivores." PhD diss. East Lansing: Michigan State University, 2009.

Pangle, Wiline M., and Kay E. Holekamp. "Lethal and Nonlethal Anthropogenic Effects on Spotted Hyenas in the Masai Mara National Reserve." *Journal of Mammalogy* 91, no. 1 (February 2010): 154–164.

Patai, Daphne. "U.S. Academics and Third World Women: Is Ethical Research Possible?" In *Women's Words: The Feminist Practice of Oral History*, edited by Sherna Berger Gluck and Daphne Patai, 137–153. New York: Routledge, 1991.

Pelley, Patricia. *Postcolonial Vietnam: New Histories of the National Past*. A John Hope Franklin Center Book. Raleigh/Durham: Duke University Press, 2003.

Peres, C. A., and I. R. Lake. "Extent of Nontimber Resource Extraction in Tropical Forests: Accessibility to Game Vertebrates by Hunters in the Amazon Basin." *Conservation Biology* 17, no. 2 (2003): 521–35.

Perkins, Mandaley. *Hà Nội, Adieu: A Bittersweet Memoir of French Indochina*. London: Fourth Estate, 2005.

Perramond, Eric P. "Oral Histories and Partial Truths in Mexico." *The Geographical Review* 91, no. 1–2 (2001): 151–57.

Petley, Christer. "Flying Away and Grounds for Concern: Mobility, Location and Ethical Discomfort in Researching Caribbean History from the UK." In *Beyond the Blood, the Beach and the Banana: New Directions in Caribbean Studies*, edited by Sandra Courtman, 15–23. Kingston, Jamaica: Ian Randle Press, 2004.

Pillow, Wanda. "Confession, Catharsis, or Cure? Rethinking the Uses of Reflexivity as Methodological Power in Qualitative Research." *Qualitative Studies in Education* 16, no. 2 (March 2003): 175–196.

Plante, E. "International Research Collaborations: Promoting International Student Research." *The ASHA Leader* 12 (Nov. 2007): 15–17.

Pohl, Gabriela, "Cross-Cultural Pragmatic Failure and Implications for Language Teaching." *SLLT* 4 (2004). http://www.usq.edu.au/users/sonjb/sllt/4/Pohl04.html (accessed on September 20, 2009).

Poole, Deborah. "Landscape and the Imperial Subject: U.S. Images of the Andes, 1859–1930." In *Close Encounters of Empire: Writing the Cultural History of*

U.S.-Latin American Relations, edited by Gilbert M. Joseph, Catherine C. Le-Grand and Ricardo D. Salvatore, 107–138. Durham: Duke University Press, 1998.

Pratt, Mary Louise. *Imperial Eyes: Travel Writing and Transculturation.* New York: Routledge, 1992.

Price, Marie D. "The Kindness of Strangers." *The Geographical Review* 91, no. 1–2 (2001): 143–150.

Pritchard, P. C. H., and P. Trebbau. *The Turtles of Venezuela.* Oxford, Ohio: Society for the Study of Amphibians and Reptiles, 1984.

Purkayastha, Bandana, et al. "The Study of Gender in India: A Partial Review." *Gender & Society* 4 (2003): 17.

Raffaelli, David. "How Extinction Patterns Affect Ecosystems." *Science* 306, no. 5699 (November 2004): 1141–1142.

Reason, Peter. "Three Approaches to Participative Inquiry." In *Handbook of Qualitative Research*, edited by Norman K. Denzin and Yvonna S. Lincoln, 324–39. Thousand Oaks, Calif.: Sage, 1994.

Redford, Kent H. "The Ecologically Noble Savage." *Cultural Survival Quarterly* 15, no. 1 (1991): 46–48.

Reiche, Sebastian B., and Anne-Wil Harzing. "Key Issues in International Survey Research." (26 June 2007) http://www.harzing.com/intresearch_keyissues.htm (accessed September 20, 2009).

Reis, Leonardo Oliveira. "Translating Questionnaires for Use in Cross-Cultural Research: Are We doing the Right Thing?" *Actas Urológicas Espanolas* 33, no. 1 (2009): 5–7.

Ritchie, Jan, Anthony B. Zwi, Ilse Blignault, Anne Bunde-Birouste, and Derrick Silove. "Insider-Outsider Positions in Health-Development Research: Reflections For Practice." *Development in Practice* 19, no. 1 (February 2009): 110.

Robinson, Chris, ed. *Doing Research with Children and Young People* (London: Sage, 2004).

Roche, Jeremy. "Children: Rights, Participation and Citizenship." *Childhood* 6, no. 4 (1999): 475–93.

Rodgers, J. "Trying to Get it Right: Undertaking Research Involving People With Learning Difficulties." *Disability and Society* 14, no. 4 (1999): 1–33.

Rorty, Richard. "Solidarity or Objectivity?" In *Post-Analytic Philosophy*, edited by John Rajchman and Cornel West, 3–9. New York: Columbia University Press, 1985.

Rutten, M. M. E. M. "Parks Beyond Parks: Genuine Community Based Wildlife Eco-tourism or Just Another Loss of Land for Maasai Pastoralists in Kenya?" London: *International Institute for Environment and Development*, Issue paper no. 111, 2002.

———. *Selling Wealth to Buy Poverty - The Process of the Individualization of Land-ownership Among the Maasai Pastoralists of Kajiado District Kenya, 1890–1990.* Saarbrucken-Fort Lauderdale: Verlag Breitenbach Publishers, 1992.

Saint Augustine, *De Civitate Dei.* B.H.S., K 1 267.

Salvatore, Ricardo D. "Local versus Imperial Knowledge: Reflections on Hiram Bingham and the Yale Peruvian Expedition." *Nepantla: Views from the South* 4, no. 1 (2003): 67–80.

Sands, Roberta G., Joretha N. Bourjolly, and Dorit Roer-Strier. "Crossing Cultural Barriers in Research Interviewing." *Qualitative Social Work* 6, no. 3 (September 2007): 367.

Sapolsky, Robert M. *A Primate's Memoir*. Touchstone. New York: Simon & Schuster, 2001.

Scheper-Hughes, Nancy. "Ire in Ireland." In *Ethnographic Fieldwork: An Anthropological Reader*, edited by Antonius C.G.M. Robben and Jeffrey A. Sluka. Blackwell Anthologies in Social and Cultural Anthropology. Malden, MA: Blackwell Publishing, 2007.

Schwartz, Joan M. and Terry Cook. "Archives, Records, and Power: The Making of Modern Memory." *Archival Science* 2, nos. 1–2 (2002): 1–19.

Scott, Steffanie, Fiona Miller, and Kate Lloyd. "Doing Fieldwork in Development Geography: Research Culture and Research Spaces in Vietnam," *Geographical Research* 44, no. 1, 2006: 28–40.

Segall, Avner. "Critical Ethnography and the Invocation of Voice: From the Field/ in the Field—Single Exposure, Double Standard?" *Qualitative Studies in Education* 14, no. 4 (July 2001): 579–592.

Segebrecht, Ray, "Undergraduate Research Aboard" (September 2009). http://www.kansan.com/news/2009/sep/11/undergraduates_research_abroad/. (accessed September 23, 2009).

Sen, Amartya. *Poverty and Famines: An Essay on Entitlement and Deprivation*. Oxford: Oxford University Press, 1981.

SIAPAC. *A Situation Analysis of Orphan Children in Namibia*. Windhoek, Namibia: MOHSS & UNICEF, 2002.

Sillero-Zubiri, Claudio, and Dada Gottelli. "Feeding Ecology of the Spotted Hyaena (Mammalia: Crocuta Crocuta) in a Mountain Forest Habitat." *Journal of African Zoology* 106 (1992): 169–176.

Sin, Chih Soong. "Ethnic Matching in Qualitative Research: Reversing the Gaze on 'White Others' and 'White' as 'Other.'" *Qualitative Research* 7, no. 4 (2007): 477–499.

Smith, Linda Tuhiwai. *Decolonizing Methodologies: Research and Indigenous Peoples*. London: Zed Books, 1999.

Smith, N. J. H. "Aquatic Turtles of Amazonia: An Endangered Resource." *Biological Conservation* 16, no. 3 (1979): 165–76.

Snow, Charles P. *The Two Cultures and a Second Look: An Expanded Version of the Two Cultures and the Scientific Revolution*. Cambridge: Cambridge University Press, 1964.

Spariosu, Mihai. "Mimesis in Contemporary French Theory." In *Mimesis in Contemporary French Theory: An Interdisciplinary Approach*, 66–108. Philadelphia/Amsterdam: John Benjamins, 1984.

Spence, Mark David. *Dispossessing the Wilderness: Indian Removal and the Making of the National Parks*. New York: Oxford University Press, 2000.

Spruce, R. *Notes of a Botanist on the Amazon and Andes*. Edited by Wallace Alfred Russell. London: Macmillan and Company, Ltd., 1908.

Starrs, Paul F., Carlin F. Starrs; Genoa I. Starrs; Lynn Huntsinger, "Fieldwork . . . with Family." *Geographical Review*, 91, no. 1/2 (Jan.-Apr. 2001): 74–87.

Stavenhagen, Rodolfo. "Ethnodevelopment: A Neglected Dimension in Development Thinking." In *Development Studies: Critique and Renewal*, edited by Raymond Anthorpe and Krahl Andras. Leiden: E. J. Brill, 1986.

———. *Ethnic Conflicts and the Nation-state*. New York: St. Martin's Press, 1996.

Steinberg, Ted. "Down to Earth: Nature, Agency, and Power in History." *The American Historical Review* 107, no. 3 (June 2002): 798–820.

Stocks, Anthony, Benjamin McMahan, and Peter Taber. "Indigenous, Colonist, and Government Impacts on Nicaragua's Bosawas Reserve." *Conservation Biology* 21, no. 6 (2007): 1495–1505.

Stocks, Anthony. "Mapping Dreams in Nicaragua's Bosawas Biosphere Reserve." *Human Organization* 62 (2003): 65–78.

Stoller, Paul. *Sensuous Scholarship*. Philadelphia: University of Pennsylvania, 1997.

Streitwieser, Berhnard and Neal Sobania. "Overseeing Study Abroad Research: Challenges, Responsibilities and the Institutional Review Board." *Frontiers: The Interdisciplinary Journal of Study Abroad*, 6.

Sultana, Farhana. "Reflexivity, Positionality and Participatory Ethics: Negotiating Fieldwork Dilemmas in International Research." *ACME* 6, no. 3 (2007): 376.

Sun, Yu-Chi. "Three Chinese Immigrant Daughters: Their Perceptions of Schooling, Family, and Identity." PhD diss., Pennsylvania State University, 2004.

Sundberg, J. "Masculinist Epistemologies and the Politics of Fieldwork in Latin Americanist Geography." *Professional Geographer* 55, no. 2 (2003): 180–90.

Sutherland, William J., Susan Armstrong-Brown, Paul R. Armsworth, Tom Brereton, Jonathan Brickland, Colin D. Campbell, Daniel E. Chamberlain, Andrew I. Cooke, Nicholas K. Dulvy, Nicholas R. Dusic, Martin Fitton, Robert P. Freckleton, H. Charles J. Godfray, Nick Grout, H. John Harvey, Colin Hedley, John J. Hopkins, Neil B. Kift, Jeff Kirby, William E. Kunin, David W. Macdonald, Brian Marker, Marc Naura, Andrew R. Neale, Tom Oliver, Dan Osborn, Andrew S. Pullin, Matthew E. A. Shardlow, David A. Showler, Paul L. Smith, Richard J. Smithers, Jean-Luc Solandt, Jonathan Spencer, Chris J. Spray, Chris D. Thomas, Jim Thompson, Sarah E. Webb, Derek W. Yalden, and Andrew R. Watkinson. "The Identification of 100 Ecological Questions of High Policy Relevance in the UK." *Journal of Applied Ecology* 43, no. 4 (2006): 617–27.

Szanton, David L. "The Origin, Nature and Challenges of Area Studies in the United States." In *The Politics of Knowledge: Area Studies and the Disciplines*, edited by David L. Szanton, 10–11. Berkeley: University of California Press, 2004.

Tatar, Sibel. "Turkish Graduate Students' Perceptions of Participating in U.S. Classrooms." PhD diss., Indiana University, 2003.

Tayeb, Monir. "Conducting Research Across Cultures: Overcoming Drawback and Obstacles." *International Journal of Cross-Cultural Management* 1, no. 1 (2001): 10.

Taylor, Edward, Elizabeth J. Tisdell, and Mary Stone Hanley, "The Role of Positionality in Teaching for Critical Consciousness: Implications for Adult Education." Paper presented at 2000 *Adult Education Research Conference* (AERC). http://www.edst. educ.ubc.ca/aerc/2000/tayloreetal1-web.htm (accessed in Jan 2007).

Tilley, Susan, and Louise Gormley. "Canadian University Ethics Review: Cultural Complications Translating Principles into Practice." *Qualitative Inquiry* 13, no. 3 (2007): 368–87.

Tiryakian, Edward A. *Sociologism and Existentialism: Two Perspectives on the Individual and Society.* Englewood Cliffs, NJ: Prentice-Hall, Inc., 1962, 115–116.

Trân Tử Bình. *The Red Earth: A Vietnamese Memoir of Life on a Colonial Rubber Plantation.* Translated by John Spragens, Jr. Edited by *David G. Marr.* Ohio: Ohio University, Center for International Studies, Center for Southeast Asian Studies, 1985.

Tuan, Yi-Fu. "Life as a Fieldtrip." *The Geographical Review* 91, no. 1–2 (2001): 41–45.

Turnbull, Colin. "Liminality: a Synthesis of Subjective and Objective Experience." In *By Means of Performance: Intercultural Studies of Theatre and Ritual,* edited by Richard Schechner, 50–81. Willa Appel. Cambridge University Press, 1990.

Turner, Victor. "Dramatic Ritual/Ritual Drama: Performative and Reflexive Anthropology." In *Interculturalism and Performance: Writings from PAJ,* edited by Bonnie Marranca and Gautam Dasgupta, 99–111. New York: PAJ, 1991.

———. "The Anthropology of Performance" and "Performing Ethnography." In *The Anthropology of Performance.* 72–98; 139–155. New York: PAJ, 1986.

U.S. Immigration and Customs Enforcement (ICE). *International Students SEVIS by the Numbers.* 2006. http://www.ice.gov/sevis/numbers/student/ (accessed on March 5, 2007).

UNDP. *Human Development Report 2007/2008. Fighting Climate Change: Human Solidarity in a Divided World.* New York: United Nations Development Program, 2007.

Valetine, Gill. "Being Seen and Heard? The Ethical Complexities of Working with Children and Young People at Home and at School." *Ethics, Place and Environment* 2, no. 2 (1999): 141–55.

Vangen, Siv, and Chris Huxham. "Nurturing Collaborative Relations: Building Trust in Interorganizational Collaboration." *The Journal of Applied Behavioral Science* 39, no. 1 (2003): 5–31.

Verhoeven, Michael, Das schreckliche Mädchen [The Nasty Girl] 1990.

Vertovec, Steven. "Transnational Social Formations: Towards Conceptual Cross-Fertilization." Presented at Workshop on "Transnational Migration: Comparative Perspectives" June 30-July 1, 2001, Princeton University http://www. transcomm.ox.ac.uk/working%20papers/Vertovec2.pdf

Waldinger, Roger D. "Between 'here' and 'there:' Immigrant Cross-Border Activities and Loyalties." *International Migration Review* 42, no.1 (March 2008): 3–29.

Warren, Louis S. *The Hunter's Game: Poachers and Conservationists in Twentieth-Century America.* New Haven, Conn.: Yale University Press, 1997.

Weiner, Douglas R. "A Death-Defying Attempt to Articulate a Coherent Definition of Environmental History." *Environmental History* 10, no. 3 (July 2005):
404–420.

Welsch, Erwin K. *Archives and Libraries in France*, with 1991 Supplement. New
York: Council for European Studies, 1979/1991.

Wiles, Rose, Sue Heath, Graham Crow, and Vikki Charles, "Informed Consent in
Social Research: A Literature Review," *Sociological Research Online* 12, no. 2
(March 30, 2007). http://www.socresonline.org.uk/12/2/wiles.html. (accessed
on January 28, 2010).

Wilkie, David S., Malcolm Starkey, Kate Abernathy, Ernestine Nstame Effa, Paul
Telfer, and Ricardo Godoy. "Role of Prices and Wealth in Consumer Demand for Bushmeat in Gabon, Central Africa." *Conservation Biology* 19, no.
1 (2005): 268–74.

Wilson, Edward O. *Consilience: The Unity of Knowledge*. New York: Vintage Books,
1998.

Wilson, Ken. "Thinking About the Ethics of Fieldwork." In *Fieldwork in Developing Countries*, edited by Stephen Devereux and John Hoddinott, 179–99.
Boulder, CO: Lynne Rienner, 1993.

Wilson, E. O. *The Diversity of Life*. Cambridge: Harvard University Press, 1988.

Wilson, Shawn. *Research Is Ceremony: Indigenous Research Methods*. Halifax &
Winnipeg: Fernwood Publishing, 2008.

Wittel, Andreas. "Ethnography on the Move: From Field to Net to Internet." *Forum
Qualitative Social Research* 1, no. 1 (2000). http://www.qualitative-research.
net/index.php/fqs/article/viewArticle/1131/2517 (accessed on April 5, 2010).

Wolcott, Harry F. *The Art of Fieldwork*. Walnut Creek: Altamira Press, 1995.

World Resources Institute, United Nations Environment Programme, and The
World Conservation Union. *National Biodiversity Planning: Guidelines Based
on Early Experiences around the World*. Baltimore: World Resources Institute,
1995.

Yamagishi, Toshio, and Midori Yamagishi. "Trust and Commitment in the United
States and Japan." *Motivation and Emotion* 18, no. 2 (1994): 129–66.

Yamagishi, Toshio. "Trust as a Form of Social Intelligence." In *Trust in Society*,
edited by Karen S. Cook, 121–47. New York: Russell Sage Foundation, 2001.

Zapata Luyo, Marco. "La dinámica glaciar en lagunas de la Cordillera Blanca." *Acta
Montana* (Czech Republic) 19, no. 123 (2002): 37–60.

About the Contributors

Lise-Hélène Smith received her PhD in Comparative Literature from the University of California, Davis, and is currently assistant professor of World Literature at California State Polytechnic University, Pomona. Her research interests include exile, hybridity, and migration as linked to race and gender in the Southeast Asian diaspora as well as in Francophone, and colonial/postcolonial literatures. She is currently working on a book project on exile, métissage, and the aesthetics of representation in Vietnamese diasporic literature from North America and France.

Anjana Narayan is an assistant professor at California State Polytechnic University Pomona. Her areas of interest are ethnicity, migration, and gender. She received her PhD in Sociology from the University of Connecticut and is the co-author of *Living our Religions: Hindu and Muslim South Asian-American Women Narrate Their Experiences* (Kumarian Press 2009). She is a recipient of the American Sociological Association Section on Asia and Asian America 2010 'Early Career Award.' She also has a postgraduate degree in social work from the Tata Institute of Social Sciences (TISS), Mumbai (India). She has been associated with a range of innovative initiatives in the field of women and development in India.

Kelly Shimabukuro received her MA in Literature from California State Polytechnic University, Pomona and holds a BA in English from the University of California, Los Angeles. Her research interests include transnationalism, interracial relationships, particularly those depicted within Asian and Asian American literature, and identity formation as presented in works by interracial/religious individuals.

David Del Testa is currently associate professor of History at Bucknell University in Lewisburg, Pennsylvania. He received his PhD in History, with a focus on Modern Europe, from the University of California at Davis in 2001. His primary research concerns the radicalization of Vietnamese and Cambodian railroad workers during the 1920s and 1930s in French colonial Indochina, and for this research he has worked extensively with Vietnamese and French archival materials in France and Vietnam. He also has an important secondary research interest in the métis or mixed-race community of the French colonial empire between the two world wars.

Mark Carey is an assistant professor of History at the University of Oregon, where he teaches Latin American and environmental history. He holds a PhD in History from the University of California, Davis, and was a Ciriacy-Wantrup Postdoctoral Fellow in the geography department at the University of California, Berkeley. He received the Leopold-Hidy Prize for the best article in the journal *Environmental History* in 2007. Ongoing research on the history of climate change, environmental sciences, and natural disasters is currently supported by the National Science Foundation. His book, *In the Shadow of Melting Glaciers: Climate Change and Andean Society*, will be published in 2010 by Oxford University Press.

Wiline Pangle is currently a lecturer at Central Michigan University, where she teaches courses in Ecology and Biology. She obtained a PhD in Behavioral Ecology in 2008 at Michigan State University, East Lansing, under the supervision of Kay E. Holekamp. Her dissertation, entitled "Threat-sensitive behavior and its ontogenetic development in to mammalian carnivores," focused on the antipredator behavior of spotted hyenas in the wild and led her to carry out data collection in the Masai Mara National Reserve, Kenya, where she resided for over sixteen months. A native of France, Wiline Pangle holds a B.S. from McGill University, Montreal, where she completed a thesis that examined the antipredator behavior of the Eastern chipmunk. She has received multiple fellowships and grants to conduct her doctoral research, including the American Association of University Women International Fellowship and the Graduate Women in Sciences Eloise Gerry Fellowship. Wiline Pangle has also been actively involved in improving science education in the K-12, including the teaching of evolution. She has worked in close collaborations with science teachers across Michigan and Ohio to develop inquiry-based activities that promote science at all levels of education.

Jack Fong is a political sociologist who focuses on issues and strategies related to a non-economistic approach toward global development, particularly the role of ethnicity, race, self-determination and nationalism in development processes. A native of Southeast Asia, Jack Fong continues to focus his research on emergent and existential identities, as well as political systems in the nation-construction projects of Thailand and Burma, as well as in the United States among the Southeast Asian diaspora and their nexus with Asian Americans. Jack Fong received his PhD from the sociology department at the University of California, Santa Cruz and is currently assistant professor of Sociology at California State Polytechnic University, Pomona.

Mónica Ruiz-Casares is an assistant professor in the Division of Social and Cultural Psychiatry and at the Center for Research on Children and Families at McGill University in Montreal, Canada. She holds a Law degree from Universidad Pontificia Comillas-ICADE (Spain), a MA in International Development from The George Washington University, and a MSc in Program Planning and Evaluation and PhD in Policy Analysis and Management/Human Services Studies from Cornell University. Building on her previous research on orphan care in the Majority World (a.k.a. developing countries), where she has traveled and worked extensively, her doctoral dissertation was the first to study the social relations and wellbeing of children heads of household in Namibia. Her main areas of expertise cover the wellbeing and protection of orphan, separated, and unsupervised children across cultures; children's rights and participation; and social policy and program evaluation. She is committed to research and evaluation that affects programs and policies to protect vulnerable children early, strengthen the capacity and efficiency of social services, and involve children in decision-making and action. She can be reached at mr225@cornell.edu.

Kristen Conway-Gómez holds a PhD in Geography from the University of Florida since 2004. She obtained an MA in Tropical Conservation and Development and Latin American Studies from the University of Florida in 1997. She graduated from Macalester College in St. Paul, Minnesota with a BA in Environmental Studies and Religious Studies. Her research focuses on rural Latin American natural resource conservation with an emphasis on community involvement in the process, from start to finish. She has conducted research in Bolivia, Chile, Costa Rica, Honduras, and Panama. Kristen Conway-Gomez is currently an assistant professor in the geography and anthropology department at California State Polytechnic University, Pomona.

Cecily Jones is an associate professor in Sociology at the University of Warwick, UK, and a former Director of the Centre for Caribbean Studies at the same institution. She holds a PhD in Sociology from the University of London. Her research interests primarily address issues of race, gender and childhood within colonial and postcolonial societies. Her recent publications include "*Engendering Whiteness: White Women and Colonialism in Barbados and North Carolina, 1627-1865;*" Manchester University Press [April 2007]; "*Oxford Companion to Black British History*," [co- editor] Oxford University Press, (March 2007, Oct 2008); "If this be living I'd rather be dead: enslaved youth, agency and resistance on an eighteenth century Jamaican estate." *History of the Family*, Vol. 12, No. 2, 2007, pp. 92-103.; "Youthful Rebels: Young people, agency and resistance against colonial slavery in the British Atlantic World," in Gwynn Campbell ed., *Children in Modern Servitude*, Ohio University Press (forthcoming).

Rebecca Sammel is an assistant professor at Ferris State University in Michigan where she teaches Writing, World Literature, British Literature, and Comparative Literature. She received a BA in English from the University of California at Santa Barbara, an MA in Medieval Studies from the University of Toronto, and an MA and PhD in English Literature from the University of California at Davis. Rebecca Sammel's work centers on intertextuality in medieval and early modern European literature in Middle English and Medieval Latin. She has studied medieval and Renaissance culture at the Universities of Oxford and Toronto, taught at the Université de Bordeaux III, France on a Fulbright Fellowship, and published articles on medieval and early modern parody.

Shweta Majumdar is a doctoral candidate in Sociology at the University of Connecticut. She received a MA in International Development from the University of Pittsburgh. She also has a Masters in Sociology from Jawaharlal Nehru University, New Delhi. Her research interests include race and ethnicity, gender, sexuality, human rights and immigration. She has been actively involved with several development projects in India and has also worked as Program Management Intern at Management Systems International, Washington D.C. Shweta Majumdar is the recipient of Taraknath Das Award, University of Pittsburgh for the best student paper on Asia in 2005. In addition, she has won two competitive human rights grants from Human Rights Institute, University of Connecticut and several research and dissertation fellowships.

Virginie Magnat holds a PhD in Drama and Theatre from the University of California, San Diego/Irvine joint doctoral program. Originally from France, she received the International Federation for Theatre Research New Scholar's Prize and her writing has been published in American, Canadian, French, Polish, and Italian theatre journals and books. Virginie Magnat's research interests include experimental and intercultural theatre, non-Western performance traditions, performance studies, cultural anthropology, performance ethnography, and postcolonial theory. She is also a performer whose training is Grotowski-based. She currently teaches both practice and theory as an assistant professor of Performance in the Faculty of Creative and Critical Studies at the University of British Columbia, Okanagan.

Sami Hanna holds a PhD in Second and Foreign Language Education from the State University of New York, Buffalo. A native of Syria, Sami Hanna holds a B.A. in English Language and Literature and an Advanced Diploma in Translation from Tishreen University, Latakia, Syria. He also holds a Master's Degree in TESOL from the State University of New York, Buffalo and has extensive experience teaching English as a Foreign Language and English for Specific Purposes both in Syria and in the United States. His research interests include nationalism and language policies, postcolonial theory, and politics of research.

Mustafa Sever holds a PhD in Education from the State University of New York at Buffalo. He received his BA degree in Educational Psychology and MA degree in Social and Historical Foundations of Education from Ankara University, Ankara, Turkey. Mustafa Sever has also worked as a school counselor and research assistant in Ankara University. His current research interests include the politics of representation in critical ethnographic research of education, education and emancipation, and history of childhood.

Index